"Dr Jennifer M. Fullerty has developed an important case study of the University for Industry in an underresearched area of vocational educational and training.

Dr Fullerty has made a valuable contribution to the literature."

Professor James Avis

*Director of Research and*
*Professor of Post-Compulsory Education and Training*

*The University of Huddersfield*

*

"Each chapter here reveals another chance for people to improve their lives. Those who have been reluctant learners at school discover their self-esteem and confidence in basic literacy and numeracy.

In particular, the Learndirect centre of computer skills offers the exciting prospect of being able to start a job late in life."

Mair E. Pinnell, MBE

*Honorary Member of Soroptimist International*
*of Yorkshire and of SI Leeds*

# LIFELONG LEARNING

## Post-Compulsory Education and the University for Industry: A Case Study

### OR

An Investigation of the Impact of the UK Government Initiative Learndirect on a Changing and Ageing Society with Implications for Policymakers, Researchers and Teachers in Terms of the Supply and Demand of Educational and Training Opportunities

## Jennifer M. Fullerty, EdD

F Street Books (Parkgate Press)
Arlington, Virginia

# Publishers Online!

For updates and more resources, visit
F Street Books and Parkgate Press online at

**www.fstreetbooks.com**
**www.parkgatepress.com**

Edited, page layout and cover design by Matt Fullerty

ISBN-13: 978-1-937056-57-5

Library of Congress Control Number: 2011926933
**Library of Congress Subject Headings:**

Adult learning--Great Britain.
Adult education and state--Great Britain.
Continuing education.
Continuing education--Great Britain.
Continuing education--European Union countries--Congresses.
Continuing education--Social aspects--Great Britain.
Education and state--Great Britain.
Vocational education--Great Britain.


[Parkgate Press: F Street Books reference number: 002]

In research the horizon recedes as we advance, and is no nearer at sixty than it is at twenty. As the power of endurance weakens with age, the urgency of the pursuit grows more intense.... And research is always incomplete.

Mark Pattison, English Educationalist, 1875

# Contents

# Introduction

This is an interpretative study of lifelong learning in the context of the University for Industry (Ufi). Its broad purpose is to attempt to explore the factors that determine the successful, or otherwise, implementation of an educational initiative.

The theoretical underpinnings of the research are an idealist ontological stance and a non-positivist approach to epistemology. The methodology lies within the qualitative paradigm and consists of a case study investigation. 'Ufi providers and their students' are the 'case' of the case study.

Data was collected during in-depth interviews—face-to-face, on the telephone or by e-mail—with two sets of people; namely, the providers of learning and the students. Each set occupies a different role within the Learndirect network. This is the Ufi's brand name for its online information and advice service, its courses, and the learning locations.

Grounded theory analysis is applied to the information given by the respondents. Theoretical findings are thus generated from this empirical evidence. It emerges that twenty-two Ufi providers share, albeit to different degrees, many perspectives on lifelong learning. Similarly, thirty-seven Ufi students have some common perceptions, of varied extent, of the Ufi's approach to lifelong learning. These induced concepts are categorized as being economic, socio-cultural, demographic, technological or educational issues. A subsequent discussion focuses on how, singly, and through their interrelationship, they signify the Ufi's implementation of a government policy.

It is argued that there exist two conflicting paradigms of lifelong learning: one espouses the critical tradition of political goals; the other considers that learning is as unpredictable as life itself. The continuance of learning is related to its supply and demand: currently, and in terms of the Ufi, supply is the dominant component. Both lifelong learning and the Ufi are committed to people's better quality of life. They take account of the diverse circumstances of, for example, age, employment status, gender, environment, health and ethnicity. Equally, they acknowledge the harnessing of technology for personal and professional development.

The notion of 'change' is the overriding factor which impacts on practice and policy in a learning society: it determines the lifelong approach to, and the multifarious delivery of, education. Collectively, these concluding remarks are indicative of the place of lifelong learning within the philosophy of the Ufi.

# Acknowledgements

Lifelong learning is a broad issue. In attempting to make sense of it in the context of the Ufi I have received unfailing co-operation from the Learndirect providers and their students who gave information to me during this inquiry. I wish to record my utmost gratitude to all fifty-nine of them.

Support has been in abundance from those with involvement in the EdD Programme at the University of Huddersfield. I particularly appreciate the help and guidance given to me by Dr Paul Oliver and Dr Roy Fisher. Liaising with my contemporaries on this course has also been invaluable.

I would also like to thank my publishers F Street Books (Parkgate Press) for all their guidance and assistance in the publication of *Lifelong Learning*.

Undoubtedly, the parts played by my family, friends, acquaintances, colleagues and academic advisors, together with the input from companies and participants, have ensured that I reached my goal in producing this book. Without reserve a huge thank you goes out to you all.

# Chapter 1
# Research and Background

## 1.1 The Research

This research is about lifelong learning and the University for Industry (Ufi). The emphasis oscillates between these joint subjects as the investigation progresses, but they are of equal importance to the outcomes of the project. The distinctive purpose of the study is to examine the implementation of a specific government policy initiative, the Ufi, and use the findings, though limited compared to educational research results in general, to draw a conclusion that will contribute to the development of lifelong learning.

Using a case study method of investigation I am aiming to tell the 'inside story' of the Ufi's approach to lifelong learning by collecting and analysing data from the people who carry out (providers), and the recipients (students) of, this educational policy. It is important to attempt to establish which factors currently determine the Ufi's successful, or otherwise, implementation. Hence, the goal of this research project is to produce the optimum relevance for professional policy makers and practitioners in the field of education.

The decision to do this research is based on two separate factors. The first is borne out of my own background. The length and diversity of my involvement in education and industry, which embraces a constant abiding concern for their development, should help me to focus the study. Fascinated to know what impacts on, or causes the extent of, the interaction between these 'disciplines', I have developed an intense interest in lifelong learning.

'The fast pace and complexity of modern society have made 'lifelong learning' more than a catch phrase' (Kasworm et al., 2003, p.vii): it is a concept. It is not static; rather it encompasses ideas, and encourages debate, about educational practice and policy—past, present, and for the future. Lifelong learning has a global perspective, and its delivery and support involves networking the economy, politics and technology, society and individuals. The government of the United Kingdom (UK) is strategically aiming for a coherent system of education through effective partnerships, and shared responsibility, for provision. This mission embodies equity, and inclusion, for the individual within a varied, flexible and diverse learning society.

Hargreaves (2004) documents some specific foundations of lifelong learning including, curriculum, assessment, advice, guidance, information and communication technology (ICT), information and learning technology (ILT), innovation and leadership. He thereby, and alongside a perspective on the process of change, attempts to 'create an intellectual framework for its deeper understanding' (p.vi).

Therefore, on an interpersonal level—interviewing participants from the Ufi—my overall research intention is to investigate whether an unceasing pursuit of learning is an existing widely-reflected phenomenon within this cohort and context. The research is designed to try to show this through exploring their perceptions of lifelong learning. The term lifelong learning has a 'strong element of tautology' (Matheson, 2000, p.196). In the learning society and in learning organizations other people's ideas have permeated the fundamental issues in learning systems, whether formal, non-formal or informal. They continue to appear in educational institutions, workplaces, communities and homes.

The second part of the rationale for this research relates to the fact that the Ufi is a government policy initiative. It is a topical subject in education and business circles alike, where, because it stimulates consensus and controversy, people want to hear and talk about it.

The Ufi was started in 1999 by the Government as a learning resource to develop education and skills principally by using technology. In its business-like way of aiming to stimulate a demand for continued learning, the company Ufi Limited was launched in autumn 2000. Hyland (2000) describes the Ufi as 'one of the more elaborate visions of the learning society . . . unequivocally directed towards those who have benefited least from the system' (p.126). In a conference document, Cowham (1999), the Chief Executive of the Open College of the North West, is less sure and asks if, on the evidence of its recent history, the Ufi is 'a panacea—an all-encompassing solution to lifelong learning; prophylactic—prevents crises and promotes solutions in meeting society's lifelong learning and training needs; palliative—is successful in increasing the uptake of lifelong learning opportunities, or a placebo—remains an expensive and unnecessary adjunct to the existing national further, higher, and work based learning infrastructure'.

On the 25th October 2000 a national network of information and advice venues called Learndirect was established in order to deliver lifelong learning. The Ufi avidly promotes itself as a key strategic partner of the Government. The latter, as a stakeholder, invested £84 million in the year 2000–2001 for the ongoing development of the Ufi's infrastructure, of which £10 million passed to its Learndirect service (Tysome, 2000). The

Ufi occupies a key role in the furtherance of education in the UK by aiming to widen access and increase participation.

Learndirect is the Ufi's 'surface' operation in the electronic (e-learning) market. A provider-led franchised system, with intentions to attract, and impact on, individuals and organizations, it offers over 500 programmes of which approximately 70% are delivered online. They are work-based, skills training, leisure and information courses in, for example, finance, customer service, ICT, supervisory management, languages, literacy and numeracy. At present they are taken by adults in more than 2,000 Learndirect centres and 6,000 UK online centres, whose target, contained in the Ufi's strategic plan for 2002–2005, is to recruit a million learners by the end date.

The subject of this research is thus a wide, well-documented concept with a considerable history—that is, lifelong learning. The research is carried out through a study of a relatively self-contained, innovative policy—namely the Ufi. This choice is purely personal for two reasons.

First, the contrasting aspects of lifelong learning and the Ufi should be interesting to explore. Secondly, my ongoing learning experiences and intermittent working life—switching between, and amalgamating, education and industry—influence the philosophical and methodological approaches to a proposed inquiry. Both these ideas, which are expanded on in Section 1.2, became channelled into a research undertaking. They ultimately narrowed to an intention to add to current and future thinking about the widely debated notion of lifelong learning by providing information about its execution within the particular context of the Ufi.

The research topic was thereby determined; a study of which could then hopefully be carried out with the benefit of some background knowledge. Its aims are to investigate the perceptions of a group of Ufi providers of the approach to lifelong learning of the Ufi, to explore the perceptions of a group of Ufi students of the approach to lifelong learning of the Ufi, and to examine the place of lifelong learning within the philosophy of the Ufi.

## 1.2 Background to the Research Topic

The introduction to this book has three primary elements: the subject matter, the theoretical stances and the researcher in person. Each part has a historical perspective. All intermingle and impact on each other throughout the research procedure. The first—the research topic—has already been outlined. The second component is discussed in more detail below.

By undertaking research I am trying to understand an aspect of the world. To explicate the diversity of the relevant concepts is no simple task. This means, for instance, that knowledge and belief, doubt and certainty, actions and events, and facts and values (Mangolis, 1973) are all dichotomies composed of philosophical problems for the human brain to try to solve.

A fundamental task in research is to create new understandings of phenomena, and to gain fresh insights backed by evidence. A vital element is clarity of transition from theory to practice. Aristotle (384–342BC) referred to the concept of practice as 'praxis'—the pursuit of good through the realization of a morally committed action. Carr (1987) agrees that judgement is needed, assessed in terms of goals and values, in all practical activities. This search for comprehension is pre-empted by theoretical ideas that can be translated into three notions: these are ontology, epistemology and methodology. The meanings that I attach to these three generic terms dictate, in turn, what is to be studied, the investigative design, and the outcomes of the research.

Ontology is the philosophical dilemma resting upon how one thinks about the world. In Greek civilization knowledge (episteme) was differentiated from belief (doxa), and there continue to be conflicting convictions of the state of being. Realism is the theory that an ordered external world exists irrespective of cognitive intervention. It aligns 'truth' to objectivity. The antithesis is an idealist world; a product of the human mind constructed from intuitive values and ideas. The various taught philosophies of idealism—theistic or modern by Berkeley 1685–1753 (Berkeley, 1910), transcendental by Kant 1724–1804 (Kant et al., 2003), absolute by Hegel 1770–1814 (Hegel, 1963), and subjective by Fichte 1762–1814 (Neuhouser, 2000)—are in agreement that the mind and spirit are more fundamental than, and do not originate in, matter.

The opposing postures of objectivity and subjectivity bear significantly on research. Objectivity claims unrestricted access to 'truth' about the world (Brown, 1984; Walsh, 1993). Also known as 'naive' realism, whereby knowledge is absolute and valid, it is a concept considered to be totally irrelevant to the personal life of the individual. There is similarity with determinism (Berofsky, 1966)—the doctrine that a human being is not a free agent to access, or to decipher, true and certain enlightenment.

In contrast, the principle of subjectivity claims that all understandings of the world are interpreted in the mind of the individual, and that beliefs are bounded by personal frames of reference (Hall, 2003). Searle (1995) distinguishes the ontological sense from the epistemic sense of the objective-subjective distinction: in the former they are 'predicates of entities', but in the latter 'predicates of judgement' (p.8).

Epistemology is the study of the basis of knowledge. Positivism is a realist scientific perspective on inquiry into human behaviour. Giddens (1974) maintains that:

> Positivism in philosophy in some sense revolves around the contention or the implicit assumption that the notions and statements of science constitute a framework by reference to which the nature of every form of knowledge may be determined.
> (Giddens, 1974, p.3)

At its extremes positivism can be called 'logical' or 'interpretive' when respectively explaining the material world or ethics. Reductionist, and driven by rigid mechanisms, a positivist stance is predictive and controlling: it rejects value judgements. The testing of scientific theory is called logical empiricism or experimentalism (Doyal and Harris, 1986).

Conversely, anti-positivism is the broader relativistic approach that declares no absolutes. It aims instead to expose and espouse different 'truths' about the universe. It is a concept akin to the subjective conditioning or reasoning of the truth: the belief is that the world is only understood within cultural frameworks. Socrates (469–399BC) had an unshakable faith that critical human reason, coupled with moral character, is the primary source of knowledge, and if aided by evidence from the senses truth would be forthcoming (Gottlieb, 1999).

The concept of reason is split—corresponding to positivism and non-positivism respectively. On the one hand there is 'rationalism' (McGuigan, 1999, p.36), a process of rational thought based on innate ideas irrespective of experience: it was laid down in the seventeenth century by Descartes and Pascal. On the other hand there is 'pure reason' which is interpreted by Kant as 'the sphere of logic is quite precisely delimited: its sole concern is to give an exhaustive exposition and a strict proof of the formal rules of thought, whether it be a priori or empirical' (Cahoone, 2003, p.49).

Methodology is concerned with operationalizing the polarized types of knowledge by selecting the mode and means to search it out. The nomothetic methods of measurement dictated by the material natural sciences—for example, surveys and statistics—systematically check data in order to explain human behaviour. Reference is made to recognized scales, notably for mental testing and academic ability. Reliance is put on a priori ideas of basic logic and deduction to substantiate, independent of experience, terms such as value and morality.

There are contrasting non-positivist procedural styles, like phenomenology and ethnography. In the former tradition, one transposes and mixes one's own stock of knowledge with the life worldview of another person. The latter approach involves trying to immerse oneself in an anthropologically strange cultural world. These ideographic methods of inquiry are guided by naturalistic a posteriori knowledge whose justification is experiential—for example, typification (Lyle, 2003) and reflexivity (Greenbank, 2003).

Invariably in research there exists a lineage between the distinct theoretical foundations, that is, from ontology to epistemology to methodology. Usually, realism leads to positivism and quantitative methods (Newell, 1986), whereas idealism engages the interpretive model and qualitative techniques (Popkewitz, 1984). Every researcher has an obligation to question their assumptions before they relate theoretical criteria to any particular study. The philosophical preferences and the choice of subject matter must be seen to interact, sustain and complement one another.

There existed a vital stage in my research planning: a time to match theory to best practice. It was my aim to organize the components of this study, and to fuse ideas, into a well-specified research design, one worthwhile in terms of its anticipated contribution to professional and educational development. Incumbent upon the ontological view I took, and the 'provisional' topic I chose, was the kind of knowledge needed to give expression to both—that is, the epistemological grounds on which the research was based. The outcome determined my selection of explicit methodological ways to acquire that knowledge, and collect information, in order to finalize my choice of research subject—'Lifelong learning and the University for Industry (Ufi)'. Hence my two thought processes were synonymous.

My ontological contention is that truth is not certain, nor consciousness extrinsic: they are not totally immaterial to human existence. Rather, subjective truth is approbated in that the philosophical question is distinguishable from the individual's relationship to it. One's entire existence can be drawn into a search for knowledge: aspects of internal validity are attainable with the aid of thinking and reason, and the evidence of the senses. This ontological view is suited to a research project the function of which is to explore concepts of lifelong learning.

My theoretical and academic interest in lifelong learning leads to a non-positivist approach to epistemology being adopted. Culture and society are not identified as structures. Instead, they are interpreted as a combined portrayal of individual codes of conduct. This is a transactional model; a form of explanation related to understanding, destined to be as close as possible to the everyday world. Therefore, I designated it to this research— a cluster of beliefs claiming that learning justifies lifelong research particularly within the context of a specific policy implementation.

The practical strategy of my project lies within the interpretive tradition and incorporates an ideographic approach to methodology. Empirical methods—specific data collection tools and a proven analytical process— are used to contextualize the findings, explain conceptual evidence, and justify subsequent conclusions. Qualitative techniques, such as observation and interviewing, allow the elucidation of theory and recognition of the value-laden nature of 'facts'. Dialectic and hermeneutic, they form a dynamic medium through which to negotiate meanings, both introspectively, and in the fieldwork setting. As adaptive tools that co-ordinate easily they can search out and cluster, and thereby aid the analysis of, attitudes to lifelong learning and the Ufi.

The epistemological foundation of the research topic and its manifestation, appropriately derived from the preceding ontological stance, lead to the relative superiority of certain methods. Overall my train of thought, from philosophical to technical issues, has affinity with the instrumentalist fallible rhetoric of Dewey (1916) who applied pragmatic principles to educational contexts. The value of knowledge, consequent upon the empirical context in which it is applied, formulates ideas to facilitate change in an impermanent world. Even so I remain mindful of being in the postmodern era and that new developments could 'save the Western world or destroy it' (Cahoone, 2003, p.1).

Since the early 1970s social changes, and shifts in political and economic practices, have been bound together by 'postmodernity'; a dominant discourse that underlies research in many disciplines. The origins of the modern-postmodern divide or transition—'that profound shift in the nature of feeling' (Harvey, 1990, p.65)—still spark intellectual fireworks.

'The postmodern house' was the title of Joseph Hudnut's 1945 article in the *Architectural Record* in which he defined the concept as:

Both a new historical category, referring to the atomic and the computer era, and an aesthetic ideal, harnessing scientific and technical advances so that they could foster the flourishing of unmediated authentic human experiences.

(Drolet, 2004, p.10)

Masters of this traditional art form—architecture—synthesized, or debated, ideas and ways to represent the complexity of daily lifestyles over the next two decades; culminating in a famous publication by Jencks (1977). Interest in a 'postmodern age' was stirred and accelerated, and in 1979 Lyotard described the condition of knowledge in the most developed countries as a breaking up of the grand narratives of the modern era, for example, the policies of nation-states and historical traditions. Postmoderism in the Western world is characterized by language games based on narrative knowledge—that which 'makes someone capable of forming 'good' denotative utterances, but also 'good' prescriptive and 'good' evaluative utterances' (p18).

Several free-floating syndromes of contemporary life—economic and social aspects, conceived or affected by change—were coming together as a movement. New concepts, encompassed by the term 'postmodern', became widely accepted. Flexible specialization became the antithesis of the rigidities of Fordism with contrasting features of 'production process, payment system, and technology' (Phillimore, 1996, p.127). Collaboration became a metaparadigm of educational and organizational change. One of seven principles of postmodern professionalism (Goodson and Hargreaves, 1996) it is 'a commitment to working with colleagues . . . a way of using shared expertise to solve the ongoing problems of professional practice (p.20).

Jansen and van der Veen (1992) expressed a different view of the developing world. They dismissed the concept of postmodernity in favour of Beck's (1986) notion of a 'risk society' in which conditions in social and biological life are modernizing themselves on an ongoing basis. Prominent features are new political cultures, technological innovations, and ecological rationality, in addition to unpredictable scientific influences and global insecurity of life. Jansen and van der Veen argue that educators cannot afford to ignore this unifying idea, known as reflexive modernization. They say:

The result will be an adult education that sticks closer to the daily hopes and worries of learners, and is more prepared to further a dialogue be-

tween conflicting experiences, interests and ideological images and to stimulate reflection in a Socratic way, i.e., raising awareness of the crucial questions to be asked instead of pretending to know the answers.
(Jansen and van der Veen, 1992, p.275)

Postmodernism today already has a history. Does it have a future? 'Whither' or not, Woods (1999) contends that 'it remains a highly contested concept, a concept in which many people are still trying to look for the new consciousness in contemporary cultural production' (p.258). In 2004, Wright was doing just that. His critique of schema for dismantling the synergy between mega-narratives—like liberalism—and modern pedagogy precedes constructive ideas for the postmodern theory and practise of education (Wright, 2004). Higher education's relative autonomy could exercise powerful control over curricula in order to attract, and retain, students in a changing and competitive field of lifelong learning.

I have argued that the instrumentalist perspective of knowledge is best suited to adapting to changes in society and improving the world. The epistemological pendulum swung away from positivism and quantitative methods towards a strong interpretive discourse and qualitative strategies. This move was exposed by the dominance of postmodernity with its need of appropriate forms of knowledge to solve the problems, and unravel the incidences, of complex contemporary life.

Qualitative research is a diverse phenomenon: it is still subject to a variety of definitions. In spite of this, it's commonly agreed distinct character can be recognized from certain key elements. These include; the perspective of the researcher and the researched, the nature of the research design—that is, the type of tools used for data generation and its analysis—and the outcomes (Ritchie and Lewis, 2003).

The above critique of the theoretical characteristics of research, and my specific allegiances therein, served to co-ordinate the practical strategy of my investigation. It also helped to clarify and analyse the research topic.

In this study, the current forms of lifelong learning and of the Ufi are derived from a historical perspective on their two main elements; namely, education and industry. After the Second World War (1939–1945) separate government ministries of Education and Labour undertook policy decisions on the basis that they were dealing with two different concepts. The former, being person-orientated, provided formal discipline bases for encouraging argument, critical thought, and affiliated tasks needing many years to accomplish. The latter focused on criterion behaviour in a work-place setting, and featured short-term objectives to equip trainees for vocational assignments.

In 1995 the two remits converged under the Department for Education and Employment (DfEE) with influences from the Departments of Trade and Industry, Social Security, and Health and National Heritage. Central statutory initiatives now developed in the wider sphere of 'learning', but were in effect supervisory because, due to decentralization, the approach was not unified. Since 2001 the Department for Education and Skills (DfES) has exercised control. Today's position regarding lifelong learning and the Ufi—both are aspects of the Government's educational policy—is arrived at via shifts in 'fashion'. These are changes that represent different frames of reference depending on the perceived objectives of the players therein.

Two key concepts resulting in, and from, the growing interest in life-long learning are 'the learning society' and 'the learning organization'. They are configured around the repercussions of globalization and post-Fordism—processes that encompass socio-economic and technical change, power, and networks. The learning society is based on the notion of lifelong learning directed via learning organizations.

The learning society is a diffuse, enveloping, and contested concept of multiple and competing definition (Coffield, 2000). Inconsistent models of the learning society accentuate the diversity of themes within: each paradigm has its own vision. The commonality is that lifelong learning represents a powerful consortium that commands a major part of a learning society, even though that society might convey different meanings, and respond differently, to different groups of people. Essentially, the basic ideological premise is that it must not alienate those who it is supposed to help. There are considerations of treatment, and of equity and justice, around gender, ethnic origin, class, disability, sexual orientation, religion and age. Every human being is unique, but they all have the same rights to develop their potentialities and live life to the full.

Some of the earliest concepts of a learning society disguised an educative society. An educative society is the product of rapid social changes and continuing education—itself the outcome of the influence of those same changes in altering the function of adult education from remedial to continuing (Kidd, 1961). However, Hutchins (2003) cautions that 'educational systems are relied on to improve the society in which they operate.

But they will not be permitted to improve it in ways or by methods [of which] the society does not approve' (p.278).

Moreover, an educative society encapsulates educational research and its concern for emancipatory change. Educative research has a political nature characterized by democratic and egalitarian interests: it seeks to contribute to, and further, those interests. This necessitates avoiding epistemological dualism by immersing the researcher in the research, thus concentrating on the consciousness-raising of problems, and the use of mutual dialogue—the language of possibility—by investigators and practitioners. Setting aside theoretical knowledge from its application in educational settings does not accomplish change for the betterment of learning. Researchers who seek direct involvement in policy debates can increase understandings, and thereby get to influence developments in a learning society.

According to van der Zee (1991) the concept 'learning society' refers to a society in which learning is the whole of life, and the whole of life is learning. Yet any wide-screen view of the learning society usually embraces nearer shots of lifelong learning. Van der Zee conforms by engaging with a learning society in which societal forces, such as an explosion in technology and an ageing population, affect learning needs. Stability in provision together with equality of access opportunities would make an ideal foundation, but these are sometimes unrealistic hopes to harbour. Nevertheless, proficiently, and productively, matching the delivery of education to learning requirements is an acute and constant goal in many complex related areas, such as basic skills attainment, employability, curricula planning and student retention.

The Organization for Economic Co-operation and Development (OECD, 2000) sees its challenge in the learning society of the new millennium as the management of knowledge. This is a concept that might be interpreted in a socio-economic context as examining factual information, understanding the principles of teaching, and encouraging and developing human skills. The role of learning in this changing paradigm is at the core of many issues.

Hierarchical and political control systems are in evidence. University 'disciplines' are usually ranked: medicine maintains a top position 'by virtue of the status of its allied profession and the cost of its research' ((Boureois et al., 1999, p.32), whereas relatively recent subjects, like business and media studies, form a lower grouping. The status of academic research and educational development is, according to MacDonald and Wisdom (2002) 'a response to a changing higher education environment at both an institutional and national level' as exemplified by 'the Quality Assurance Agency through its subject and academic review process, codes of practice and other frameworks' (p.5).

Integrating the use of information and computer technology into teacher training and curriculum development programmes ensures that students of all ages benefit from enriched learning experiences (Wentworth, Earle and Connell, 2004). Palacios Lleras (2004) insists that investment in human capital is vital because education, if defined as the growth in productivity following training, has economic value. He also argues for alternatives to traditional funding—the 'pure state supply side model' (p.31)—to take the form of human capital contracts, and options involving private financial markets.

It is established, therefore, that learning is a powerful force in society. It follows that its organization presents a persistent challenge for educationalists and policy-makers, especially on two counts—how to collaborate, and where to respond to more diverse learning needs.

Learning organizations must themselves learn, and be capable of changing their behaviour and responses to the environment. This is part of an organic view of the implications of rapid change in global society. Hence, fluidity, adaptability and attitude are key features: achievement has more relevance than attainment in attracting individuals into a dynamic, not passive, relationship with learning.

Organizational culture has repercussions for learning in that it can take place at any age, in numerous ways, and in a variety of settings. Learning might be formal, informal or incidental—in each sphere many associated matters arise. Formal learning conforms to a set curriculum facilitated by professionally planned objectives and a definite location. The informal kind is usually self-directed, experiential, non-institutional, non-certificated, and has unpredictable outcomes. Unintentional, incidental learning can occur during social interactions—for instance, as a quiz team member or playing the word-forming game 'scrabble'. Learning locations may be public, private or voluntary/charity aided: they include educational institutions, the workplace, the community and the home. All are environments that impact on the positive or negative image of lifelong learning and its integration into society.

Schools are traditional establishments for the delivery of compulsory education. On the other hand, nurseries, colleges and universities function for the 'voluntary' pre-school and 16+ sectors, and it is in this context that the pursuit of lifelong learning predominates.

The success of a school in a learning society is based on an integrated, non-prescriptive curriculum taught by teachers who are lifelong learners themselves (Quicke, 1999). The rationale for the 'curriculum for life' is derived from an analysis of contemporary society and 'what needs to be done to realize democratic goals in that society' (p.160). The remit of professional educators to teach the competences required by statute—for example, numeracy and literacy—can be made compatible with the life skills of autonomy, and a capacity for critique, yet respect, of others. Glover and Law (2002) believe that matching teaching approaches to learning styles is educationally effective and economic. A report by the Learning and Skills Research Centre (2004), that critically reviewed literature examining thirteen models, disagrees. In either event, pupils' good experiences of their schooling, complemented by good professional practice by teachers and facilitators, should prolong interest in learning beyond the compulsory boundary.

The principal aim of a nursery is to nurture early childhood development. It strives to assimilate and accommodate behaviour, and reduce egocentrism to heteronymy, then autonomy, in line with Piagetian theory (Piaget, 1973). In tandem it fulfils practical demands like 'minding' the children of busy and working parents. These same adults often become involved as helpers or committee members, and later as school or college governors, sharing, and acquiring, knowledge and skills while learning alongside every age group.

Colleges of further education (FE) are organized to supply a mostly local cohort of 16+ learners with education and training packages to satisfy their wants and requirements. Predominantly they need to get qualifications, access or return to the job market, develop professionally and gain promotion, or learn for pleasure and self-satisfaction. Potential students can attend an open day to discuss informally a learning programme tailored specifically for them, and to receive appropriate details of the ancillary services available, such as fees and careers advice.

FE colleges might 'reach out' to promote learning through a campus-share project with sixth-form colleges, especially in localities where, for a variety of traditional reasons, people have shied away from lifelong learning. Also, a college might be a licensed or associate college of a named university; a status which acknowledges its competency to deliver higher education (HE) that upholds the standards of that university. At this level, accreditation of prior experiential learning (APEL) might soon be possible: guidelines are under review by the Quality Assurance Agency (QAA, 2004), as lifelong learning becomes part of its emerging agenda for HE.

Traditionally the main aim of a university education is to stimulate academic growth and research acumen, but it also serves other purposes. It is 'a means to upward social mobility in a meritocratic system' (Bourgeois et al., 1999, p.28), and the institution's activities are crucial for innovation (van Weert and Kendal, 2004)—'the very bedrock of good governance' (p.32). Whilst acknowledging a suggestion from the Dearing Report that a university should 'sustain a culture that demands disciplined thinking', Pike (2005) contends that 'part of that discipline should be to curb wilful literal interpretation, emotionalism and uncritical relativism' (p.15). Therefore, on the basis that a university's current main market is the cohort of multifarious learners, it is these students' diverse needs that require meeting the most.

The tremendous growth in scale of universities, with their associated claims on revenue and limited resources, invites speculation (Levis, 2003) about the merit of adopting a business model as an agenda for success—this the reward for strategic proficiency, like treating students as customers, and making teaching a core competence. Wolf (2003) disagrees; emphasizing with the title of her article that each domain should 'stick to core functions . . . universities can't produce completely 'work-ready' employees any more than workplaces can take over education' (p.13).

The changing nature of work has ramifications for its organisation. Workplace training is an arranged practice intended to produce learning and, in many cases, to guarantee specialist vocational skills or pathways to promotion. There are many reasons for setting up a learning organization. It might be to interplay the component learning parts therein, individual and group, with the outside environment in order to benefit the whole establishment; to engage in total quality management and learning initiatives—for instance, Investors in People—or to establish a Learning Company in response to changing industrial relations practices (Tight, 2002). Hence, innovative workforce development programmes usually become a condition of directive executive management to ensure that productivity targets are achieved, audit requirements can be satisfied, and quality standards maintained.

In 2001 a radical change took place in the workplace with the introduction of Joint Investment Plans (JIPs) to maximize the chances of inclusive employment, with guaranteed equality of opportunity for disabled people who wish to work. Therefore, in terms of harmonizing lifestyle, learning and work, there remains an important question. Is a knowledge-driven economy essential, or are policy makers re-designing the education system to meet an imaginary demand for learning from employers? Only research into the initiatives and organizations themselves can deliver the answer.

People tend to congregate in natural interactive environments to share, and acquire, knowledge and skills while befriending, supporting, and acting as mentors to, one another. Local voluntary and community organizations are usually specifically orientated by faith, sport, hobbies, youth/retirement, charity care or fundraising. Most are regionally, nationally or internationally affiliated—for example, the Mothers' Union, Local Authority Leisure Centres, the Women's Institute, the National Trust, the Workers' Educational Association, the Boys'/Girls' Brigade, Age Concern, the National Society for the Prevention of Cruelty to Children, and Rotary Clubs: all encourage static and outreach provision of learning. Moreover, their present activism, drawn from past best and worst experiences, can be the forerunner of, and prolong, neighbourhood renewal in impoverished areas. Continued learning stimulates decision-making and leads to the challenging and modification of policy.

Learning enhancement in the home has always been possible even though its purpose and structure has progressively changed. Books and journals—while still comparatively expensive—are ever more available, but it is the personal home computer that occupies the increasing proportion of free time in most people's lives. The computer age is upon us. Every-thing is getting faster, and those who cannot cope may be left behind. So is the home environment the ultimate, flexible, comfortable setting for the individualized learning organization—self-directed learning? Maehl (2000) outlines the complexities of the idea and asks if it is:

> A process or a goal . . . compatible with institutionalized learning . . . ? Is individualization or learner control appropriate for all learners? What is the role of the teacher or facilitator? Does the individual focus overlook cultural and sociological factors that affect education? Is self-direction possible if knowledge is socially or culturally constructed . . . or is it a deceptive charade whose goal is to accommodate learners to prevailing social or political beliefs while carrying on an illusion of individual control?
>
> (Maehl, 2000, p.51)

All these aspects have been the object of research, and continue to invite clarification.

Many service agencies, such as Homestart UK, the Basic Skills Agency and the Money Management Council, liase to actively support family learning. This form of education centres on activities that involve children, parents, grandparents, distant relatives and carers in learning to understand, communicate with, and look after, each other. Organizations encourage all family members in their responsibilities towards parenting, play, health/diet, drugs, credit/debt and the legal system. Alexander and Clyne (1995) regard family learning as *Riches beyond price*—the title of their paper that discusses good learning practices. Regularly interacting with relatives does have educational significance, in that, home-school harmony is dependent on keeping pace with sociological change. By fine-tuning quality assurance, and concentrating on staff development in this field, then the 'creativity, industry and good humour of family learning will leave an impression on learners for years to come' (Haggart, 2000, p.82).

There are many critiques about the phenomenon of 'change'. Chaney (2002) sees cultural change in everyday life in the late twentieth century as 'both something accomplished and made manifest in the routines of ordinary experience' (p.11). He claims that it is 'sociologically' understood through forms of interpersonal interaction, citing a proliferation of the means of entertainment and expansion in leisure time—for example, the multi-cinema complex and cheaper foreign travel—as being indicative of cultural diversity in the modern era. Although Chaney regards cultural change as a conception of modernity, his interpretation is synonymous with the post-modern approaches that I discussed earlier.

Other perceptions of change include digital evolution (Kanter, 2001), urban planning (Ward, 2004), and globalization (Wolf, 2004). According to Holton (2005) globalizing trends are 'transnational'—'a range of evolving processes, relationships, and institutions that are not contained within the borders of nation-states' (p.294). Change can mean that transformational activities of empowerment are in evidence, including managing culture and building teams (Lee, 2001). Similarly, interprofessional education (IPE) arises because 'changes in workplace practices now require members of different professions to work together' (Ashford and Thomas, 2005, p.124).

There are also critical pedagogies—'ways in which practitioner researchers can break into their habitual ways of seeing things with a view to considering alternative understandings of their practice' (Brown and Jones, 2001, p.169), or 'a shift of power and an emphasis on meeting the needs and rights of people who are often marginalized' (Adams, 2003, p.31). Accountability is widely discussed, in terms of after-school care and freedom at work (Romm, 2002). Statutory national standards for monitoring, assessment, recording, reporting and accountability, referred to as MARRA, relate to learning and underpin the professional practice of teaching (Headington, 2003).

Not all change is progress; someone, somewhere, at sometime, is against it. In education it does not always impact favourably—a fact borne out by the constancy of changes to syllabi. Proposals in the Working Group on 14–19 Reform Final Report (Tomlinson, 2004), and the consequent DfES White Paper (2005), include new national standards for basic skills, and a diploma framework for current academic and vocational qualifications with a statutory pre-condition for work-related learning.

In industry, there is a view that global adverse economic factors, not the skill levels of individuals, have caused the demise in British manufacturing bases and service provision; so that many are relocating, or setting up outlets, overseas—respectively for example, electronics to Taiwan, and banking to India. Contrary opinion steadfastly puts the blame on the individual, emphasizing that people must use their capacity to invest in themselves (Woodhall, 1997); 'the concept of human capital has dominated the economics of education' (p.219). In this respect, flexible learning is championed as the means to motivate people to take on creative roles and to expect the unpredictable.

In a learning society people's learning lives can be identified in terms of their transition through learning organizations in the life-course. The expertise within successful institutions and companies, and of academics and professional managers, can combine to form 'Partnerships with people' (DTI and DfEE, 1997) which give advice to sustain the prolongation of learning in society.

Similarly, in order to meet the requirements of adults in the community, the 2002 Education Act gave widened powers to schools enabling them to become local learning centres. One suggestion was that 'Local Education Authorities should incorporate learning in school settings in both their Adult Learning Plan and their Education Development Plan' (Summers, 2002, p.3). In reality, despite new initiatives, the Government's policy directives and measures for lifelong learning continue to be ventures that divide learning into categories on a funding basis as support, or not, for courses that lead to various types and levels of certification, or do not. One of my intentions for this project is to try to find out if the Ufi is an innovative by-product of this policy.

Overall the background to the research could be construed as an anomaly. This is due to the fact that it is presented as a combination of conditional philosophical discourse, concepts of lifelong learning, and details of political initiatives, with the addition of a personal perspective. The autobiographical influence is now explained.

## 1.3 The Researcher

Lifelong learning is a concept which does not presuppose any course, curriculum or route through available educational provision. On the contrary it provides a wide range of freedom for the individual learner to select their preferred style and content of learning.

I am a lifelong learner who chose to engage in research and undertake a case study of lifelong learning and the Ufi. Having lived through some key changes in education I appreciate that my background, like that of all other learners, is unique: it is instrumental to my continued learning. The concepts of reminiscence and life review (Coleman and O'Hanlon, 2004) allow for reconciling the past and present. The development of memory stimulates adaptation to change, and is therapeutic in respect of 'social relevance, creativity, spirituality and generativity' (p.74).

Moreover, personal knowledge is, according to Goodson (2003), becoming an influential form of inquiry. He says:

> Storying and narratology are genres which allow us to move beyond (or to the side of) the main paradigms of inquiry—with their numbers, variables, psychometrics, psychologisms and decontextualized theories. The new genres have the potential for advancing educational research in representing the lived experience.
> (Goodson, 2003, p.33)

I have therefore written a small autobiographical reflexive account that has relevance for others because it shows that 'education permanante'—a synonym used for recurrent education (OU, 1995) – is based on human adaptability and the lifelong capacity to learn. (See Appendix 1.)

# Chapter 2
# Literature Review

## 2.1 Prologue

This literature review shows how the research undertaken fits into a wider body of knowledge. It also provides a firm foundation for the design and development of the investigative process. The review comments upon, and explains, the subject matter of the research by drawing together contributions about key issues from specialists with views and experience in each particular named domain.

My principal aim is to provide a brief summary, then analyse literature about lifelong learning and the University for Industry (Ufi). Publications relevant to the former are abundant, whereas information on the latter is comparatively scarce. Such a situation does however allow for a search of the literature. In effect, lifelong learning can be located within the distinct context of the Ufi: simultaneously, Ufi policy impacts on the varied concepts, and diverse aspects, of lifelong learning.

The reader is now taken through a sequence of subsections, each one being indicative of a specific theme within the spheres of lifelong learning and the Ufi. Initially each of the two main subjects is treated independently: an attempt is made to establish the meaning of lifelong learning, and then to forge an understanding of the Ufi. Secondly, questions are asked about the beginnings of lifelong learning and the Ufi, and their subsequent progression. Likewise, where do they occur? Next, consideration is given to analyses of the motivation and support networks for lifelong learning and the Ufi. Finally, literature that predicts their future prospects is discussed.

Overall this review seeks to present a comprehensive and coherent guide to the contemporary literature. The focus, while fixed on the interrelationship between lifelong learning and the Ufi, is intertwined with an overview of the thinking that underpins the case study investigation.

## 2.2 What is Lifelong Learning?

Most of what is written about lifelong learning falls between polarized viewpoints. As Green (2000) points out, 'visions of lifelong learning and the learning society differ markedly in means and ends' (p.35).

Is learning a personal endeavour on the basis that no other person can make one do it? Bill Lucas, Chief Executive of the Campaign for Learning, believes that it is. He says:

> As a child, you can be taken to a school and play intellectual truant through all of your classes. Or, as an adult, you can be sent on a training course and refuse to absorb what you are offered. And you can resolutely resist taking an active part in DIY of any kind!
>
> (Smith and Spurling, 2001, Foreword)

Conversely, is lifelong learning directly correlated to a continually changing learning society? Field (2000) argues in favour, saying:

> Its (the learning society) key features are surely that the majority of its citizens have become 'permanently learning subjects', and that their performance as adult learners is at least in part responsible for determining their life chances. By these standards, our learning society is already well-entrenched, and the challenge now is to adapt it so that it fits our needs more closely.
>
> (Field, 2000, p.38)

In his capacity as the first professor of lifelong learning in Britain, Field is clearly supportive and committed to a study of the concept in its entirety. His two-pronged definition of lifelong learning maintains firstly, that all human beings 'learn new facts, skills, ideas and emotional capacities simply by virtue of enrolling with that permanently instructive institution the University of Life' (p.vii), and secondly, that lifelong learning provides the framework for educational policies, which are themselves determined by significant factors; economic flexibility and social control being just two amongst many others.

Certainly there is no absolute definition of lifelong learning. The notion that learning is not restricted to childhood but continues through life has long been subjected to wide interpretation by academics, sociologists, industrialists and politicians. Hence, to disseminate and discuss the literature surrounding lifelong learning is inevitably a complex task. It is a contested concept; considered to be an essential requisite for finding a link, if any, between economic prosperity and personal, and professional, development, or political policy and cultural division.

Gray and Griffin (2000) rationalize the link between post-compulsory education and the competing, equal needs of young people wishing to improve their job prospects and employers looking to employ highly trained workers. They conclude that for many students commitment to a vocational curriculum depends on their perception of it leading to a good job. Gunn (2005) uses the concept of globalization to connect political and socio-cultural perspectives of learning. He affirms that the speed of global change and communicative networks allow for an international education system. Whilst arguing that learning models and practices are transferable between nation states, Gunn nonetheless maintains that for maximum effect this process is conditional upon the modification, or changed method of application, of educational policy to suit profound cultural differences in terms of race, religion and class.

Further detailed debate about these issues is abundant throughout a book by Longworth and Davies (1996). The authors, who have extensive, combined experience in education and business, are dedicated to the proliferating strategies and principles of an era of lifelong learning. These include 'the avoidance of apocalypse in the near future' and 'liberating the mind, and sometimes the soul, from ignorance and doubt' (p.8). They challenge individuals and organizations to action their commitment—for instance, liaise with someone from a different sort of organization to establish the joint knowledge and skills; discussing these attributes, and then creating a list of other talents and experience needed to grow both organizations into lifelong learning communities.

Each chapter heading of the book signals a different aspect of learning; in turn espousing the merits of the power of learning for understanding, earning, survival, developing human potential, and enhancing the quality of life. In this way, Longworth and Davies provide substantiating evidence to support their overall claim that, if lifelong learning is 'enjoyable and of tangible benefit' and 'freely available for all groups', then it is successful—as defined 'in terms of increased income or better employment', and/or in 'personal fulfilment gained from the acquisition of knowledge or from an enhanced ability to contribute to society' (p.138).

Whilst acknowledging the existence of these beliefs Coffield (2000) is manifestly doubtful about them. Concerned about the intrinsic and extrinsic value of education, he remains consistent in his view that lifelong learning is merely a phenomenon for shifting the cost and responsibility of learning from the Government onto the unsuspecting and willing individual. Coffield charts the passage of his enquiry into lifelong learning through overlapping phases that he calls 'romance, evidence and implementation' (p.1). There is a comparative link between these three periods and those that Stock (1993) discusses and names as romanticism, modernism, and the future.

A book edited by Hodgson (2000) likewise expresses the interest of its eleven individual contributors in the historical development of lifelong learning. It records and analyses past and current lifelong learning policies and politics, then discusses a learning system for the future. Hodgson interprets these facets as; latterly 'the education of adults', currently 'an umbrella term for post-compulsory education' (p.vii), and then forward-looking to a notion of lifelong learning based on 'all-throughness' (p.199). Commenting on this conjecture Spours (2000) says:

> This inclusive interpretation of lifelong learning can also provide a means of relating relatively separate and fragmented education debates, so that those involved in early-years education can see themselves as much a part of the debate about developing lifelong learners as those in post–16 education and training already do.
>
> (Spours, 2000, p.ix)

Here, whilst acknowledging the separateness of the issues analysed in different chapters of the book, Spours is arguing that they are all interdependent and related to lifelong learning. It is a viewpoint endorsed by Williams (2000) who links lifelong learning to the question 'Who pays for it, how and when? (p.80), and concludes that a comprehensive financial scheme of life-cycle earnings and savings involving individuals and commercial enterprises is the answer. Spours' version of the concept of lifelong learning instigates the question 'when does lifelong learning begin?' An attempt is made to find the answer in the next section in this literature review.

In 2003 Hodgson and Spours retain their shared vision for the future of education while examining the complexities of the reform of 14–19 qualifications outlined in *Curriculum 2000* (UCAS, 2000). They blame certain weaknesses on political compromise, citing 'piecemeal' implementation and structural problems. It is, they say:

> Focused on qualifications rather than curriculum . . . the Government's desire to show that A levels continued to exist and that it was improving

standards in vocational and applied qualifications through the extensive use of external assessment.

(Hodgson and Spours, 2003, p.50)

The authors contend that the programmes of study should instead be conceptualized as 'a stage to a unified and all-through system for lifelong learning' (p.27).

The perspectives on lifelong learning continue to be numerous and diverse. They are likely to differ according to the discourse within which they are voiced. I define 'discourse' as the established language use by which we present, and make sense of, the material world, with a view to changing it. At this juncture, therefore, I will examine some differences between the literature currently available and that published approximately a decade ago. At that time most educationalists and sociologists tended to concentrate on exploring one specific aspect of the changing world.

A strong overriding theme recurring in the literature is 'change'. In many texts it is, therefore, demographic, economic, technological and/or socio-cultural change that predominantly is argued to herald the need for lifelong learning.

Writing in 1993, Schuller and Bostyn attempt to place a discourse of the 'third age' on the provision of learning opportunities. They emphasize that demographic projections of an ageing population must lead to the preparation of an education policy for older learners. In four detailed case studies Pilley (1990) discusses the integration of older people with education and community development. He concludes that much depends on the cognitive and psychological accessibility of the individual.

Edwards (1991) believes that a sound skills base is an essential pre-requisite for economic success. He refers to an explanation of Fordism by Murray (1989)—in short, the manufacture of standardized products for a mass market—before claiming that the criterion is defunct due to advances in information and communication technology. He interprets learning as the delivery of education and training according to post-Fordist principles, especially evidence of a multi-skilled, flexible workforce governing the economy. By 1997, however, Edwards is less clear in his view of the changing world as he tries to unravel the diverse discourses of lifelong learning.

The Further and Higher Education Act 1992 promotes the idea of the 'consumer'. Post–16 students move in a marketplace of learning where corporate institutions, sixth-form colleges and private agencies offer a complex array of learning programmes. Some courses are certificated, notably those within the National Council for Vocational Qualifications Framework. A predominant response to changes in the global market system is to put overwhelming pressure on people to learn new skills and techniques in order to secure work in hierarchical companies (Hart, 1992).

Field (1994) suggests that the consumer culture is correlated to changing trends in society: consumption is a process that greatly influences the provision of learning opportunities. He believes that building market principles into adult education is strategic investment in the social well-being of both individuals and the nation. According to Tett (1996) there is a definite impetus towards reconstituting formal providers of education and training as businesses, with a greater emphasis on advertising and marketing.

In 1992 Bridge and Salt produced a bibliography of literature about continuing education and training. The same material, arranged in alphabetical order by authors' surname or the name of an organization, is categorized in the 'Introduction' and the 'Index' under seven headings. Five of these are concerned with issues of access and delivery, referring to, for instance, special needs and transferable skills. The final two relate specifically to Northern Ireland and Scotland.

The supplement that followed three years later (Crain, Davies and Morgan, 1995) differs in format. No issue is deleted, but one theme, 'women', shows a comparative increase, particularly with respect to equal opportunities in the workplace, and three new headings, 'Refugees, Wales, and Europe', have been added. One might argue that this indicates the increasing interest in a wider sphere and interpretation of learning. Interestingly, in a more recent book Field (2002) discusses European dimensions in lifelong learning.

Like Field, many authors, for example Tett and Edwards, are continuing to re-visit all aspects of lifelong learning. The emphasis may alter, and new perceptions are included, but the phenomenon, therefore, remains as intriguing and debatable as ever. Tett (2002) has widened the domain of her interests, albeit within the same geographical boundary of Scotland. Her writing endorses a lifelong learning agenda that promotes community education as the means of renewing social justice and inclusion, rather than solely meeting the needs of the economy. The related issue of culture struggles for serious exposure in an arena dominated by economic forces. Thompson (2002) says that 'present-day enthusiasts for lifelong learning still have to argue passionately in favour of art for art's sake because of the increasing pressure to deliver job skills' (p.7).

Reeve, Cartwright and Edwards (2002) have edited a book whose contributors support lifelong learning through the notion of organizational innovation and competitiveness. The consensus is that organized learning is equally necessary in educational and industrial settings, social networks, and the community to contend with a 'supercomplex' world (Barnett, 2002)—'a situation in which different frameworks present themselves . . . multiply and are often in conflict with each other' (p.9). This often leads to knowledge management, itself a complex concept; the idea being that because the learning process gives meaning to the creation and application of knowledge this becomes a product, the tangible outcome of a learning organization, and thereby referred to as intellectual capital (Marsick and Watkins, 2002).

The nature of demography is increasingly affected by longevity. In order to comply with this change, the aim in a learning society is to facilitate learning across the length and breadth of life (Smith and Spurling, 1999). Although the cultural construct of a pervasive ageism might marginalize older people, they are increasingly capable of overcoming social and biological pitfalls, and thus opening up their learning lifespan. The contrast with Ball's (1989) way of thinking is clear. In spite of extolling the benefits of lifelong learning, he only accepts it as being an extension of education beyond the compulsory stage.

It is evident, from the relevant literature, that because lifelong learning now has so many components, they are unconsciously, or automatically, overlapping. It is not surprising that no author appears able to concentrate on one issue without engaging another. Carruthers and Smith (1997) suggest that lifelong learning is facilitated in a world connected by an 'Information Superhighway' that allows for recent developments, such as telephone banking and electronic mail. At the same time, however, the writers warn that this could exacerbate the creation of a two-tier society—a state whereby a new underclass emerges in which people are disadvantaged because they lack the means of access to information.

Within the time-scale of the last decade, the interest in learning has escalated and intensified. Knapper and Cropley (2000) convey the increasing popularity of the term 'lifelong learning' since their first edition in 1985. They stress, however, that, seen as an 'approach' to higher education, the goals of lifelong learning are as valid as ever; as is the need for considerable resources and the requirement to change. These criteria are often satisfied by theoretical studies and innovative teaching practices, which have remained in abundance, if not always in unison. Goodson (2003) argues 'that so much educational research has seldom seemed useful to the teacher' (p.8). Through the reflective mode of their teacher's life and work he explores the notion of professional knowledge; concluding that it is necessary to merge this modality with the theoretical and contextual implications of practice in order to effect educational improvement.

Many writers are concerned about lifelong learning policy and the implementation of corresponding innovations. Both these conditions are engineered by political aspirations. Plewis and Preston (2001) concentrate on assessing the outcomes of work-based learning for adults and lifelong learning interventions—for example, the New Deal programmes which 'may be achieving some success in moving young people from benefit and into work' (Hodgson and Spours, 1999, p.49). The authors also interpret the measurement of the impact of incentives for learning—for example, Individual Learning Accounts and basic skills initiatives—on communities, family life, the labour market, and organizations.

Similarly, Reeve et al. (2002) insist that educational policy and practice should be designed in direct response to a particular relationship between learning and work. In 1996 Tett had foresight, and one business of the type she identified is the Ufi. It is also significant that Fryer (1999) starts a list of 'Key Initiatives in Lifelong Learning' with 'Establishment of Ufi Ltd' (p.5).

## 2.3 What is the University for Industry?

The University for Industry was conceived in 1994 by Gordon Brown (appointed Chancellor of the Exchequer in 1997) as part of the Government's policy for education and training; namely, the Welfare to Work programme. A publication from the Institute of Public Policy Research (Hillman, 1996) critically explores its proposed operation as a national learning network accessible via technology, such as the Internet, in various places—for example, the home, workplace and social environments. A year later the Ufi's anticipated success is placed alongside the proven success of the Open University (OU) as the provider of a 'second chance' of higher education: Brown (1997) suggests that the thirty-year difference, between the start-up of the one and the other, represents technological advances in learning facilities. Recently, another link between the Ufi and the OU has unfolded. The former is paying £25,000 for a three-month franchise to distribute an existing OU Careers Service publication *Knowing Yourself* under the name *Your Hidden Talents*. It will be interesting to see if their partnership is extended.

For politicians the Ufi constitutes a way of interpreting the concept of lifelong learning. It is considered to be a vitally important part of their strategy for ongoing education. In a Government Green Paper, lifelong learning is defined by Blunkett (1998) as 'the continuous development of the skills, knowledge and understanding that are essential for employability and fulfilment' (p.11). He names the University for Industry as being one initiative to carry out this approach. Coffield (2000) disagrees. He maintains that the state is not taking proper responsibility for learning because it relies too much on, and over-simplifies, 'human capital theory' (p.11). Support for this view comes from Riddell et al. (2000) who argue that lifelong learning policy in the United Kingdom is 'portraying individuals as driven by economic rationalism' (p.63); hence excluding some social groups, notably people with learning difficulties.

Literature about the Ufi is monopolized at present by policy documents. Because the Ufi is a somewhat recent government educational initiative there is ample self-promotion of what it can offer in terms of learning. This leads to a word of caution for the reader of this review, in that, the majority of the information I appraise about the Ufi is taken from its own publications, and confined by its disciplinary paradigm. It is difficult to establish, therefore, whether the Ufi's claims are supported by empirical evidence or are based on unquestioned assumptions. The literature has not been subjected to critiques from a sizable, wider, independent published audience or literary authority. In time, it is likely that the situation will alter when reactions increase, and opinions are expressed, regarding the implications of the Ufi, and the impact of its Learndirect operations, in the field of lifelong learning.

By virtue of its unusual name the University for Industry invites interest in its purpose and structure. How are 'university' and 'industry' linked? It appears that they are not, in the true sense of meeting the legal criteria for university status—for instance, awarding degrees. Currently, therefore, only the initials Ufi are permitted for public use, and a brand name 'Learndirect' has been devised for the business as it acts as a broker linking providers and students. The Ufi is a limited company administering the distribution of lifelong learning products and services; this fact accounts for the 'industry' connection.

The conference paper given by Dr Anne Wright, Chief Executive Designate of the Ufi, at the University of Sunderland on the 9th December 1998, is entitled 'New models of learning: the University for Industry—not a University and not just for Industry'. In fact at no time in the paper does she explicitly clarify the final phrase; choosing rather, as a means of explanation, to outline the concept, aim, mission and character of the Ufi. Wright presents it as a model for learning with a corporate plan (subsequently the Strategic Plan 2002–2005), and describes the key elements, including 'learning routes which could lead to awards' (p.9).

It is possible, however, to review the work of some authors—for example, Robertson (1998), Hodgson and Spours (1999), and Morrison et al. (1999)—who have a keen interest in the ethos, implementation, impact and progress of the Ufi. The exercise of comparing and contrasting the individually published contributions with that of the Ufi's written strategy is intended to be an informative element of this research.

*Transforming Learning; Changing Lives* is the pronouncement fronting the Strategic Plan 2002–2005 of Ufi Limited. This is indeed an indomitable proclamation. The document has no shortage of rhetoric and clichés: often used side by side, they include 'Learners are at the heart of everything we all do. . . . Their stories are moving testimonies to the transforming power of learning' (p.6).

Has 'The pledge to learners' (p.10), which promises learners, amongst other things, 'the opportunity, on completion of a set of Learndirect learning materials, to present evidence of their achievements for credit towards the widest range of nationally recognised qualifications', actually led to that practical end? In only one of the eight 'people profiles' portrayed in the Strategic Plan, that of Tony Peake (p.39), is a recognised qualification mentioned. This is the European Computer Driving Licence (ECDL). Even here there is ambiguity between 'work towards achieving it' and 'proven accreditation within a national framework'. No qualifications are named, let alone credit towards them.

The Ufi's projected plan is purposely ambitious. By design it outlines staged objectives, calling them building blocks, performance indicators, and targets. The Ufi aims, for example, to 'build the Learndirect brand to be the most well-recognized and clearly-defined lifelong learning brand' (p.21). With regard to one indicator—the number of course enrolments—it intends to increase the 2001/2002 target of 400,000 to a 2004/2005 target of 2 million (p.27). The attention that the plan might attract and receive could vary—between scepticism and cynicism, to support—as its roots grow. With hindsight I realize that the Ufi has been similarly reviewed since its inauguration.

Robertson (1998) examines the background of the Ufi, and the learning context into which it expects to slot. Significantly his scrutiny of this policy initiative reveals salient elements that correlate directly to those of the 'change' paradigm illustrated by the aforementioned literature on lifelong learning.

In relation to demographics, Robertson notes that the United Kingdom, if compared internationally, has 'massive under-qualification amongst older workers' (p.9). This he attributes to a combination of economic and socio-cultural factors. Both individuals and employers show a reluctance to invest in vocational training, undeterred by the grandiloquence of a need for basis, key, and technological skills. He says:

> This situation is further exacerbated by the reluctance amongst SME's and some larger firms to undertake employee development, and a culture of disbelief amongst lesser-skilled workers and adults that education and training produce any worthwhile pay-off.
> (Robertson, 1998, p.14)

In addition, he suggests closing the generational gap through 'urgent incentives to employers, and public awareness campaigns to encourage parents of younger children and other adults to negotiate access and training in the new technologies' (p.20).

A concept of social exclusion remains from a significant link with the concept of selection. Ford (1969) found that selection under the 'tripartite system' implemented by the 1944 Education Act, and later streaming in comprehensive schools, emphasize social class differentials in educational opportunity and achievement. It is possible that inhibitions do linger from this culture, reflected in the general malaise that some people have about learning and work. They lack self-motivation and personal flexibility (Haughton, 1993). This is due perhaps to a dislike of competition, such as continuous assessment and meeting targets; or their inability to respond to change—for example, new learning technologies, shift-work patterns and extra travelling.

Robertson is not convinced that the Ufi, despite its huge financial backing—it was launched with £160 million from the European Union— is a policy that can meet the learning criteria for life. He argues at length that the Ufi is doomed on the basis that 'too much reliance continues to be placed on supply-side initiatives rather than demand-led strategies' (p.9). He also chastises the political short-sightedness of experimenting in an arena of less-successful initiatives, such as the Training and Enterprise Councils (TECs).

Furthermore, Robertson asserts that 'learning on demand'—a phrase attributable to Hillman (1996, p.24)—is not a feasible foundation on which to build the Ufi, simply because of the lack of demand for skills training from individuals, and, in particular, small to medium enterprises (SMEs). Rather, success at providing learning is only attainable when its demand is evident and proven, as in the case of the Open University, through which adult learners increasingly seek to add to their knowledge and improve their educational status. From the first applicants in 1970, to 70,000 students in 1980, there are currently 150,000 graduates—70%in full-time employment—and 11,000 people studying for OU Higher Degrees (OU, 2005).

The Ufi strives to meet its huge expectation role as a national guidance service and commissioning agency. I suggest that in doing so it seems to concentrate too much on content at the expense of a model for learning, a point of view substantiated by Hodgson and Spours (1999). In their appraisal of the educational agenda of the Labour Government elected in 1997 they admit that perceptions of the term used to describe it—New Labour—are confusing; for instance 'people are asking about the precise nature of its strategy for education and training' (p.1). They decide, nevertheless, to place the University for Industry firmly in the context of skills, training and the world of work, quoting that 'by 2002 there is a target of 2.5 million people or businesses using the Ufi's services every year and 600,000 pursuing learning programmes' (p.76). Additionally, Field (2000) draws attention to the fact that the University for Industry was possibly never intended to be synonymous with the 'University of Life' (defined earlier on page 26), and Robertson concludes that the only thing that the Ufi does not provide directly is learning.

The pilot project for the Ufi took place in 1997 in the north-east region of England. Morrison et al. (1999) are co-authors of a subsequent report evaluating aspects of the Ufi in the North East. It is a Department for Education and Employment (DfEE) publication, but the views expressed are claimed to be solely attributable to the writers. The achievements of the scheme are classified as positive, or less positive, with regard to nine objectives, before recommendations are made. To précis the objectives; they can be labelled in one of four ways, as follows: training to meet companies' needs; strategies for marketing; learner motivation and support; technological, partnership and collaborative development. The recommendations include a call to 'reassess the rhetoric of intentions and the reality of outcomes' (p.39), and to concentrate less on accessing learning, but more on encouraging its longer-term engagement. Notably, these points are not dissimilar to those made by Robertson.

The writers of this report make a valuable contribution to literature about the Ufi, and show that it has an affinity with lifelong learning. However, two things should be remembered: it is an appraisal of a pilot scheme, and it is based in a specific geographical area. I acknowledge that lifelong learning is endorsed, yet I question if the time-span of learning can possibly increase without the continual reinforcing of access issues. One must await the full story of the national Ufi.

Another DfEE publication discusses the contribution of higher education to the University for Industry. Written in 1997—before the official start-up in 1998—it not only predicts what the Ufi will be, but aims to stimulate interest within organizations that might become involved. The paper exalts the advantages, in terms of experience, expertise, innovation and resources, of having higher education institutions as providers. Their suitability for meeting the demands of the six functions of the Ufi is stressed by quoting the current situation in particular universities. The common denominator for being 'an example of practice' (p.5) is apparently the usage of technology and online facilities.

The debate continues about the nature of the Ufi's impact on both higher education and the furtherance of lifelong learning. Open to argument is its degree of compliance with their broader objectives. These encompass teaching and awarding in accordance with national and international accreditation frameworks, and instigating, then sustaining, research projects. Further discussion surrounds the meaning and idea of a 'contemporary' university. The Ufi is an 'adult' university in the sense that it is accessible only to those aged over 19 years. Bourgeoise et al. (1999) claim that the adult university has a wider role to play in terms of access and social inclusion for a newly emergent 'underclass' of people who need cultural capital—that is education for social awareness and re-employment. In carrying out my research I hope to find out whether or not the Ufi can meet that criterion.

## 2.4 Lifelong Learning and the Ufi: When Do They Begin?

For learning to be a lifelong process, it must begin at birth and end with death. It is difficult to find writers who come close to embracing this interpretation. Most refer instead to learning that takes place after compulsory education. A search of the relevant literature exemplifies this situation.

Tight (2002) draws the subtle distinction between the genesis of the concept of lifelong learning and its tangible beginnings. It originated in the early twentieth century with Dewey and Lindeman. They dismissed the idea that education finished in early adulthood in favour of learning required, and available, throughout life. Tight agrees that education is a fundamental human process: one is never too old to learn. His explanation, for the accelerated interest in the concept since the mid–1990s, is that it re-names adult education and training, and hence provides a 'useful label for policy-makers' (p.39).

With the premise that lifelong learning stretches across an entire life-time, Smith and Spurling (1999) discuss the 'four ages' during which biological influences affect people's use of the lifespan for learning. The corresponding perceptions of continued learning result from the interac-tion with socio-cultural forces. With regard to early learning, the authors say:

> If it is handled well, it can make lifelong learners virtually in the cradle; if it is handled badly, it can blight learning prospects for decades—if not permanently.
>
> (Smith and Spurling, 1999, p.87)

In early child development a basic instinct is learning. The theories of two educational psychologists help in the understanding of how, and when, children learn. Piaget's interactional model (1973) maintains that children learn through active experience. Vygotsky's social-constructivist model (1978) insists that they construct skills and learning scenarios, known as the zone of proximal development.

Influenced by the above theories, further insights come from Bruner (1987). He believes children learn when they revisit key ideas, engage the mode of pretend play, or use talk as a catalyst for learning through other children, adults, and the intervention of the teacher at the child's learning threshold.

Some learning in infancy may be culturally specific; some is universal (Collins et al., 2002). The 'model for life' that they describe incorporates interactive, interdependent, reciprocal and interpersonal learning, with shared control of the process itself, in a responsive environment.

Longworth and Davies (1996) are of the opinion that lifelong learning begins in schools, but are critical of its nature—the preoccupation with passing on information and memorizing facts at the expense of nurturing personal values, such as flexibility and tolerance. They argue that school children are unaware of the 'need to invest in a lifetime of learning' (p.39), and suggest, therefore, that schools should prepare pupils for continuous adjustment to a rapidly changing world of, for example, 'information overload'. A lifelong learning school featuring ten main characteristics, one of which is 'stimulates home-school co-operation' (p.43), is their preferred solution for encouraging lifelong learning from an early age.

Greany (2003) also concentrates on the school environment in his attempt to find out what makes an effective learner. Believing that the skills and dispositions required are not necessarily implicit, the Campaign for Learning—which, in part, promotes learning as 'an increase of skills, knowledge, understanding, values and a capacity to reflect' (Fryer, 1997, p.16)—has undertaken the Learning to Learn in Schools project in twenty-five schools over a two-year period. Despite being the Policy and Information Director, Greany does not refer to the kinds of schools or their locations. He discusses, however, the study's outcome which is a model for good learning: it integrates five new Rs; namely, readiness, resilience, resourcefulness, remembering and reflectiveness. Greany claims that when children are taught these attributes, which complement the established three Rs, lifelong learning becomes effective from an early age.

Therefore, a significant amount of the literature emphasizes the nurturing role of parents and extended families, and the importance of effective teaching, in guiding infants' and children's future learning capacity. Adolescence too, is deemed a vulnerable time when biological and educational matters bear upon physical and emotional development. Smith and Spurling (1999) warn that any resulting lack of self-confidence and academic underachievement can be extremely discouraging in terms of lifelong learning. Maintaining that during young adulthood and middle age a different concept of learning becomes apparent, they note a specific two-fold trend borne out of a changing society.

When a family lives together the children tend to take priority as regards time and educational requirements. Many parents can no longer rely on their own experience and knowledge in order to help their children, because they themselves would need to learn new skills, particularly technological and communicative. However, when children grow up and leave home an opportunity presents itself for adults to respond to innovative policies, like the Ufi, that outline and emphasize the benefits of time spent learning and so attract them as participants.

As people reach the age of fifty they enter the 'Third Age'. Even though the biological constraints on their learning are reduced, demographic change results in an increasing proportion caring for elderly relatives. Smith and Spurling define the 'Fourth Age' as the period of final physical decline coupled with a lack of aptitude for learning. They conclude that for this stage continuous learning would delay its start, add longevity and increase fulfilment.

A major theme in education, 'Third Age Education' (Jarvis and Griffin, 2003, Vol.1), covers education for aging (Frank, 2003), and the obsolescence of the educational system (Laslett, 2003). Ageing can bring with it feelings of unhappiness, resentfulness and neglect. Some people are burdened by poor health and limited finance. Western society is late in its attempts to ease such deprivation. Frank says:

> Increasingly in the future we may hope that during the middle years, especially in the 40's and 50's, men and women will engage more frequently in various activities that will keep alive their capacity for new and enlarging interests. And this includes revision of their ideas so that, as they grow older, they will not become progressively out of date.
> (Frank, 2003, p.342)

Alternatively, 'the primary concern must be relearning' (p.344). Arts and crafts courses are safe occasions, compatible with personal dignity, where individuals can master new skills while engaging in group discussion and personal reflection.

In the conventional educational system, people in the 'Second Age' teach those in the 'First Age' to succeed them, and emulate their values. There is no comparative function for Third-agers. However, the capacity of older people to develop intellectually is illustrated by The University of the Third Age (U3A). This organization is solely the preserve of its voluntary paying members who teach, and learn from, each other. Moreover, the success of recruiting and retraining older workers is portrayed by their acquisition of new skills, knowledge, confidence and wisdom, based on experience. Laslett (2003) suggests that 'the educational system can be judged as obsolescent now that the Third Age is of such importance' (p.377).

Carlton and Soulsby (1999) introduce their policy paper on learning in later life by quoting testimonies from some people aged between 57 and 87 years about the impact and implications of their continued education. Although their articulations are individual, there is an indication that the advantages of learning are linked. Physical and mental stimuli interact: success as a writer, qualifications that secure a place at university and valuable skills to gain employment lead to confidence, independence, and self-discipline. Life takes on a sense of purpose or new meaning—a feeling of citizenship, dignity or enjoyment. These comments suggest therefore that, no-matter when it begins, learning is always rewarding.

The authors proceed to put a case for continued learning in old age. They move on from the recent past of the 1980s—a time sustained by models for entitlement and opportunity in later life from Jones (1981), Midwinter (1982), Groombridge et al. (1983), Age Concern Scotland (1984) and Harrison (1988)—to follow demographic trends embedded in issues of economic activity, health, wealth, gender, ethnicity, participation and barriers; all of which determine the making of provision for age related learning. Ultimately, Carlton and Soulsby offer practical recommendations. They suggest that to 'develop equitable and coherent policies on fees and concessions available for older learners' (p.83), and to 'work with the University for Industry, and the National Grid for Learning to develop new themes and programmes accessible by digitalized ICT, ensuring access by older people' (p.86) are two means of shaping successful lifelong learning.

Withnall (2000) presents the theoretical arguments in the education and training of Third-agers, simultaneously developing from the mid–1980s onwards. About activity theory he says:

> Activity theory sees later life as a time of potential individual growth and renewed social relationships. The purpose of educational activity is to provide solutions to the problems of how to achieve successful aging through the preservation of a positive, healthy and active lifestyle or through adaptation to a socially acceptable role.
> (Withnall, 2000, p.291)

He also scrutinizes the moral dimension of older people's rights of access to educational opportunities, based on the 'relative deprivation and structured dependency characteristic of later life' (p.292), and argues for current issues of ethnicity and intergenerational equity to be taken into account. Withnall further refers to the work of Glendenning (1997)—a critical educational gerontologist—who seeks to situate a discourse about later life within a new strong paradigm in order to unravel the thinking behind such marginalization, and free older people to take charge of their lives.

Literature about learning in the Fourth Age is less abundant than for the other 'ages'. This is, according to Jarvis (2001), because 'it has been necessary for society to adjust to having a large physically and mentally active retired population for the first time' (p.127). Research into learning at this advanced age is minimal. For this reason, it is difficult to ascertain the true variable proportion of those with, to those without, the inclination to acquire new knowledge. Whilst Jarvis's book covers aspects of learning in later life in common with previously mentioned publications (Carlton and Soulsby, 1999; Withnall, 2000), it also focuses on learning to retire, and after retirement. The writer has the added capacity to look at 'learning to work with elders' (p.139) from other angles.

Physical disability is no bar to continued learning. Face-to-face recreational courses, such as artwork, are available in residential care homes; the OU offers *The Openings Programme* comprising 600 hours of distance study designed to attract new learners from under-represented groups, and there is the opportunity to learn online due to the conception of the World Wide Web (www). Life histories are a significant outcome of learning in the Fourth Age: reminiscence is a valuable element. Confusion and dementia are not to be dismissed as totally detrimental to learning. The guidance of skilled teachers and carers ensures that people can re-learn and regain independence. Jarvis (2001) is emphatic that 'lifelong learning really is lifelong' (p.137).

The Ufi begins when—according to Young (2000)—the Green Paper (DfEE, 1998) 'stresses that lifelong learning is too important to be left to individuals on their own and requires the intervention of government' (p.97); the Ufi being the main strategy to promote it. Its procession through the last five years has undergone several changes, and to date the main media coverage of when these take place remains the Learndirect website.

Since the Ufi's inception, Learndirect advice, Learndirect business and Learndirect corporate have been launched: details about them are given on the Ufi website. 'Advice', launched in 1998, offers free advice from over 200 advisors and 'information on over 500,000 courses' (6th February 2003). 'Business', launched in 2001, offers 'innovative online corporate training solutions for organizations of all types and sizes' (17th February 2005). 'Corporate', launched in February 2002, uses the same learning infrastructure to supply employer-beneficial products simultaneously giving employees an 'unparalleled learning experience' (17th May 2002). From April 2000 to December 2004 Learndirect reached almost 1.5 million learners: in total they took over 3 million courses.

In asking the question 'when do lifelong learning and the Ufi begin?' I am implying the existence of chronological boundaries. Through reviewing the literature, it appears that many authors indicate 'when' they take place while exploring the contexts in which they are active. Therefore, it seems reasonable to answer that the process of learning is a continuum.

## 2.5  Lifelong Learning and the Ufi: Where Do They Take Place?

Locations for learning are many and varied. It appears that learning, whether formal, informal or incidental, can occur almost anywhere. However, the majority of the literature about lifelong learning and the Ufi takes a certain venue as the core element for discussion about other components of this research subject. The centres of learning, whether they are educational institutions, the community, the workplace, urban cities or rural countryside, are sites that impact on the authors' different interpretations of lifelong learning and the Ufi.

Educational institutions are traditional seats of learning: pupils are taught in nursery, primary and secondary schools. Post-compulsory education and training is catered for by colleges—including school-affiliated, sixth-form colleges—and universities. The concept of 'lifelong' learning joins these divisions 'so that the process of learning for older people creates a society in which the compulsory stages of education for younger people can flourish' (Oliver, 1999, p.4).

By the age of five children are 'institutionalized' as they learn. They are required by law to attend school full-time and adhere to the National Curriculum framework until they reach sixteen years of age. Using interviewing as his research tool, White (2000) elicits how people feel about this physical and mental context at the early stage in a lifetime of learning. The bulk of his book records their responses to give a varied insight into that unique environment—school—which everyone passes throughout, and where learning takes place therein.

Comments from some Year 11 and sixth form pupils of today are compared with those from pupils of the same age, thirty years ago. Alistair's view is, 'you've got to have schools because otherwise you'll be thick. If you haven't got an education, you won't get very far in life' (p.16). Donna believes that 'school is full of experience it's not just the learning' (p.45). In 1969 Richard said, 'everything learnt is second hand if it comes from teachers, and very often out of date if it comes from books' (p.31).

Six prominent figures from the educational world also reflect on their schooldays. Two anecdotes, one from Dr Nick Tate, formerly Headmaster of Winchester College, and the other from Professor Ted Wragg, School of Education, University of Exeter, read respectively; 'I had a pretty standard state elementary education. Very large classes: very heavy concentration on the three R's. Hardly a broad and balanced curriculum' (p.123), and 'I didn't like Infants. I remember my first day well. I sat next to somebody who was threading beads onto a piece of cotton, and I thought, 'If this is school, count me out'' (p.130).

A book by Wallace (2001) is written primarily as an aid towards achieving the Further Education National Training Organization (FENTO) qualifications endorsement. It concentrates on how teaching and learning can be balanced to operate successfully within institutions. Wallace sets out the criteria required for both processes. She passes on to the reader practical ideas reinforced with illustrations—for example, how to reflect by keeping a journal (p.25), plan ahead through lesson preparation (p.38–39), and systematically measure achievement with an assessment framework (p.67). Moreover, managing and facilitating learning in an FE institution, in terms of students' needs, can be communicated by case study research, as the result of her interviewing a particular student named Barry reveals (p.96).

Learning in an HE institution (HEI) is mentally challenging. The students, lecturers and management face the day-to-day pressures of economic, socio-cultural and political change that affects how it functions. Universities compete for potential 'clients', financial provision for learning resources fluctuates, and the Government insists on relevant HE systems plus accountability from individual institutions. The consequences, King (2000) argues, include new learning methods for the duration of lifelong learning spent in HEIs, especially 'the development within graduates of an agreed set of generic attributes in addition to content mastery' (p.142).

The report of the Universities Association for Continuing Education (UACE) Annual Conference (1998) details some lifelong learning issues appertaining to specific HEIs. Representatives from forty universities presented papers in four different workshops under the general heading 'University Continuing Education in Partnership for Development'. No contributor expressed any partnership links with the Ufi. One study, by Murphy and Fleming (1998), about full-time degree mature students on Third Level Allowance, found academic excellence on a par with traditional students; their levels of motivation equally volatile. Harrison and Sunderland (1998) presented a paper on a pilot project to promote employee-led development undertaken by the Access and Guidance Unit at Sheffield Hallam University. The report authors' target audience for 'Employee Development and Learning Providers' is SMEs. Admitting to initial uncertainty they say:

> Universities are HE providers . . . employees engaged in ELDs almost exclusively access lower level education and training. This factor posed a major credibility gap which we recognised must be bridged at an early stage, and focused attention on the key 'selling points' of SHU and its ability to offer an ELD 'product' relevant to individuals' development needs.
>                                    (UACE, 1998, p.102)

The Ufi, as the Government's main policy vehicle for lifelong learning, aims to move primarily in work-orientated locations. SMEs do not have a good background of investment in education and training. Matlay and Hyland (1999), recognizing the absence of specialized research within that sector, carried out a national survey. Telephone interviews and a semi-structured interview schedule were used to gather the opinions of owner-managers about the Ufi, and appraise its chances of success.

The authors find that learning 'Ufi/Learndirect style' might find a location in the workplace but overwhelmingly all decisions about it are attributable to the employer. Thus remains 'the perennial difficulty of attracting those SME owner-managers and employees who have never participated in learning since learning school' (p.258). Significantly, the larger the company the more likely it is to know about the Ufi: the firm with under fifty employees has little understanding of the initiative.

A book by Clarke (2000) aims at helping SMEs to capitalize on past experiences and adjust to change, and thus simultaneously maximize the potential of their workforce. Based on the method of open learning, Clark advises on how to set up and manage a learning centre. He stresses the importance of outreach alongside the evaluation and marketing of learning materials—in this connection, acknowledging the Ufi's permission to use their 'Learners Charter' (p.34).

Lifelong learning is an increasing dimension of the world of work, but opinion varies about positive links between education and commercial ventures. In favour, Clark (2001) maintains that the business that becomes a learning organization is distinguishable from its traditional counterpart. In the pursuit of excellence it continuously develops; having a facilitator delegating responsibility to staff, instead of following a fixed business plan to achieve targets with a director controlling fixed job descriptions. Less enthusiastic are Keep and Rainbird (2002) who caution that companies conscious of profit margins, and fearing that competitors will poach their skilled employees, think of training as an unnecessary luxury.

However, there is no doubt from the Learndirect website (2003) which displays 'an exciting new concept from Learndirect' called *Learning through Work*. This introduces their partnership with some educational institutions—for example, the University of Central Lancashire, and Chester College of Higher Education—which enables workers, without taking time off, to achieve recognized university qualifications. This method of delivery of lifelong learning is not in fact new.

Jarvis (2000) tells us that in 1996 'the Management Consultancy Business School entered into an association with the University of Surrey in order to get its masters degree programme validated' (p.57), and the British Aerospace Virtual University was established in response to its own need for specialist information. What we can learn from this is that, in the postmodern learning society, academic, commercial and industrial institutions should expect, and be prepared, to amalgamate or reciprocate some of their functions to supply different or more sophisticated kinds of knowledge. Kimball (1998) warns, however, that when—in most cases—distance learning technologies are used they need careful management: she says that 'it is really teaching strategies and styles that have the most impact on the quality of learning' (p.25).

Longworth (1999) attaches an additional meaning to 'work'. After explaining his commitment to eternal lifelong learning for all seasons, characteristics of which are adaptability and flexibility, he introduces the 'learning city'. For Longworth a learning city is synonymous with a learning community. 'True learning cities are outward looking' (p.111): a model for the future. Since the 1980s, when Edinburgh took part in an Organization for Economic Co-operation and Development (OCED) project and became an 'Educating City', over 100 UK cities, among them Liverpool, Southampton and Sheffield, have achieved the same status.

The European Lifelong Learning Initiative (ELLI) defines a learning community using key words, each precisely expanded upon, for example, 'vibrant—a dynamic environment which hums with co-operative activity, and vital spontaneous energy' (Fig. 8.1, p.112). A virtual reiteration is its 'Charter for Learning Cities' (p.206). According to Longworth the ten commitments therein are encompassed by the concept of lifelong learning.

He selects a case study of Kent for special mention as a region of community learning, appraising its effectiveness against the aforementioned criteria. Though as a county Kent consists of towns and countryside, as well as cities, the study highlights the significance of learning concentrated within a geographical boundary.

Learning takes place in the community in both a territorial and a collaborative way. Collins et al. (2002) explain what collaborating in a learning community means. It is a process whereby people are encouraged to take account of personal differences, like age and gender, as they work towards a common educational goal. Activities such as thinking, reflecting, reading, researching, debate and discussion are thus exercised.

The authors go on to explore some other properties of collaborative learning, and claim that it is productive, non-competitive, and affects hierarchical relationships, all of which can lead to better understandings in a learning community. They find that knowledge is socially acquired through teamwork or interdependence, the acceptance, trust and understanding of oneself and one's peers, and the effective management of the balance of power between teachers and learners. This model of learning not only involves social communication and practical co-operation, but also necessitates confronting issues of power and authority, in the sense of trying to change or remove 'structures that we believe to be antithetical to learning' (p.135).

In this respect, the collaborative ethos is itself empowering for some learners. Those adults who maybe feel mentally and physically constrained in formal educational surroundings—for instance, a classroom—find that interdependence in a community allows them to develop emotionally. They feel valued as individuals and for their mutual, influencing contribution to ongoing learning.

Thompson (2002) examines the creative potential of lifelong learning. Her work shows the significance of those people who actively engage in learning culture and the arts. Thompson mentions especially the Green Candle Dance Company. As part of 1st Framework in the Voluntary Arts Network, this group toured five different regions, spending ten days in each. She argues that by:

> Working together with a rich mix of local arts organizations, schools, colleges, community groups, brass bands, dance groups, special needs centres, asylum seekers, community choirs and older people, they were able to build up a production that was unique to each place.
>
> (Thompson, 2002, p.74)

A learning community, therefore, is where people discover ways to help themselves. They take control of, or change, their lives instead of being seen as casualties of fate relying on experts to help them to cope with situations.

Tett (2002) 'seeks to examine whether community education can make a difference to people's lives by challenging these 'victim' discourses' (p.48). Her investigation reveals the positive influence of partnerships between schools, parents and community educators, and of social movements—for example, the Zero Tolerance campaign against domestic abuse. She also prioritises citizenship, in terms of active participation in creating community projects, as a stimulus for learning to flourish.

A commonality of interest in lifelong learning in rural communities is evident from the thirteen contributors to a book edited by Gray (2002). By combining their diverse knowledge, experience, and personal and professional interests, the publication provides a detailed insight into current learning issues, and active projects, in countryside contexts.

At the outset Gray tells of the countryside in crisis: he discusses numerous reasons for this, including 'BSE, and Foot and Mouth . . . closure of banks . . . withdrawal of buses . . . genetically-modified crops . . . proposed hunting ban . . . agricultural subsidies' (p.3). All of these are urgent matters that affect people's livelihood and, because they take precedence, are factors that impact on the neglect of rural lifelong learning, and its associated educational research and policy development. Gray emphasizes the necessity to change this situation. He advocates a critical investigation to find out how social, economic and political controversies, and deficiencies, can be solved or rectified in order to improve the lives of country dwellers and workers.

Approximately one third of the book's content deals with the wider themes of rural learning. Social change, exclusion, adult guidance and continuing education are issues relevant to the countryside life in general.

Ryley (2002), in each of two articles, connects social exclusion to economic change. First, he gives a detailed factual account of how agricultural employment is falling, and attributes its decline to changes in rural life. The large-scale mechanization of farming practices usually leads to fewer, but larger, farms. Diversification into leisure and light industrial activities, however, rarely brings advantages, due to the poor infrastructure and high transport costs. In addition, demographic change —'a clear drop in the number of school-leavers up to the mid–1990s' (Haughton, 1993, p.130)— shows a decreasing proportion of the rural population are young people, many of whom are permanently leaving their homes to study or find more suitable work, and social activities, in larger centres.

Consequently, Ryley appears to be claiming that groups of learners in dispersed rural communities are difficult to sustain, if not enrol. It may be that this analysis is valid on the basis of experiential evidence (Eisner, 1998), because Ryley later reports on a widening provision project to secure the concept, presence, and future of lifelong learning in such environments. In 1995, using a grant from the Higher Education Funding Council for England (HEFCE), the University of Hull carried out 'Towards a University of the Moors' to prioritise partnerships, new centres, dispersed delivery and open learning in the extensive geographical area of North Yorkshire.

Key issues of poverty, lack of education, and unemployment are clarified further by Pester (2002). People living in rural areas are an underrepresented group in HE, and are at risk of social exclusion. She stresses their need for a professional adult guidance service to inform, advise, facilitate, assess, enable, advocate, give feed back, teach and network for the learning community.

Davidson (2002) justifies the increase in flexible modes of learning delivery—exemplified by modularization, and credit accumulation and transfer—in terms of equality of opportunity, access to provision and consumer choice. This has relevance for rural providers of continuing education because it facilitates, and promotes, distance learning.

The remainder of the text is devoted to a more in-depth assessment of particular activities in precise areas. Nicholson (2002) tells how an understanding of science and technology is stimulated in targeted areas of rural Norfolk and Suffolk through programmes devised by the University of East Anglia. Similarly, Askham (2002) describes how a third-age rural learners' project in Bedfordshire and Hertfordshire, under the auspices of the University of Cambridge Board of Continuing Education, holds courses in venues such as church halls and small museums. This learning programme is devised to 'relate to the putative students' frames of reference in the local community and draw heavily on local landscape and history' (p.135).

## 2.6 Motivating and Supporting Lifelong Learning and the Ufi

Participation is a theme that recurs throughout an extensive proportion of lifelong learning literature. The extent and value of participation in learning varies directly according to the degree of motivation and support for learning. These two concepts, which embrace, amongst others, academic and pastoral understandings, connect individuals' needs with incentives and initiatives in order to facilitate active and beneficial learning projects. Some authors present an integrated overview of motivation and support: others choose to concentrate on different practical or emotional aspects, or refer to experiences in specific settings.

Through an increasing analysis of the literature on lifelong learning it appears that many authors regard the concept as solely 'informal'; that is, directed at non-traditional students, and often non-certificated. Several writings of this type are collected together by Richardson and Wolfe (2001).

Jeffs (2001) evaluates the historical shifts in balance between informal and formal approaches to education; but finds no history that he considers adequate enough to influence present principles and practices. He suggests that all present educators should not focus on the differences between the two modes of delivery, but develop a shared role in promoting lifelong learning. Jeffs does not, however, adhere to his own argument when he maintains that it is the dialogue inherent in informal learning that engages people in democratic discourse, and they thereby get 'the opportunity to identify the knowledge they value and to negotiate their own learning pathway' (p.46). In a similar way, Wolfe (2001) explains how lifelong learning is generated by the voluntary and open-ended nature of conversational relationships. Participants share their experiences and perceptions, resulting in the emergence of changing views and new understandings of, for example, educational and social issues.

Banks (2001) explores the meanings of values, in respect of human rights, multi-cultural society and religion. She indicates conflicts between personal, professional and agency standards of behaviour, by quoting the reaction of an Irish catholic voluntary youth centre worker aged sixteen to a fourteen years old pregnant girl who asks him for advice (p.70). France (2001) discusses the notion of evaluation, especially judgement against standards, and knowledge-backed and increasingly participatory elements.

Rees et al. (2000) combine qualitative and quantitative approaches in an investigation of participation in the learning society. They use a questionnaire survey to collect empirical evidence of 'types of learning episodes throughout the life course' (p.175). The data is analysed into different concepts of lifelong learning that represent people's pattern of involvement resulting from their social background and personal desire. A final set of five lifelong learning trajectories are derived. Statistics are produced which show that the frequency (that is, the total number of times each particular survey result per trajectory occurs) of lifelong learners is virtually equal to that of non-participants: together they represent nearly two-thirds of the cohort of 1,104 education and training histories. These research findings illustrate why policymakers who are committed to the ethos of lifelong learning continually try to devise new ways to widen access, move boundaries and break down barriers, in order to increase participation rates.

Therefore, it is a massive task for stakeholders, and practitioners, in education to produce successful and satisfied participants in lifelong learning and the Ufi. An inevitable demand is to sustain learning through motivation and support.

An advice document (Fryer, 1999), from the National Advisory Group for Continuing Education and Lifelong Learning (NAGCELL) to the DfEE, focuses on stimulating demand by creating learning cultures related to contemporary social change. This kind of change is characterized by new political agendas for race, gender, disability, environment and transport. In addition, the social divisions concerning access to income, employment, housing, health care, education and information are examined with a view to their elimination, or, at least, narrowing. The publication signifies that lifelong learning 'constitutes a key resource in enabling people to participate in shaping society, and to take advantage of social change, rather than being its possible victims' (p.7).

Tett (2002) embraces the concept of democratic renewal as implemented in Scotland in terms of inclusive education. She proposes that attempts to fuse the existing boundaries between the interests of the state, the market and civil society will result in understandings that lead to positive changes. This idea does not operate easily, possibly due to each party's different expectations from education, or some ambiguity in government policies. Tett says:

> One the one hand, there is an emphasis on the improvement of people's skills and individual capabilities whilst, on the other, there is a wider focus on the economic and social forces that exclude people. This debate is clearly visible in state polices about lifelong learning and social inclusion.
>
> (Tett, 2002, p.60)

Nevertheless, in line with others, such as Bartlett, Rees and Watts (2000), and Gilchrist (2001), Tett is clear in her belief that the formation of partnerships acts as both a motivator and a supporter of learning, facilitating access and widening participation throughout the lifespan. Bartlett et al. (2000) interpret 'partnership' as the co-operation of adult guidance services; a crucial common factor, in five countries in the European Union (EU), for 'the enhancement of economic competitiveness, the avoidance of social exclusion and the fostering of a 'learning society'' (p.4). The funding of career guidance is found, generally, to be a divisive issue, and one of five resolutions suggested is finance through local partnerships involving public, private and voluntary sectors—as in France and Italy. By contrast, those in the UK—Information, Advice and Guidance for Adults Partnerships—are centrally funded. Evidently this is a political decision, and therefore subject to change.

Gilchrist (2001) narrows the concept of partnerships to informal learning networks within the context of a community. She argues that personal needs, like access to information and support, are met through human social interaction in groups sustained by trust and respect. One could quickly regard this approach to education as too restrictive, so it is reassuring to read that Gilchrist accepts, and subsequently discusses how to overcome, the limitations of the parameter of community organizations. She says that 'informal educators are often in a position to bring together various 'stakeholders' to develop a joint strategy for solving the initial problem' (p.111).

Tett (2002) is emphatic that if community educators make political and ethical choices, and are self-critical of their practice, then socio-economic advantages do emerge. Families become learning units and sites; an outcome illustrated by a literacy programme to tackle family discord, which has a curriculum of child-adult conversations, budgeting, and writing timetables. Social exclusion is reduced as communities, parents and schools co-operate to create their own projects, and active citizenship replaces the polarity of client and consumer.

The difficulties of the task are borne out by a scheme to improve a multiple disadvantaged urban area. Its two aims are; first, to encourage parental involvement, hence increasing children's educational attainment, and secondly, to foster partnerships between home, school and community. In reality, a fulltime community educator prepares courses in response to local need. Help is given to adults to run before-school and after-school clubs; thus inspiring decision-making and autonomy. Parents soon become assertive in questioning the school's practices: the result is conflict between the different purposes, and the interpretation, of the 'supportive role'. Tett comments on this outcome:

The headteacher wished to see more emphasis in the programme being placed on the educational development of children, and thus raising of their academic standard. The community educator on the other hand felt that the parents' right to challenge the school's way of doing things should have priority.

(Tett, 2002, p.50)

The OECD (2000) published a report of its empirically-based study about how eight countries, including the UK, encourage lifelong learning. Initial discussion centres on the importance and nature of motivating students. Raising educational standards and preventing student dropout are deemed essential aspirations. These are achieved by dealing with physical and psychological factors, such as health and nutrition, self-confidence and reward.

The writers subsequently cover the wider dimension of recent policies and approaches that affect young people. They explain some present and longer-term problems, and their solutions, in tandem. For instance, they argue that demoralizing anti-social behaviour, like bullying and truancy, can be replaced by motivating aspects of learning—maybe computer skills—through the integration of educational initiatives devised from a holistic stance. After exploring further educational issues, such as student-centred assessment, counselling services and the powerful role model of the teacher, the OECD concludes that these are fundamental supportive factors of lifelong learning. They suggest that out-of-school centres, like the '100 that operate under the YOUTHREACH scheme' (p.45), provide an excellent psychologically motivating learning environment, based on the positive impact of learning—in terms of the acquisition of skills, trust and respect—on self-confidence. This is a common theme in much of the literature about lifelong learning. Dench and Regan (2000) quote from a study of mature women (Cox and Pascall, 1994) whose continued learning 'imparted an almost mystical quality in search of self-fulfilment' (p.8).

In the context of the UK, the report provides evidence of hostility towards education from many teenagers and some factual information is presented regarding the continuing inequality of access to FE and HE. Concern is also expressed about an emerging gender divide. It appears that the academic accomplishments of boys is comparing unfavourably with girls' achievements. The boys' tendency to be less well motivated has led to research to uncover the causes (MacDonald et al., 1999; Mahoney, 2003). In the context of adult education and training, McGivney (1999, 2004) suggests that educational practitioners and employers must together devise effective strategies that encourage men to be lifelong learners.

The report proceeds with details of three separate case studies located in Barnsley, Chesterfield and the London borough of Barnet (pp.183–189). In each instance, steps are being taken to stimulate lifelong learning. They include, respectively: the SNAPT programme of specialized and self-esteem training for assistants, aimed at improving the motivation of pupils with learning and/or behavioural difficulties (p.183); the Thirty-Nine steps initiative, a model tailored for building knowledge, commitment and understanding via work experience; the strategy for change devised by one particular school, illustrated by adopting a new name, individual student feedback interviews and staff review meetings.

Overall the publication gives a varied account of what works in innovation in education, in terms of how to encourage participation in lifelong learning. However, in closing, it states that 'it is notoriously difficult to measure motivation' (p.189).

Another report about lifelong learning, by Plewis and Preston (2001), prioritizes different aspects of the concept. It evaluates the benefits of learning, and presents a framework that 'emphasizes the formal aspects of lifelong learning, in particular post-compulsory education in all forms and at all ages' (p.2). Using a classification of lifelong learning policies (Hillage et al., 2000), the writers cite the Ufi, through Learndirect as its broker of learning materials, under 'changes to partnership and brokerage arrangements'—in other words, a provider initiative linked to purchaser demand. Yet this link may be tenuous. Like all promoters of learning the Ufi must attract, motivate and support participants in order to exist.

Hodgson (2000) explores the challenge of widening participation. As background information she mentions two points. The first is that, for 16–19 year olds, participation and achievement rates were in 'system slowdown' (p.55) for five years prior to the millennium, after which there was a level trend. The second is that, participation in full-time education is strongly linked to socio-economic group.

Hodgson contends that participation in learning can be widened by breaking down major internal and external barriers within, and beyond, the education and training sector. Resulting from her qualitative research, she finds that these mostly comprise practical issues. 'Internal' embodies timetabling, contracts, traditional teaching practices and types of learning accommodation. 'External' incorporates lack of money, course incompatibility for academic, general vocational and vocational qualifications, and the ill-defined link from the last of these to the job market. She nonetheless remains convinced that widening participation is achievable and argues for an 'infrastructure' of ten key challenges. The most predominant is how to identify, and cope with, learner support issues. Two of the others are, how to understand the potential and limitations of information and communication technology (ICT), and how to provide adequate financial support.

McDonald and Edwards (2000) edit a book of articles about widening participation through the Ufi. Its particular dimension is ways in which libraries support lifelong learning. At the beginning, Wright says:

> Ufi is about easy access to information and learning opportunities, in learning places and spaces that are both virtual and in friendly physical environments with helpful supportive staff and support. Well, that sounds like libraries to me.
>
> (Wright, 2000, p.12)

Law (2000) develops this vision while contributing to creating a networking information society that will facilitate learning through a combined political and technical agenda. In his capacity as a Library and Information Commissioner he knows that ample money is readily available from the Government for library training—for instance, from the New Opportunities Fund. Law urges the setting up of cross-sectoral and collective working practises, such as local Metropolitan Area Networks, which 'will make local resources even more available because they do not actually require you to go physically to other people's libraries' (p.23).

Further support for the Ufi's perception of libraries as a facility paramount to enabling learning through life is given in a case study report of Birmingham Library Services. Rogers (2000) maintains that 'through our lifelong learning-related activities we fully support the Ufi concept' (p.35). Drawing on her experience as the manager she lists some library-based activities that exemplify the connection—early learning with leisure, family literacy and homework clubs. In addition, a partnership in the Ufi ADAPT European Social Fund Community Initiative sustains a high-quality learning centre for SMEs based in business information services in the Central Library.

Reiterating such views is Hogg (2000) who represents the City Library and Arts Centre, Sunderland. She commends the Ufi for its unique and simple registration procedure which 'makes the return to learning as easy and uncomplicated as possible (p.43). On the other hand, Parker (2000), the

Independent Library Learner 1997 Award Winner, while giving a personal insight of the therapeutic effect, more often reveals the negative experiences of using a library.

Lore and Hurd (2001) concentrate on a collection of writings about lifelong language learning. They aim to identify recent changes within the context of educational institutions. Collectively the book's authors draw a parallel between the need to maintain motivation, and the means of support and expertise during language learning. Lore maintains that tutors are themselves lifelong learners, reflecting and adapting learning in a common purpose with students. Both parties are also in an intricate relationship with the organization, hence 'creating the learning environment in which teaching takes place' (Fig.1, p.12).

The chapters by Woodin (2001), and one by Walker (2001), focus on the practicalities, and the underlying theoretical principles, of language teaching and learning. They likewise suggest that tutors and students go through similar processes, such as planning, skills development and resource management. Murphy (2001) extends these ideas by highlighting the role of the reflective practitioner. She regards giving support as enhancing one's own practice through continuing professional development (CPD); meaning, therefore, that subject knowledge and linguistic skills are updated, research is undertaken, and self-evaluation critical analysis—using available models (Figs.3–5, p.193)—is engaged in.

The teaching of language is augmented by the use of information and learning technology (ILT). But how far does this tool support the independent learning process and its intended outcomes? In an extensive section of the book, Wright and White (2001) investigate ILT's general role before explaining the computer-based applications, their usage, and their incorporation into curricula. The authors pose pedagogical and practical questions for people to ask prior to becoming obligated, for example, 'How interactive is it?' and 'Is it value for money?' (pp.100–101). Ultimately, evidenced by rapid and sophisticated technological change—like ubiquitous computing—they forecast a lifetime of learning opportunities.

Support, not always ambition, is the key to participation in lifelong learning. Women learners in particular are often not supported by those closest to them. Family members who have come to rely on a woman's maternal and home-making skills can feel threatened if some time is withdrawn to concentrate on learning (Morrison, 1992). More crèches; foundation courses that incorporate study skills, tuition techniques and understanding assessment; modular, self-directed, part-time and flexi-time learning; APEL: all of these are facilities or measures that could result in learner retention rates rising, and reasons for drop-out diminishing.

Auto/biographical work by Thompson (2000) widens this view; bringing it up to date by elaborating on 'how informal learning and formal education have both helped to shape our lives' (p.1). She maps out literary journeys of reflection about working class women's determination to alter unacceptable conditions and tensions allied to class and gender identity. Warning of the increasing polarization of women in British class society, she argues, on behalf of academic feminism's remit to inspire, social analysis and change, that educational institutions should promote collaboration between women that is 'democratic and egalitarian, critical but inclusive' (p.105).

Using excerpts in 'illustrations' about Northern Ireland, Trade Unionism and Ruskin College, Oxford, Thompson's book chronicles individual women's experience of, and critical thinking about, motivation and support for learning. In the first scenario of the Women's Group, which meets in the Rosemount Resource Centre in Derry, interaction brings about solidarity, mutual support and persistence to make up for lost time. A group member Winnie, born one of twelve children, her schooling seriously interrupted, and now divorced for seventeen years, says, 'I feel I have got a second chance to further my education, I have built up a lot of friendships doing this which has brightened up my life a lot' (p.117).

To try to understand technology is to help to widen participation in learning. Word processing, communicating, internet access to information, and computer-based training packages can all motivate education almost anywhere at any time.

The Ufi considers information and communication technology (ICT) to be a priority learning support mechanism. Learndirect centres and dispersed online learning environments use specially commissioned open learning materials (Clark, 2000). The National Institute of Adult Continuing Education (NIACE) believes that ICT is the new basic skill: it increasingly permeates work, education and leisure pursuits. Individuals who become proficient in ICT reduce their risk of exclusion from society (Clark and Englebright, 2003). Yet people with little money cannot afford the 'luxury' of ICT. Lack of finance has repercussions for lifelong learning in that not everyone who wants to study gets the opportunity to do so. To alleviate this situation Robertson (1998) favours vouchers, training credits and individual learning accounts as incentives—all have been activated.

Action to redistribute public funding through these means is, say Smith and Spurling (2001):

> To target support on family and community issues, and to tackle the problems of social exclusion and the low participation in post-compulsory learning of disadvantaged and deprived social groups.
> (Smith and Spurling, 2001, p.120)

Further recommendations are highlighted by Fryer (1999). They come from a working group convened by Finn and its ensuing paper 'Lifelong Learning and the Benefit System' (p.18), and result from an analysis of how the said system impacts on participation in learning.

Perraton (2000) and Williams (2000) both explore some monetary aspects of learning. The former is interested in who benefits, and who pays; the latter addresses financial problems and possibilities.

Perraton stresses that education is a human right. In response to public demand, and because it creates socio-economic advantages, governments pay for education. They are unable to satisfy all learning requirements through the conventional system, so open and distance learning at tertiary level has become the inevitable additional supply route. On the premise that a fundamental concept of lifelong learning is the individual's right to be educated further at any stage of life, Williams argues that one should be able to delay all, or part, of initial compulsory, government-funded learning until a time of one's own choosing

## 2.7 The Prospects for Lifelong Learning and the Ufi

For many advocates of learning the new millennium marks the beginning of its future. All the contributors to a book edited by Green and Lucus (1999) embrace the overall idea of realigning the further education (FE) sector for the twenty-first century, whilst individually putting the emphasis on its different factions. Educational policy and practice, management criteria, curricula guidelines and professional development are some aspects of learning that they choose to investigate.

Young (1999) thinks that the UK's qualifications system is out of date. As the principal determinant of the curriculum in most educational institutions it needs reform 'based on greater unity of academic and vocational learning, more flexibility of choice for students, inclusiveness, and learner coherence' (p.200). With a view to the prospects of a new century, Guile and Lucas (1999) describe the 'learning professional'. They allude to research about the demise of the traditional concept, and to 'five shifts of knowledge' (pp.216–217)—one being, teacher-centred to learner-centred pedagogy—then stress the resulting requirement for responsible obligations to ongoing economic, social, technological and educational change.

Guile and Hayton (1999) appraise, against theoretical, or practical, past and present trends, the potential of information and learning technology (ILT). They outline the learner-centred emphasis of the 1980s in line with different perceptions of experiential learning—namely, andragogy, the 'outcomes' model, and open and distance learning. In order to expand this approach, the writers cite later initiatives aimed at the FE sector. Critically assessing a government policy document (DfEE, 1998), they say it 'assumes that a clear link exists between access to information via ILT and increased interest in learning . . . also assumes that colleges have a key role in supporting the objectives of the University for Industry (Ufi)' (p.121).

In conclusion, Guile and Hayton warn about the necessary rethinking of learning as a social process compliant with the required dual usage of ILT as an information search tool, and a resource for collaborating with others to create new knowledge. Only then can ILT become an effective part of the future agenda of lifelong learning.

Green and Lucus, by writing the book's first and final chapters, chart the FE sector's intricate and fragmented historical background, especially the lack of cohesion of voluntary and technical education, and respective funding. They argue that, despite the establishment of a national funding strategy, the situation is unchanged.

Green and Lucus subsequently suggest that a future crisis of identity could be avoided if colleges have 'a clearer definition of their function and clientele' (p.231)—in essence; exact boundaries, explicit missions and minimal competition. The recommended realignment is that FE colleges become solely 18+ institutions for all sub-degree provision; 16–19 year olds being catered for in a school sixth-form or sixth-form colleges. Thus, their hope is for—subject to changes of control and funding—an eventual comprehensive tertiary sector for 16–19 year olds within the wider context of lifelong learning.

Field (2000) sees a future for lifelong learning within a new technological paradigm, driven at speed by global competitiveness and primarily organized around the policy consensus of intergovernmental agencies. He warns though of ambivalence towards this trend from adult educators who, while appreciating the recovery from neglect of FE and HE, believe it presents a fragmented view of learning.

Field himself is confident that 'lifelong learning will not go away': of its impending, and ultimate, state he adds:

> But while the term may be replaced, the disparate bundle of concerns and challenges that have been given the label are so deeply rooted in contemporary economic tendencies, social processes and cultural patterns that there is no prospect of their disappearing.
> (Field, 2000, p.33)

Murphy (2001) is also forward-looking. She questions how language needs in Europe can be realistically met in an information age beset by increasing globalization. At the same time, she monitors the transition of ongoing programmes. DIALANG, a research project about language proficiency assessment, is informative. Equally so is the European Commission funded Socrates II (2000–2006): it incorporates subsidiaries, of which one is the Minerva Action on Open and Distance Learning. Consequently, Murphy is confident in predicting future trends.

Greater numbers, and a wider range, of personnel will engage in work-related and work-based language learning. There will be shorter non-specialist courses aligned to Institution Wide Language Programmes (IWPP) and reflecting a vocational bent. These changes represent the challenges and implications ahead for the lifelong learning of language students and tutors alike.

A long-term, broad motivational strategy for lifelong learning would be to mix economic interests with socio-cultural dimensions (Smith & Spurling, 2001). Material values should balance the intrinsic worth of the human being.

According to Nomura (2000) the principles of the theory of lifelong integrated education consist of the combination of human renaissance, co-existence, and the creation of a new civilization. She believes that lifelong learning is aimed at people's holistic development 'with the earnest hope of contributing thereby even in a small way to building a brighter future for the world and its children' (p.142).

Media announcements about conference venues may indicate concern about the future of learning. In 2003, for example, the demise of judgement and the decline of the rigorous study of intellectual ideas were two issues under debate by academics, journalists, novelists, scientists, artists and activists at the Institute of Ideas and Goodenough College, London—

a venue specifically dedicated to improving understanding and tolerance in the contemporary world. During the same year, 'From term time to life time' was the theme of a conference in Birmingham where discussion centred on a strategy for the future of volunteering in HE. This is a matter prioritised by government, and encouraged by the availability of £27 from the Higher Education Active Community Fund.

The final report of the Skills and Enterprise Agenda in the United Kingdom and Northern Ireland (1999, p.49) mentions points in line with the Ufi's own publicity as regards building a lifelong learning system for the future. Ann Limb, the Chief Executive, emphasizes the Ufi's experience in stimulating demand, supports the concept of working in partnership with high street banks to reinforce the drive to improve skills development, and vows an active role in delivering the initiative (www.ufi.com). The Ufi Press Office regularly updates the Strategic Plan. Releases include: 'Ufi/Learndirect welcomes the Chancellor of the Exchequer's budget announcement of a packaged advice and training aimed at SMEs, and looks forward to working as a member of the steering group set up to take the initiative forward' (2003), and 'integrated national and local Integrated, Advice and Guidance (IAG) services to launch later this year' (2004).

## 2.8 Epilogue

I hope that this exploration of the literature will have provided detailed coverage of all aspects of lifelong learning and the Ufi. Not least is the relationship between the two. I am aware that, being a lifelong learner myself, I must remain impartial and objective while appraising the work of others. I am a virtual participant observer in the field of lifelong learning and the Ufi. The sources I have examined, and discussed, provide historical background, research findings, ideas and opinions. Reference to published work also suggests that this particular case study can be related to previous research.

By design, the review has compartmentalized the literature on lifelong learning and the Ufi. At the same time, however, the reader is made aware of the interplay between many facets of the research topic—for example, a discussion of libraries applies equally significantly to the motivation and support for lifelong learning and the Ufi, as it does to establishing where they take place. Throughout the review the notion of 'change' has played a pivotal role by being ascribed to numerous interconnecting themes in the complex worlds of lifelong learning and the Ufi.

The literature has highlighted the authors' arguments, reasoning, and supporting evidence and illustrations; hence suggesting that the research topic is multifaceted. It was purposefully selected from the substantial amount available on lifelong learning, in order to analyse the concept. Contrastingly, few writers independent of the Ufi have published work about it, either as a sole or integrated topic. The tendency instead is to repeat, then interpret in their own words, part of the Ufi's own literature, and thereby reinforce an argument. For example, McKie (2000), in her exploration of adult viability in a technological world, quotes 'Networks of guidance and support are the central mission of the University for Industry (Ufi)' (p.279) as one illustration of supporting lifelong learning.

Overall, some foundations for building a progressive lifelong learning system, of which the Ufi is part, have been laid by the work of the authors featured in this review. The scope of the literature has revealed that, learning and learning innovations, whether occurring within homes or institutions, by individuals or cohorts, require motivation and support from their inception to conclusion. Only the true futures of lifelong learning and the Ufi remain an enigma.

The final understanding drawn from this literature review is that the Ufi is not merely context specific, but is a dynamic educational synthesis. Characterized by constant activity and change it is a medium through which to explore the concept of lifelong learning. The scene is now set for me to expand on, and explain, all the further dimensions of my research.

# Chapter 3
# Methodology

## 3.1 Introduction

The object of undertaking this empirical study is to attempt to establish what factors determine the successful implementation of a named policy—the University for Industry—within the field of education. Specifically, the study aims to ascertain and judge the effectiveness of the Ufi within the framework of lifelong learning, and vice-versa. This chapter contains descriptions, explanations and deliberations about the overall investigative approach that I used as the means of satisfying the aims of my research.

Methodology is important because it 'shapes which methods are used and how each method is used' (Silverman, 2000, p.88). Its fitness for purpose is essential, in that, the methods must be a workable means of enquiring into the subject matter of the project, thereby ensuring that the maximum amount of valuable and reliable data, relevant to the research focus, is gathered. My choice of methodology was deliberate, based on the expectation that it could be effectively used to study, represent and analyse the particular research phenomena.

The ontological and epistemological positions behind the research have been decided: they were outlined in Chapter 1. Guided, therefore, by my understanding of these preliminary theoretical concepts, I am using a qualitative research approach to carry out a case study within the non-positivist tradition.

I am also influenced by the definition of postmodern theory as an attitude to history in its broadest sense—that is, the relationship between the past, the present and the future (Breisach, 2003). In addition, I accept that postmodernism is a condition that includes all forms of change—cultural, political and economic (Kumar, 1997). Combining these two interpretations of the concept keeps me aware throughout my inquiry that change is relative, and, though not instantaneous, is increasingly rapid.

I am critical of ontological objectivity—an ideal known as veridicality (Eisner, 1992)—whereby things are seen as they are; their actual features are revealed. I would argue instead that one's knowledge of the truth is never direct; it is always mediated. By carrying out a practical investigation I am aiming to demonstrate that the concept of truth depends on frameworks of perception.

Research is a construction: all the people involved, including the researcher, are interacting to build meanings. Thus, through direct access to the research context, data becomes available for analysis. The results of this procedure help in establishing the authenticity of the subject matter. A kind of 'symbolic truth' is found as its unique character is captured in the unique words of those with experience in, and perspectives on, the case.

The fieldwork involved the use of a pre-prepared interview schedule as the research instrument. Interviewing individual participants resulted in two sets of data being collected: one came from Ufi providers, and the other from Learndirect students. Each set reflected the respective respondents' understanding of the Ufi's attitude to lifelong learning. The data was audio-recorded and subsequently transcribed verbatim. The transcripts then became the constituents of a reasoned qualitative analysis. This involved me in the development and testing of all of the data gathered in the fieldwork. The work culminated in the generation of themed interpretations of the interview data by using grounded theory. Hence, the total methodological strategy was appropriate for drawing a conclusion from the research findings.

## 3.2 Case Study Method

Historically, case studies, whether individual, cumulative or comparative, have been associated with many branches of knowledge. They have benefited academic disclosures, and been widely used during professional development and policy decision-making. Hamel et al. (1993) say:

> In the midst of such diversity, however, is the categorical singularity of case studies. The research aim may be on describing, understanding, or explaining, but it is the focused n-of-one character that sets a case study apart as a method amongst methods.
>
> (Hamel et al., 1993, p.v)

Thus there is no rigid definition of case study research. Rather, it is a strategy that embraces both philosophical and disciplinary perspectives, and shifts between the experimental scientific paradigm and the rival naturalistic model. It is the 'all-encompassing method—covering the logic of design, data collection techniques, and specific approaches to data analysis' (Yin, 2003, p.14). In writing about the design and methods, and the applications, of case study research Yin (1994, 2003) emphasizes, yet differentiates between, its descriptive, exploratory or pilot, and explanatory salient elements. In fact, as separate criteria, these can classify whole studies or be applied to different parts of the same study.

The scope and variety of this type of empirical inquiry will usually be determined by the selection of a topic, referred to as the 'case': it might be singular or plural, an event or individual, policies or organizations. The case must correlate directly to the purpose of the research, which could be to help solve behavioural problems or influence curriculum policy in education. The inquiry process is managed with a specific aim in mind—that knowledge in the said discipline will be increased. To this end, data is gathered. 'Data are nothing more than ordinary bits and pieces of information found in the environment' (Merriam, 1988, p.67), but the usefulness of their 'type' is conditional upon the 'type' of the case study. This influences the choice of collection instrument; for example, an interview schedule in a qualitative study and a survey in quantitative research have different, but equally significant, bearing.

In order to comply with the interpretive canon of research, the basic premise of doing a case study is to examine in detail a few situations; often just one—as I do in this study—having regard for the uniqueness of the case. The single-case study design is appropriate because the interrelationship between lifelong learning and the Ufi is distinct. For Stake (1995) case study research is an art; a human skill applied to a unique case. It is the accomplishment of many facets, such as asking questions, collecting, analysing and interpreting data, reporting and reflecting. 'A good case study illuminates the context in which the phenomenon is studied, as well as the phenomenon itself' (Raffe, 2003, p.ix).

Once the case is identified, literature relevant to the subject matter and its context, whether it is a published research database or a non-database written critique, will act as background information. At the same time, the appropriate theoretical orientation steers and permeates the whole interactive process, enlightening further choices that may lead to the detection of new theory.

While conducting holistic inquiry in the 'real' world, naturally occurring data is captured about experiences and attitudes. Producing detailed descriptions and 'rounded understandings' based on the perspectives of the respondents in their typical setting is a prime feature of this method. The approach is to take the 'emic' (Stake, 1995) perspective whereby people are studied by penetrating their frames of meaning: the researcher sustains empathetic neutrality; that is, uses personal insight while taking a non-judgemental stance. A further aspiration is to eliminate complexity in the case by establishing relationships between happenings and concepts.

Inevitably all forms of data collection technique have to stop and lead on to analysis; again varied in orientation. In a quantitative study, handling data from the physical sciences may involve descriptive or inferential numerical calculations, summaries to include totals and ranges, and technical manipulative methods like chi-square and probability. These can also support a qualitative study. Bassey (1999) concentrates on the educational 'theory-seeking and theory-testing case study' (p.3), a model which claims that data analysis nurtures professional discourse, and, in turn, reforms practice and policy. A particular characteristic is the progression to non-collaborated general statements, known as 'fuzzy generalizations' for pedagogy. Accordingly, it bypasses the alternative traditional route expected of the experimental and survey approaches of positivism with their need to concentrate on the validity and reliability of the findings before generalizing to, and across, populations.

Research analysis is the means by which to arrive at the claims and, or, findings from the collected data: it involves the sequential sorting of the same. Discourse analysis produces 'readings of talk, text and contexts . . . that are warranted by attention to the detail of texts and that lend coherence to the discourse being studied' (Gill, 1996, p.147). In a case study, analysis is first applied to the 'case' then, in order to draw conclusions, it intensifies and widens to take in the focus of the project. The common denominator of the three by-products of this evaluative stage is convincing evidence.

Just as empirical findings are peculiar to the case, then reciprocally the 'analysis has also to be appropriate and not a straightjacket that deforms your findings' (Gillham, 2000, p.25). Sometimes, interest may lie in the single case studied for itself because it has general significance—perhaps national or global. Alternatively, the conclusions may display some ambivalence towards generalizability; the conceptualization of which has attracted an abundance of alternative terms (Schofield, 1990). These include: 'comparability'—the aim is to compare by criterion, norm or personal referencing, as in the case of examinations by pass mark, age group or past performance; 'transferability'—the process of spontaneously associating the results with a different case; 'naturalistic generalization'—a ubiquitous feature of the human tendency to try to make sense of, and be guided by, everyday occurrences; 'fittingness'—grounded theories 'fit' if they are recognizable and of relevance to those studied (Glaser and Strauss, 1967).

Yet among qualitative investigators some consensus does exist. They agree that 'thick description' which, according to Richardson (1996) was introduced by Geertz (1979), describes 'detailed, contextually sensitive, meaningful research' (p.27). It is 'an effort aimed at interpretation, at getting below the surface to that most enigmatic aspect of the human condition: the construction of meaning' (Eisner, 1998, p.15), and it is essential to add 'richness' to research reports. Distinctive terminology, like 'looking cool' and 'the macho lads' (Mac an Ghaill, (1996, p.144), is used to capture the complexity of aspects—here for instance, demeanour—embedded in a precise case. It may be that qualitative researchers dismiss the idea of making laws for universal application, but accept that, if the crucial element of thick description is present, then what arises from one study can be transported to impact on other situations.

The concrete end product of the case study method is the report. Although it endorses a complete academic work, there is no set format. Diversity of writing style usually corresponds with the relationship between researchers and their respective sponsors. This interaction is responsible for allocating reporting space to, and balancing discussion of, each component, be it literary background or methodology. Also, some authors of research, aware that the distinction between findings, claims and conclusions is vague in their work, opt to combine these elements in the final summary.

In relating my own case study I am aiming for clarity of expression and purpose in order 'to provide an in-depth picture of a particular area of the educational world, chosen because it is relatively self-contained' (Drever, 1995, p.7). The basic conjecture is that everything learned from executing my research will be documented.

## 3.3 What is the case of the case study?

The unique 'case'—the phenomenon about which data is collected and analysed—is the 'Ufi providers and their students, in the north-west region of England'. Hence, my research is clearly defined in situation, the fieldwork being located in fourteen Learndirect learning centres within the jurisdiction of different 'hubs' in this particular geographical area. A hub is committed to linking providers and students: the former establish nuclei, offer support, and set up networking services; thereby assuring the latter of a high quality, accessible and secure point of entry into learning.

I am trying to ascertain the views of Ufi providers by gathering information from the appropriate people in all of the centres. These are individuals occupying a similar role within the Learndirect network. A concerted effort was made to contact providers, and subsequently students, in a broad spectrum of settings—educational, recreational, commercial and industrial—as a means of securing valid and reliable feedback. The fourteen centres, twenty-two providers, and thirty-seven students/clients are described using details amassed from observation during my visits to the locations, and through my personal contact with the respective individuals or their minder. Although the centres are all named Learndirect centres, they are exclusive.

Details about the particular centres, followed by an account of the role of every affiliated person who gave me information, is presented according to the chronological order in which data was collected. All the names are fictitious to protect people's privacy and guarantee anonymity. They deliberately resemble, and begin with the same letter, as the 'real' ones; a strategy I devised to constantly jog my memory, and to aid accurate recall of the fieldwork. In addition, the providers and the students are coded for future reference—(P1, P2, P3 etc.) and (S1, S2, S3 etc.)—in sequential order of their respective interviews.

At this juncture I will deliberately deviate sharply from my previous style of writing, albeit temporarily over the next section. 'All writing is founded on effective description—the basic literary draughtsmanship that allows you to express your sense impressions clearly' (Cusick, 2000, p.3). The academic content lies with the 'descriptive theory' (Yin, 2003)—that which 'covers the criteria of what needs to be described' and is 'openly stated ahead of time' (p.23). In line with this descriptive element of case study research, and to emphasize and verify the illustrative character therein, my intention ahead is to give the reader a 'living image' of the fundamental aspects, such as the logistics and timing, of doing fieldwork.

The data collection process was an interpersonal phase of my research. I gathered information according to a straightforward fieldwork plan. It is appropriate, therefore, to write about its execution in a simple way—by using description. I supplemented this process by writing my reflective thoughts in a diary. Everything that happened was given expression in a more atmospheric colloquial way, a familiar everyday conversational style.

Walford (1991) refers to a genre of qualitative research reports (Bell and Newby, 1977; Roberts, 1981; Mac an Ghaill, 1988) that 'give accounts of the 'backstage' research activities and unveil some of the idiosyncrasies of person and circumstances which are seen as being at the heart of the research process' (p.3). Similarly, in order to present a realistic account of some of the practicalities of this particular study, I am going to include parts of my 'researcher's log'. This form of writing serves to explain to the reader how Learndirect centres operate and, at the same time, allows them to explore my method of collecting data. However, I remain ever mindful of the need for the subsequent academic interpretation of that data.

The fieldwork began in the month of September, with the first two weeks spent securing the providers' co-operation for this exploratory phase of the project. A pre-arranged telephone interview became the starting point of the data collection process; this the preferred mode of the initial participating centre, Kinesmere Learndirect. Drawing from the information thus given: it is a private limited training company based in the Lantinshire hub where it occupies a purpose-built suite of informal classrooms in a converted mill, in a town once at the heart of the thriving cotton trade of the early twentieth century. The building houses other small commercial enterprises, some of which are clients of Kinesmere paying for instruction in ICT.

I spoke to an executive director of the company, Catherine Harris (P1). Her role is to sell and operate skills improvement courses, principally to the self-employed and independent business sector, in order to sustain a profit-making existence for the Learndirect centre. She answered the questions openly, only hesitating when reference was made to financial matters. However, Catherine denied me access to the centre's students/clients by referring to certain clauses of the Data Protection Act (1998).

The first centre that I actually visited was at Hanes College in the Cherfield and Wallis hub. A traditional 16+ educational institution built in 1963, it is conveniently located on the main 'A' road through Widding, adjacent to the Town Hall and Central Police Station. The college draws learners from an approximate twenty-mile radius of this industrial town, where previous heavy manufacturing has given way to the provision of service sector employment.

John Spence (P2), a Training Advisor who works for the Training and Development Directorate, provided me with information about Learndirect. At his suggestion the interview took place in a small annex of the Main Reception. There was a learning centre on the 'Level Four' equipped with three dedicated Learndirect computer assisted set-ups, accessible between 9.00am and 9.00pm Monday to Thursday, with an earlier finish at 4.30pm on Fridays. However, no invitation was extended, and thus no apparent opportunity became available, to see this actual working area. There were no Learndirect students in the college at the time; therefore interviewing this cohort was impossible. Also, the fact that Hanes College had decided that very morning to sever all connections with the Ufi and Learndirect, made it unrealistic for me to seek access to students' information via this particular provider in the foreseeable future.

Four days later I visited Wilken College, part of the Wilken and Leerton hub. Compared to others within the North-West Region this hub is very small geographically, but has a high concentration of people. A purpose-built Learndirect 'flagship' centre occupies a prominent position at the entrance to this traditional 16–19 college; itself situated in the town centre and serving an urban area. Practical features of the centre are a crèche, disabled facilities, a lift, parking and long opening hours—weekdays 9.00am–8.00pm, plus Saturday mornings. Its main function is to oversee the college-based Learndirect venues—one in each Wilken campus, two at Leerton, one at Russell Road, and one at Marsh Street. Two outreach centres also come under the same remit.

I interviewed Alex Foden (P3), the Centre Manager. An unemployed welder at the age of forty he came back to college to study, then got the job, and now prides himself on the fact that ten years later his personal experience helps him to identify with student 'returners'. The second interviewee was Ann (P4), a Skills for Life (SfL) mentor previously based in the said department of the college. She had transferred full-time to oversee the tutors, and to integrate SfL provision with Learndirect. Agreement to the use of a small tape recorder was made before each sitting, and no notes were made; an arrangement I carried over to my subsequent conversation with Winnie (S1), a 'third-age' student who does courses on at least three mornings a week.

The third negotiated invitation to engage in fieldwork had come from a Learndirect Centre run by Vactrum Disability Services (VDS), a registered charity. I was welcomed there on 24th September. As an Access Point, based in the Cherfield and Wallis hub, the centre occupies a suite of three rooms on the ground floor of a modern unit close to the County Council building, the market, bus station and combined commercial-shopping area of a semi-rural town. It was set up less than a year ago with a view to attracting physically disabled adults in the local community into coming out of their houses to attend a welcoming venue and try out very specifically tailored courses. It is not a traditional setting for learning. Rather it aims, in terms of transport, physical access and adaptive equipment designed to cater for various impairments, to provide a comfortable environment conducive to creating a feeling of aspiration, empowerment and belief in their own abilities, for its users.

I interviewed four members of the management and administrative team. Carol (P5), the Chair of the Board of Governors, and Geoffrey (P6), the Centre Manager, jointly contributed information during an interview, mostly about why and how the centre became established. Geoffrey followed this up the day after by contributing further facts and his own ideas in an extensive e-mail. Martin (P7), the Senior Tutor who specializes in ICT, and David (P8), the Outreach Worker currently employed in a nursing residential home in Winton, responded in similar, but separate, face-to-face question and answer meetings with me. Martin also explained some courses he had designed for specific disablements, and demonstrated how to use the correspondingly adapted computers.

The students are not mainstream learners. Due to their various impairments a conventional interview was never expected of them. However, one young man, Stuart (S2), conversed 'through Geoffrey' and highlighted much about his life and learning. After the visit I sent a 'thank-you e-mail' to Vacrum Learndirect and included a request for information from other students, at the discretion of the provider. No specific questions were asked; instead I outlined areas of interest. There was no reply.

Later the same day I received further data regarding the Ufi and Learndirect from Mersha Partnership, a Learndirect Access Point. This centre operates in a seventeenth century building, located in a very historical area of a small urban town. The partnership has two other centres within the Knollenden area of the county of Mershire: the county geographically coincides with the jurisdiction of the Mershire hub. During a telephone conversation with me the previous day, Jane Dean (P9), the General Manager, had expressed a preference for details of my inquiry to be e-mailed to her. Using the same method of communication she fulfilled the fieldwork requirements, responding quickly with a supply of facts and associated comments. Exactly two months later I contacted Jane again, this time asking if she could provide information from her students/clients about their attitudes to lifelong learning and the Ufi. She agreed to present my questions to a small focus discussion group. The data came back by return, due to the combined efforts of Learndirect five students (S3–S7).

The following day I travelled to the physical limit of the North West Region, into the Cirus Plus and Stinton hub. Ripley Dane College, a traditional FE institution presides over three learning outlets; namely Cherwen Campus, Mappen Campus and, mid-way between them, Hollins Mill. All are in the confines of the Metropolitan Borough of Stinton and bureaucratically answerable to the local education authority. The first two sites are indicative of the habitual college educational environment for 16–19 year olds, whereas Hollins Mill promotes its unconventional setting for adult-only learning, and so attracted my research visit.

This centre effectively operates as a small business offering courses in ICT and affiliated training. Learndirect is just one sector; others include the ECDL and Barclays University. The centre is easy to reach, being signposted from the large free car park to a third floor suite divided into several rooms. The well-appointed infrastructure embodies wheelchair access, cloakrooms, a bistro, a lockable reception area, boardroom, staff-room, offices and teaching areas. Everywhere is newly furnished and equipped with up-to-date apparatus. Some rooms and facilities are also advertised to hire for meetings or video conferencing.

I had an appointment to jointly interview two members of staff—Hilda Fielding (P10) and Sheila Kelly (P11). The former is the Development Manager with overall responsibility for the successful execution of the centre's economic, educational and social policies, concerning, for example, budgeting, teaching and networking. The latter's title is Senior Facilitator: she supervises one tutor who works full-time, two 'part-timers', and presides over an IT suite of twenty-two machines. Preceded by coffee and an informative chat the interview session was held at the large boardroom table. As it ended Hilda gave me permission for one person only, due to time restraints, to be interviewed. Sheila chose from the teaching room Phyllis (S8), an elderly student, who readily obliged to give an insight of how she thinks the centre translates Learndirect's mission. This one-to-one informal episode took place in the boardroom after the members of staff had left. One month later I e-mailed the Hollins Mill learning centre with news of my research progress, and, hoping to re-engage their co-operation, attached a questionnaire seeking more client feedback. Within a week I received by post individual answer sheets from five anonymous students (S9–S13)—not even identifiable by gender or age.

The following day I made a pre-arranged telephone call to CCA Services, its purpose being to interview Keith (P12), the Senior Tutor. When I made the initial request to visit the centre he had not been in a position to grant it, due to the Manager's absence, and agreed instead to this alternative means. Our conversation proceeded as planned, and produced useful information. Lines of communication with CAA Services were kept open and resulted in Sherrie Rowan (P13), a director, becoming available. I met her one week later.

This learning venue has certain commonalities with the previous one. Its origins are in the Cherfield and Wallis hub. A Learndirect centre started three years ago at Mid-Cherfield and Wallis College in Crowsthorne, a town renowned as a light-manufacturing base mostly for the rail industry, still operates for 16–19 year olds. CCA Services, a Private Limited Company, subsequently evolved as a 19+ Access Point at Alterton, a suburban residential town integrated with some light service industry, in the Cirus Plus and Stinton hub. Run on a commercial basis the business offers training by making available learning technology and associated support mechanisms. Its premises consist of a main room which houses computers and accessories, plus an adjoining staff office, on the upper floor of Oakley House, a Victorian mansion converted to satisfy the local need for commercial space to rent or buy. The property is conveniently placed for using many of Alterton's amenities, especially the bus and railway stations, motorway network, car parks, schools, market, library and shopping area.

In the period of time between the separate sessions of data collection from the aforementioned centre, I was a guest, on consecutive days, at two learning venues, in the respective small towns of Longslin and Askmore, both in the Wilken and Leerton hub. The first, solely a 19+ Learndirect centre, occupies a relatively small annex of Longslin High School; in effect one large room entered from dedicated parking spaces in the school's car park, but with a connecting door to the school for toilet facilities and a canteen. It is open from 8.00am to 1.00pm.

For Josh Bellamy (P14), the Manager who gave an interview, the main aspects of his job are engaging with students as their course advisor or facilitator, and working as an administrator under the auspices of the Ufi. Josh was keen for a student to be interviewed, and selected 82 year old Jack (S14) to participate. Jack was equally eager to oblige. He fulfilled the role admirably, telling of the changing learning experiences in his long lifetime, and expressing his opinion of Learndirect in relation to this particular centre.

The second centre that I visited was Yarworth Training Centre in Askmore. It shares a similar type of general environment, features of which have undergone dramatic changes over the past two decades. Full employment in traditional industries, like mining, has given way to a lack of replacement work, culminating in physical and social problems for this small conurbation. Factories fall into disrepair and the infrastructure declines: inevitably, young people leave or commute for better prospects in wealthier places. The centre was purpose-built in the 1960s and affiliated to the Young Men's Christian Association (YMCA). It was founded specifically to serve the ongoing needs of the local community, and is run by a Chief Executive and the Board of Governors. The current prime focus is on education and training—namely, Learndirect and Modern Apprenticeships—but it also functions as a Youth Club, a Luncheon Guild, and holds recreational classes in, for example, drama and first aid. The learning centre, which incorporates service areas for parking, childcare, eating and disabled people, is open between 9.00am and 9.00pm from Monday to Thursday.

Jayne Cleen (P15) was the interviewee. She became the Manager a year ago having previously worked as an ICT trainer in a large company. Her interest in learning retains a bent towards work-based topics, especially employment law. At its inception in 2001 this Learndirect centre stood alone in the locality, whereas it now competes with centres in two nearby schools and the public library. Jayne's part-time job entails securing and processing client enrolments, in addition to stimulating and maintaining students' interest and attendance—tasks more easily achieved in the days of Yarworth's monopoly. On the morning of my visit it was impossible to get any student perspective on Learndirect because not one came to use the machine room—apparently due to a systems breakdown. I agreed with Jayne to wait two weeks before e-mailing some questions for her to pass on to students. This did not, however, entice any responses.

The next day, I was again in touch with CCA Services by going to Alterton to interview Sherrie Rowan in her capacity as the Manager responsible for two centres. The information she provided was extensive. The business's primary function is investment in training for learning, especially in the increasingly electronic world of global communication. Sherrie explained how this happens. The core of attention here is on learner achievement, and to this end the company uses Learndirect products. This provider's enthusiasm to co-operate in the fieldwork extended to her continued e-mailing to me of appropriate published literature.

The client viewpoint at this centre came from Suzanne (S15). Abiding by the Manager's request not to tape an interview, I instead made notes during our conversation about lifelong learning and the Ufi. This more cumbersome method engendered less useable data, so I made no further effort to involve other students in situ on this occasion. However, a month later I formally applied to Ms Rowan, according to the desired vetting terms of the CAA Services, for additional student feedback via a prepared research questionnaire. I received no acknowledgement.

By prior arrangement, I spent the next morning in an exploratory meeting with the proprietor of Bespoke Training, another commercial nucleus for learning within the Cirus Plus and Stinton hub. Stuart McHugh (P16), the sole owner of the business, employs two full-time and five part-time staff. He set up the centre to provide training courses for SMEs and individuals who were prepared to pay fees. The company then moved in a divergent direction to become a franchise with Learndirect, offering free training to anybody over 19 years of age. It has since undergone three annual audits.

Bespoke Training is positioned at the heart of Salton, a suburban area five miles out of a large city: it is surrounded by large retail stores, small specialist shops, public or private offices, professional surgeries and leisure clubs. These amenities create a vibrant vicinity for the training centre and help to draw people into its well-advertised premises—through a ground floor security-tailored foyer—during its weekday opening hours of 9.00am to

5.00pm—extended on two nights until 9.00pm—plus Saturday mornings. Facilities for childminding, disabled people and parking are not, however, available.

The centre occupies the whole first floor level of a private commercial block. This area is designated two-fold. One section is open-plan with reception furniture that incorporates a drinks facility leading to forty well-spaced machine stations. The other part is Steve's office where half the space is newly altered to cater for the recent addition of language courses to the company's portfolio.

Steve reacted positively to giving an interview, despite the demands on his time and his pivotal role in the business—made obvious by the numerous interruptions to the taped conversation to answer the telephone or deal with urgent queries brought to his desk by other personnel. He imparted a great deal of knowledge about his own and the centre's work, stressing the wider implications for learning. His strong beliefs came across on many issues, including the contrasting survival and demise of Learndirect courses, certain Ufi directives and the competitiveness within learning provision. Rather less, though equally important, information came from Patsy (S16) the client that I interviewed immediately afterwards—simply because she happened to be in the language room. Other people were too busy to take part on this occasion, so, after a few days, I e-mailed a questionnaire about Learndirect to Bespoke Training with a polite request for Steve to vet, approve, and distribute it at his discretion, to five clients. I added that the answers could be returned at any time, by any means of communication, and be would gratefully received for the benefit of the research. Hitherto, nobody from this centre has made further contact with me.

Having accepted an open invitation to spend a whole day with Ecolmount College Business Endeavours (ECBE) to look at their learning outlets, I kept this date on the 10th October. Ecolmount College has a home-based learning unit and an Access Point in each of three public-sector buildings, called the Antelope, the Cobbles and the Littleshaw. The first two belong to a National Health Service Trust; the third is a residential and day care unit for physically disabled people. Also in ECBE's control is a venue called Variations, a 'point of delivery' for learning in a long established private textiles company that has installed six computers. College staff will rotate to visit this outlet on a weekly basis.

Business Endeavours has a Managing Director and a Company Secretary. They are the Principal and the Vice-Principal of Ecolmount College respectively. The company and the college do exchange business in the field of training and learning: they integrate their commercial and educational ideas and aptitudes for the benefit of their clients and students.

The lead, original pilot, site for Business Endeavours is a structurally modernized single story building that was once part of the general fabric of a traditional FE college. As an 'altogether' learning and training centre customized for the 19+ age group, and with an emphasis on ICT, it attracts students to 'drop-in' anytime between 8.30am and 4.30pm from Monday to Friday, and 10.00am to 2.00pm on Saturday. Approximately 72 square metres of floor space, designated for Learndirect opens straight from the parking spaces into a reception/common room furnished with armchairs and large coffee tables. Along one wall are information displays, drinks vending machines, telephones, and physical equipment for disabled people, such as ramps, trackball, and voice recognition software. On the remaining three sides of this rectangle room are doors through to a computer-room of thirty-two workstations, a utility block housing the kitchen, janitor's cupboards and toilets, and an office shared by the Learndirect Manager, Teresa Shaw (P17), and the Deputy Manager, Jenny Watson (P18).

My data collection recording session with Teresa was redirected from a formal to an informal setting due to a non-timetabled management meeting in her office. The interview was conducted while she and I were sitting on adjacent computer stools in the machine-room. Jenny was not present, but joined in the general conversation that followed during a tea break: I later made notes about of her contribution.

My attention turned next to the students and, with Teresa's permission, I sought out interviewees. Two women of mature age, Joan (S17) and Teri (S18), were quick to volunteer. Each, in turn, quickly and confidently acknowledged the nature of the activity— answering questions, reacting to prompts, quoting facts and personal experiences, and expressing their opinions, hopes and anxieties about lifelong learning and the Ufi. Sandra (S19), a disabled student, became my third respondent during this, her first, trip to Business Endeavours. George, the outreach worker who goes to the Littleshaw Day Centre once a week, had recommended ECBE as more befitting her intellectual capabilities. Sandra was accompanied at the interview by her mother, who afterwards, while allowing me to make notes in the fieldwork diary, gave reasons for her own refusal to be persuaded to enrol for any courses.

Time was by now limited so I left a short questionnaire for Jenny to administer at her convenience. It was in a table format of four questions—1.) What do you like best about Learndirect? 2.) What do you like least about Learndirect? 3.) Why do you come to this centre? 4.) What does 'lifelong learning' mean to you?—interspaced with room for a few full sentence answers. In December, shortly before the year-end vacation, and with apologies for the delay due to the preoccupation with audits, an e-mail from Teresa delighted me with its attachment of individual sets of replies, from three men and one woman (S20–S23).

The next item on the fieldwork agenda was my 14th October outing to Silken Summers Learning Centre: it is a branch of the Age Concern—a federation of registered charities. In compliance with the organization's charter, and regulated by the Community Legal Service, the centre incorporates the provisions, dexterity and powers of Age Concern to inform, advise, mediate for and help older people (aged 50+) in matters of welfare, education and law.

Silken Summers was the first unit I saw on turning off a main road into a trading estate on the outskirts of Harewold, a rural village in the local authority of Valley Rose Borough Council (VRBC). The original floor plan has been altered to form a less utilitarian, though just as purposeful, structure that has a comfortable welcoming ambiance because its fabric and decor are maintained to a high standard. Silken Summers Learndirect started here, in a learning suite with eight computers, during a pilot project co-ordinated by VRBC. It is in a partnership of six: the remaining centres are VDS, (previously visited), one in Frimer for younger people, the Northirsk Group for families, and two meeting places for people living in Winton, where one—The Jungle—was intentionally established in the town centre to encourage 'dropping in'.

The scenario of gathering information was enjoyable. It was pre-orchestrated for my ease by Age Concern staff. A relaxed and friendly, yet professionally handled, interviewing sequence took place in private, over coffee, in the meeting room. Alice Mason (P19), the Manager, was interviewed first. In essence she was anxious to have this opportunity to talk about Learndirect from a provider's perspective. Her job description is to deal with day-to-day occurrences, and direct everything and everybody within this local centre. To fulfil this obligation she widens her scope, actively liasing with organizations that have proven worthy credentials in the learning zone—for example, Probus, the Women's Institute and the U3A.

Sheena (P20) a tutor was interviewed next. She freely admitted her difficulty in divorcing the techniques for learning she employed while a secondary school maths teacher from those currently expected for the delivery of Learndirect courses to older people. Nonetheless, the well-balanced and thoughtful responses she proffered were a valued addition to the data collection programme.

The only student in attendance that morning was Lana (S24); considered by Sheena to be her most diffident student. This gave useful background to my recorded conversation with Lana, who 'rose to the occasion' and expressed her views from a learner's standpoint very precisely. Although Peter, the Learning Co-ordinator, was on leave that day, he later agreed via e-mail, to pass on to students a questionnaire about Learndirect. Five anonymous hardcopies of feedback (S25–S29) arrived post haste at my home address. When I received two more (S30, S31) a couple of months afterwards, I fully realized Silken Summers' ongoing interest in lifelong learning and the Ufi.

The pre-planned fieldwork concluded in a different and somewhat personal—yet nonetheless objective for the research—setting. My hometown of Wallis is focal point of the Chirfield and Wallis hub, and the site of the Ufi's North West Regional Headquarters. A Learndirect Access Point for Wallis Collegiate Institute is based in each of the district libraries of Stormer Head, Birkstead and Lyle. These were the final venues in which I obtained information about Learndirect. All offer free 'basic' courses. Their catchment areas are similar in that they rely on members from surrounding private residential estates, plus a large Comprehensive High School/Sixth-Form College with an attached sports arena.

Mary Lees (P21) is a tutor who works three days per week allocated between the three centres. Students can phone her for help, and she makes her 'timetable in situ' known to library staff. On 27th October Mary's working day was split between Stormer Head and Birkstead. At one point she travelled 10 miles from the former to the latter, and back, to enrol a new student (the candidate failed to keep the appointment, and offered no explanation). By joining Mary on the outward journey I could listen to her ideas and opinions about Learndirect. She provided more factual data in the already arranged interview at our destination. Also here, with the bonus of extra time, I was given the opportunity to undergo the student experience by logging on to a Learndirect course. As no student interview materialized, we agreed a rendezvous for the following week—at Lyle.

On this occasion one woman and two men were using the Learndirect facility; in reality, five computer stations set up against a wall of the main library. Albert (S32) and Tom (S33) who are both retired—the former from air traffic control, and the latter from a bank—agreed 'on the spot' to record, solo, a dialogue to formally express their 'student' thoughts about this online learning tool.

In a final attempt to find out what students think about Learndirect I enlisted the co-operation of Wanda (P22), a colleague. She is a part-time Learndirect online tutor who divides her work between three centres in the city of Lemes, in the Yoringshire hub. Her home telephone number is used as a helpline. I sent Wanda a set of ten questionnaires to pass on to students. Completed copies from one male and three females were posted back to me within a month (S34–S37). I received no more.

(Fullerty, 2003)

The varying lengths of my accounts about the different Learndirect centres signifies, to some extent, the degree to which I was able to penetrate the layers of the subject matter. The general aim has been to give the reader a straightforward portrayal of the data collection context of this case study. Fieldwork is a serious activity. Its successful outcome is dependent on the combination of well-organized practicalities, and tactful—that is, non-constricting for the participants—approaches to seeking information. In fact, at all times throughout my respective visits, and the incorporated provider and student interviews, I was conscious of the principle of precision. I tried to quickly link the focus of the inquiry to the participants' interests, judge the right moment to stop interviews and cease data collection, and at every instant to uphold their rights.

## 3.4 Planning the Research Process

Research is a process of making choices, arrangements, amendments and renditions, be they simple or sophisticated. These elements unfold at every step along the way from the decision to start the study, to the sight of the final published word. Confined by the parameters of undertaking a case study, this section of the methodology chapter deals with my mental and physical planning since I entertained an original research idea.

'A primary distinction in designing case studies is between *single-* and *multiple-*case designs' (Yin, 2003, p.39). Choosing the former was easy because I decided to study the Ufi, which is a unique case. From the outset I made the necessary arrangements. Presenting a formal proposal acceptable to the stakeholders in my research was essential to ensure its feasibility. I included a working timetable. This is vital in terms of containing the scale and sense of order of any research project intent on satisfaction of purpose by reaching its final goal.

Throughout the inquiry process I cautiously sought direction from my written proposal before amending the methodological procedure, on occasion wanting solace to deal with frustrating practical situations or unravel complex ideas. I initiated and co-ordinated the search for, and collected then analysed, data about the subject matter and its associated or interconnecting issues. I moved from describing them to exploring them, to explaining them—or in other words, rendition from 'what is the case' to 'how it is the case', to 'why it is the case' of the case study.

The preparation for this case study cannot be called 'a pilot' because it does not actually mirror some of the facets of the actual study, for example, practical fieldwork or data interpretation. It does, however, legitimately serve as an exploratory stage of the research, effectively informing successive phases, and thus regulating the progression and pace of the whole project.

The main research instrument—an interview schedule—was written, and my next course of action was to find interviewees. I purposely chose to communicate by telephone with prospective candidates because it was quick and easy for me to personally explain the rationale for the study, and encourage their interest. Initially, I limited my introduction to requesting an informal meeting/conversation with a provider, hoping that this would eventually lead, through their capacity as a 'gatekeeper', to access to students/clients. The exercise proved fruitful.

On pragmatic grounds I could argue that conventional interviews in different locations are more arduous than those by telephone or e-mail. Still, for whom? Surely it is the participants who deserve first choice in the matter, on the basis that they are effectively enrolees and, as such, their anonymity must never be jeopardized. One relies totally on their goodwill. Likewise, the extent of their co-operation in, and level of commitment to, the research project should not be judged; both are rooted in functional issues, or a respondent's own philosophy on research. People are usually more confident when they are given alternatives and control of the method of inquiry—for instance, in the extreme they can stop the tape-recorder, walk out, put their phone down or ignore an e-mail. However, their demeanour and responses are most often of a better quality given the relaxed terms on which they elect to input information. Securing respondents, therefore, is a very thoughtful undertaking.

This being so, the providers' preferences were established, and I became immersed in the fieldwork. Primarily it involved travelling to see the varied characteristics of the catchment areas pertinent to the Learndirect centres, because I was convinced that extra benefit for the data collection process would be gained in-situ and in-house. The logic of carrying out differently administered single interviews with 'individual' respondents in distinctive locations is that an assorted array of data becomes available. I relished the prospect of going into diverse environments for face-to-face meetings, with the opportunity to 'see for oneself', make notes and record data.

The interview in case study method is like a conversation: the stream of questions is fluid rather than rigid (Rubin and Rubin, 1995). The interview schedule is an essential component designed to aid the dialogic process. This tool acts as the investigative core of the inquiry: it guides the interviewer and regulates the dynamics of the interview. Specific elements of the schedule, however, require particular attention (Drever, 1995). Notably, the preamble, the questions, the prompts and the language require formal devising. The anticipated reward is a multiplicity of perceptions and profound thoughts about the research topic.

Hence, the applicability of the research instrument to the 'case' of the case study was my prime consideration as its design evolved. By working within my preferred (aforementioned) theoretical and conceptual framework, and devising knowledge-based questions, I produced a schedule for a 'moderately structured depth-interview'—a design that has ample balance of 'a passive receptive style and an active assertive strategy' (Wengraf, 2001, p.154). Here, therefore, this investigative tool is not working alone, in the sense that the interviewer and the interview itself are the central probing ingredients of the research. Moreover, the interviewer and the interviewee meet as peers mutually committed to penetrating, and enhancing, the understanding of the research phenomena: the former, having created the interview situation, is expected to steer a balance between guiding and being attentive to the latter.

In my research the strength of this three-way combination lies in the 'richness' of the interactions made possible—the reward for the amount of time and effort I spent in written, verbal and electronic communication, and the ensuing transcribing and analysing. In an orderly fashion I fastidiously planned the number, and the accessibility, of locations, contexts and respondents. The records of the actual face-to-face meetings give some semblance of my delicate handling of issues and people, in order to guarantee and maximize valuable feedback. During every single interview session, I gathered data, got a statement of opinions, and explored the perceptions of the respondent. Their individual experiences, as well as new, diverse and potentially influential ideas, count for so much. Inevitably, this method of inquiry proved to be an abundant source of valuable data, thereby allowing me to halt the process when the pre-estimated sufficient amount of relevant data had been collected to sustain its analysis.

Every interview, whether face-to-face, in a telephone call or by e-mail, followed a pattern laid-down in the printed table on the interview schedule (See Appendix 2). There were certain impossibilities in the last two modes of delivery—for example, no body language, no prompting and no follow-up questions. Such omissions can in fact be advantageous in research should an interviewer be inclined to be too subjective in outlook or make value judgements. Besides which, I believe it is reasonable to accept that my three modes of interview produced first-hand and comparable, as far as being credible and reliable, data for analysis.

By way of introduction, I talked to each interviewee about the way the semi-structured interview can satisfy the purpose, and occupy a prime slot, in the process of research. I thanked the respondent ahead of their contribution because it seemed a genuine and smooth way of establishing rapport. The audio-recorder was demonstrated, especially how to stop it: it pauses automatically when no-one speaks. Any general queries were invited and calmly dealt with. Well-phrased interview questions that are not too obvious or demanding, but flow naturally through the topic, allow the respondents to spontaneously express ideas and opinions in their own words.

The interview continued through a thematically connected sequence of five main questions:

1.
Thinking generally about the University for Industry and Learndirect—what are the main features?

2.
Would you tell me about Learndirect in this centre—the reasons for using it here, and your own involvement with it?

3.
Can you think of ways in which Learndirect changes and affects people's learning experiences?

4.
Consider for a moment 'lifelong learning'—overall what do you think it means?

5.
What would be your perception of the approach to learning of the Ufi?

These open-ended core questions had been fashioned with a 'hidden' agenda. I made simple adaptations along the way to suit the recipients' reactions, striking the balance between guiding and being attentive. Non-verbal cues were useful—for instance, making eye contact—but I took care to avoid too much. As issues emerged through different dimensions in an answer I explored them by introducing words, such as cost, time, support, age and gender to prompt the respondent to elaborate. At the same time psychological mobility was engaged, that is, thinking on one's feet to avoid closure.

In order to extend the conversation if areas of sensitivity or hesitancy appeared, responses were never forced. Instead I used leading questions: 'why do you think people carry on learning' was a typical example. These also served to 'check repeatedly the reliability of the interviewees' answers, as well as the interviewer's interpretations' (Kvale, 1996, p.158) because random variation may influence the stability and consistency of the research results. According to Morse and Field (1985):

In order to conduct valid research, it is imperative that the researcher be aware of personal cultural perspective, bias or agenda.

(Morse and Field, 1985, p.13)

Hence, by using a phenomenological approach I was minimizing the methodological threats to the validity of the data. I had reached out for the informants' subjective views of reality, and I accepted all the responses as working equally towards enhancing the validity of that qualitative procedure.

It takes skill to bring an interview to a close. With practice I recognized the signals to wind down the interview for the mutual benefit of both parties: lack of time, enthusiasm or information were the most common. It was then easy to say to the interviewee, 'we seem to have covered every aspect . . . would you like me to clarify anything . . . do you have any questions?' To mark the official end definite physical signs were best used. I switched off the tape-recorder, stood up, and reiterated my appreciation of the effort afforded. However, on several occasions this acted as an indicator for people, usually providers, to relax more and, whilst 'chatting', a whole new area of data emerged. I took advantage of this, though not in a covert fashion, by repeatedly starting then stopping the recorder to preserve a further memoir of some impromptu useful and interesting material.

Planning fieldwork is an important design issue, about which Lewis (2003) says:

Many research studies involve only one episode of fieldwork. This would be appropriate, for example, if the focus of the study is on the current manifestation of the research subject, if what is being studied is expected to be reasonably stable. Even if there is a dynamic or changing quality to what is being studied is expected to be relatively stable.

(Lewis, 2003, p.53)

I collected all the data during a four-month period of 'condensed field-work'. This is a method for use within a democratic mode of research that 'takes us even closer to the endemic problems of case study research, especially the problems of reliability and validity, confidentiality, consultation, publication and control over data' (Walker, 1980, p.43).

The initial stage of interviewing occupied the first two months. Individual face-to-face, in-depth semi-structured interviews were conducted with eighteen Ufi providers within twelve centres. I also carried out two telephone interviews, and one e-mail question and answer session, to gather data from a further three provider respondents. In addition, by soliciting the attitudes and opinions of Learndirect students/clients across the range of post-compulsory education, other aspects of the Ufi's approach to lifelong learning were discovered. Twelve Learndirect students at nine centres acted as the sole respondent in face-to-face interviews with myself.

At a later date, when the interviewing period was over, extra data from different students was sought and amassed by e-mail. I contacted two centres where lack of time, and students being absent or too busy with courses, had constrained my visit. I tried to extend co-operation in three more venues where the hospitality of the host had been similarly curtailed. It was essential that this process should comply with the requirements of the Data Protection Act (1998), and permission to ask for information from this cohort was sought via the Learndirect centre managers. Certain providers replied positively, and the resulting data from twenty-five students/clients came back to me in e-mails. However, others did not acknowledge my request.

Whilst one can develop an interview schedule using theoretical knowledge and writing skills, engaging in successful oral communication is reliant on the preparation, and the unpredictable naturalistic issue of one's own personality and rapport with the interviewee. In practice this becomes increasingly evident. Therefore, with hindsight I mentally monitored each interview: although differences were evident, common features were also present. Respectively for example, the providers' attitudes corresponded to the dissimilar functions of the centres, and in all locations the majority of the student interviewees were older people (aged 50+).

The explanatory phase of the case study began with the transformation of the gathered data into a suitable format for its analysis. Wengraf (2001, p.209) advocates 'instant interview debriefing', and this was adhered to. As soon as possible after a meeting with a respondent I played back the recorded interview tape and transcribed it. This was done in totality and verbatim. Although time-consuming the exercise was very worthwhile research 'grounding'; an initial systematising of the data, both mentally and physically, it released my re-collective thoughts, and produced an accurate record of every interview.

As I became drawn to certain ideas arising from the content I halted the playback to add relevant notes/links, using brackets within the transcription. For example, (P2) saying 'I work in the training and business department, part of our Business Directorate, which actually looks to develop business outside of the college normal confines for more mature people in industry or in the homes' was registered as (economic—educational—demographic—environmental). In other places, details indicative of the interview or interviewee—like the ambiance and continuity, or their tone of voice and facial expression—were chronicled.

The extensiveness of the beginning period of thematic analysis allowed for memories to flow and develop while still fresh in my mind. As I listened to each recording in turn, then transcribed them, and subsequently enhanced the process by jotting theoretical asides, it became increasingly obvious that a multifarious function was being fulfilled: the data forthcoming was splitting itself naturally into groups of unifying ideas. In the light of this, I realized that this was akin to an early stage in the process of generating theory from the collected data. 'Memos are the theorizing write up of ideas about codes and their relationships as they strike the analyst while coding' (Glaser, 1978, p.83). Academic writing should contain a spiral of reflection, and this was being reflected in the iterative stance of grounded theory analysis; 'the 'flip-flop' process between the data and the researcher's conceptualizations' (Pidgeon and Henwood, 1996, p.88).

I constantly thought about the impact of other aspects of my study while applying the methodology, so at this juncture certain interesting incidents, issues and features that occurred during the fieldwork are recalled. Identifying how the strengths, limitations and implications of this practical phase were addressed serves to indicate what is expected and possible as any research inquiry continues. There were ethical dilemmas for me as the process evolved and, even now, about how I can faithfully express my reflective thoughts. I am ever mindful of the need for integrity.

The way in which the interview schedule was executed was altered after the first face-to-face interview. Two particular aspects of the interview situation had been unsatisfactory. (P3) had selected the college Coffee Shop for the interview. Noisy and crowded, with obvious built-in difficulties for transcription, it was not a fitting atmosphere for serious conversation and recording. Also, ahead of the interview I had given a copy of the main questions to (P3), my motive being to steadily ease the meeting. The result was detrimental for the schedule. It created imbalance in the interaction, with the interviewee dictating the pace of responses and the interviewer unable to moderate the trend. On future occasions I manoeuvred, or politely asked for, a quiet private area in which to hold the interview, and was successful, or always obliged. The previewing of the questions was never repeated.

Overall, I can recall only a few instances of 'unsuccessful' data collection. Some providers did not keep promises: their intentions never materialize, with or without reasons. One insisted he would willingly help with any request for data, but he did not. Another, who agreed in a telephone call to receive questions by e-mail, was adamant that his responses had formed an attached word document in his reply e-mail, but neither seemed to exist. And a third, despite profusely declaring on the telephone her delight at being invited for interview to convey her centre's total commitment to Learndirect, cancelled the appointment and afterwards left two polite follow-up e-mails from me unanswered.

My research strategy engaged triangulation—a medium of validation of method. There was more than one source type of information, and more than one collection technique. Yin (2003, p.11) says that 'you can even do a valid and high quality case study without leaving the library and the telephone or Internet, depending on the topic being studied'. My case study exemplifies this point. The workings of the research tool—interviewing in the 'field'—were combined with observation and the research diary entries of its key exposures. Overall, the process was carefully organized so that the threats to reliability and validity operating on the collection procedure could be recognized and assessed. The fieldwork was restricted in scope yet focused on producing the maximum amount of plausible, dependent and honest information relevant to the subject matter of the research. It may be that, judged on the basis of these academic concepts, the data is likely to be valid.

In order for it to be plausible, information must be implied by, or at least not contradict, what we take to be common knowledge. It is dependent on the researcher recognizing reactivity—whereby people act in a way, or say things, they think are expected of them instead of the way they usually do—and then addressing the issue of whether the reactive effects distort the data. Finally, honest information is produced after the researcher has fully considered the constraints under which the fieldwork occurred, and the danger of misperceiving or inferring what took place.

The completed transcriptions confirmed that the total interview-recording period had produced too much data, in that it was irrelevant or repetitive. This amount had been purposely collected to secure the maximum analytical choice while knowing that some would need discarding. I deleted, therefore, (P21) saying 'I do a little for Linton because my husband works there, so if he's got an appointment I just go and sit in, and sometimes I sit in for my husband, because one Learndirect officer is much the same as another'. I removed the low level description attributable to (P9) of 'We face the grounds of a vicarage, which is tree landscaped with squirrels. It has a cobbled pedestrian path to the front entrance', and I ignored some vague comments e-mailed from individual students, for instance, 'You get a lot about what your doing and it helps you out, it's OK. The place is all right. The stuff's all right. Nothing's bad'.

Substantial data remained for analysis of a qualitative nature. In effect, planning the research process had now reached an important staging post. The descriptive and exploratory foundations had been laid, and the initial explanations yielded, in readiness for the major evaluation of the data in anticipation of significant findings.

## 3.5  Grounded Theory

As a strategy for qualitative research, grounded theory methodology owes much of its popular use and promotion to the work of Glaser and Strauss (1967). Their development of a method for drawing theory and empirical research closer together gives priority to the generation of theory with lesser concern for its verification. The systematic procedure of theory construction, applied by means of a general constant comparative analysis of the data drawn from empirical work, continues to impact on the research world of the present day.

In the interim period the methods have also been updated. Glaser (1978) uses 'theoretical sensitivity' as an umbrella term for necessary and cultivated analysts' talents 'by which they can render theoretically their discovered substantive, grounded theories' (p.1). The essential controlling component is theoretical sampling: this involves the researcher in simultaneously, and repeatedly, collecting, coding and analysing data in order to develop theory as it emerges. The 'constant comparison' method is applied; whereby 'the data is closely examined for all instances of phenomena that seem to be similar, whether or not there is a fit with the developing category' (Morse and Field, 1985, p.130).

Substantive and theoretical coding differ: in the former process codes conceptualize the empirical data, whereas in the latter, the codes—which are always implicit—conceptualize how the substantive codes may be interlinked and thereby help to build the theory. Writing theoretical memos on codes draws out the analytic properties of the research. The aim is 'to theoretically develop *ideas* (codes), with complete *freedom* into a memo *fund*, that is highly *sortible*' (Glaser, 1978, p.83). When coding is saturated, the sorting of memos by the analyst becomes the basis for the integration of a theory, and ultimately the writing of grounded theory.

Strauss and Corbin (1990) further enhance theoretical sensitivity with techniques designed for both the early and later analytic stages. Respectively, they suggest the use of questioning 'to open up the data: think of potential categories, their properties and dimensions' (p.77), and back the use of 'far-out' comparisons with concrete examples (pp.90–92).

Grounded theory methodology is 'in tune' with doing a case study, 'providing modes of conceptualization for describing and explaining' (Glaser and Strauss, 1967, p.3). Many skilled published researchers have carried out grounded theory method in order to impact profoundly across sociologically-based practice in, for example, medicine, politics and business (Charmaz, 1994; Konecki, 1997; Howell, 2000). Empiricism is inherent in grounded theory. Drawing from her study of the experiences of chronically ill men, Charmaz (1995) illustrates the use of this method. She enthuses about its simple appeal; routines which 'allow novices and old hands alike to conduct qualitative research efficiently and effectively because these methods help in structuring and organizing data gathering and analysis' (p.28).

In this project I used grounded theory to critically analyse the accumulated raw data about the research phenomena. I applied it in accordance with the conviction that:

> In discovering theory, one generates conceptual categories or their properties from evidence; then the evidence from which the category emerged is used to illustrate the concept. The evidence may not necessarily be accurate beyond a doubt, but the concept is undoubtedly a relevant theoretical abstraction about what is going on in the area studied.
>
> (Glaser and Strauss, 1967, p.23)

Throughout the process I was conscious of the presumed impact and intrinsic value of 'the researcher's self'. Theorizing is rooted in, and develops into new theory from, the investigator's escalation of insights from the start to the end of a project: it is a reaction to personal instincts and the plausible experiences of other people. Not that existing theory should be ignored. On the contrary, if that specific to the field of enquiry is fostered to aid, but not overshadow, that produced by the grounded approach, then the best qualitative outcome can be expected.

The perspective's inductive style of theorizing fits into the postmodern qualitative interpretive framework (Golding, 2002). It avoids logical deduction based on a priori ideas, like directing information into assumed objective groupings. Information is not primarily sought out in order to prove already established theory. There is a reverse mechanism—theory is instead inductively derived from empirical data to give precise expression to the situation being investigated. In other words, from the material supplied by participants in the research situation concepts, then categories, emerge, and these are used to develop theory that is grounded in the activity it purports to explain. The process is not linear, but is discharged by intermingling definite steps of data collection, and category formation, with the generation of theory.

The fieldwork of this case study produced raw data. It was subsequently converted to a suitable form—a full hard copy of all the interviews—for sequential analysis using grounded theory methods. The transcripts and my research diary became the constituents of qualitative diagnosis. This procedure was malleable for developing and testing interpretations of the interviews. Their content was subjected to concept and theme analysis. Insights leading to new theory were generated from the organized information. The assimilated data, bound together from the specific views of the research interviewees, namely the Ufi providers and their students/clients, was interpreted as a powerful discourse on lifelong learning.

The narrative structure within the context of this case study has resonance for analytical inquiry, and by using the grounded theory tool any ambiguity between explanation and description can be prevented. Each characteristic of the case can be convincingly understood and, or, implied within the same frame of reference as all its other features.

The intention was to conduct the analysis in a logical, integrated and succinct manner, feasible in proportion to the scale of the whole study. From beginning to end there was generation of theory; a routine that evolved while all the varied facets of data collected in the fieldwork were being comparatively analysed through consecutive, yet distinct, phases.

Time spent in the preliminary phase was to ponder and tentatively prepare the data for the primary analysis. A temporal sequence of reading, attachment of meaning and annotation of text, it involved repeatedly sifting through the reproduced interview manuscripts, examining the observation field-notes, and trying to rearrange the unstructured information into a simplified coherent form of classification to work with further. There was progressive focusing; that is, exploring the data as it accumulates in transcription to ascertain what kinds of issues are arising. Linked strands in the data, and connections to literature on the research subject, were sought and found. By becoming more immersed in the data, relationships between conspicuously independent ideas eventually surfaced. Besides marking the pertinent points in the text with highlighter pens, new notes or additions to those made during transcription were written in the adjacent margin. Time 'stopping to memo' is never wasted.

At the primary stage of analysis I soon noticed that certain elements of the data were significant. Particular words, attitudes, experiences and observations emphasized the nature of the absolute topic as perceived by different people in an array of contexts. Now encouraged, and somewhat adept at recognition, I mounted a determined hunt for conceptual and thematic content relevant to the research focus. Thus, recurring data, such as the participants' problems and visions, and key aspects of policy, became encased in mutually related or integrated themes derived from the natural source—the fieldwork. Every conceptual element was designated a theme 'name': the task coincided with substantive coding which was 'run open' through the data—for example, 'crèche available = support (supp.)' and 'friendly atmosphere = environment (envir.)'. Hence, at this elementary level there was some importation of theory, and the formation of themes from concepts was taking place.

In the second stage the task entailed grouping the themes in a way that connected to the research title. Then, according to particular criteria each thematic group was assigned an appropriate category name. In other words, some of the information imparted by the respondents was recognized as core material ripe for organizing in such a way as to determine their perspectives on, and perceptions of, a relationship between lifelong learning and the Ufi.

Hence, a coding system became the analytic tool used to work patterns uncovered in this data into broader thematic groupings. I joined concepts together to make the main categories. For instance, data specific to 'finance, workplace, accountability' were assigned to a category entitled 'economic'. In this manner secondary analysis saw the whole database ordered in a systematic way for future marshalling into a fitting major category. Four more categories were established; namely, socio-cultural, demographic, educational, and technological. All the categories displayed a common factor—'change'. It was universally present, and therefore 'change' naturally emerged for selection as the core category at the nucleus of my serious construction of grounded new theories. Singly, and in unison, the five aforementioned, now subsidiary, categories became the theoretical components essential for developing the overall theory of a model of 'change': theory that should help mankind to make sense of a changing world.

At no time did I move any piece of the transcript unless it remained in context. The accurate interpretation of an informant's quotation was always protected. Once all the data had been physically consigned to separate categories these were taken, one at a time, and 'written up' more fully as explanatory sections; eventually forming the bases of consecutive chapters in this book—leading with Chapter 4 'Economic Issues Arising From The Data Analysis'. To this end the original recordings, and a copy of the full transcript, were always available for cross-checking against the transferred sections. Backed by my memory of the interviews I hoped that there could be little, if any, distortion of the original meanings. Hearing and seeing each named individual's contributory performance, and other ancillary concrete details about, for example, context and location, helped to ensure my honest reporting of the fieldwork.

The third stage of analysis involved the creation of theory. Theoretical sampling was undertaken. I looked back at the data, working through the transcript over and over again to ensure that all possible categories had emerged. This persistent and continual referral means that the emerging themes are simultaneously controlling the theme collection, coding and analysis of the data. Theoretical coding denoting the categories, attended by theoretical memo-writing, helped the subsequent re-allocating of data therein, or new allocations of concepts that surfaced after further theoretical sampling. Every piece of transcript could be assigned to one of the five categories, each item of data in each category to appear under the appropriate sub-heading or theme 'name'. Nevertheless, it was a difficult decision to streamline some data in this way. Where does one find the most relevant landing for 'multi-themed' perspectives? Confidence in the methodology cannot be compromised and, therefore, to accommodate these a sixth 'linked' category was added.

The escalation of insights into the data thus directed the analytical process onward until the point of theoretical saturation was reached. The meticulous job of building theory from the ground up—all the data integrated into a comprehensible set of assumptions that tries to explain lifelong learning and the Ufi—was deemed complete.

The methodology of evaluation is a serious endeavour. I concur with Bassey (1999) that the analytical process equates to 'an intellectual struggle with an enormous amount of raw data in order to produce a meaningful and trustworthy conclusion' (p.85). It is important to take time to think the various features of the collected data before trying to categorize the material in a mechanical way. One must be alert to the fact that fieldwork data is the product of human nature—the content conveyed in personal vocabulary and body language—and not interpose it with ideological assumptions about its meaning. Having followed this dual course of action, I can move forward to present and explain the inducted findings within the paradigm of change that convey understandings of, and correlations between, lifelong learning and the University for Industry. Before doing so, I now consider the subjective impact of the methodology that might occur, and should be avoided, when conveying the research results.

## 3.6 Ethical Issues

The right to research needs to be balanced with the responsibility to do so considerately. The boundary between ethical and unethical practice is blurred. However, there are key principles linked to the general good conduct of educational research. They frame the design, execution and final report, informing and influencing one's approach at each stage.

Ethical considerations and methodological matters are interdependent. At the start of this project it was incumbent upon me to outline the clear purpose of the research, and to draw up a working plan. There is a public right to information, but notions of integrity must permeate the investigative procedure. Two key concepts in democratic evaluation are 'control' and 'negotiation' (Elliot, 1984). Qualitative inquiry recognizes the ethic of giving control over public access to private knowledge to the researched and not the researcher. Intrusion into people's lives is negotiable, and therefore 'highlights the social researcher's responsibility to render the activities of 'insiders' publicly intelligible without misrepresenting their private meanings' (p.23). An ongoing ethical code, according to Bassey (1999), entails the rigorous administration of respect for democracy, persons and truth; the last of these being renamed trustworthiness.

For the autonomous privilege of total freedom to execute the data collection tool, analyse its proceeds and publish the result, I abided by a definite code of practice that avoided conflicting interests, deception, and the chance of presumed value judgements. I had to 'fine-tune' skills of social management in order to facilitate access to respondents whom I anticipated would possess a genuine spontaneous interest in lifelong learning and the Ufi. These were people who had chosen to be either Learndirect providers or students. Before being recruited as participants they were told what the study was to be about, promised the safekeeping of their input, and assured of their anonymity in the research report. They would also act with the ongoing right to stop their physical involvement and, or, withdraw any contribution. In return they gave their 'informed' consent. In effect, any agreement made between the main parties—the researcher and the researched—at the outset of the fieldwork to use any or all of the data provided during this intricate exercise for the research report is tenuous in the least.

Before undertaking an interview study, Kvale (1996, p.119) advises asking oneself a series of ethical questions, among them 'What are the consequences of the study for participating subjects?' in terms of, for instance, therapeutic issues. In order to optimize the fair potential of fieldwork, Spradley (1979) advocates using ethical guidelines akin to the 'Principles of Professional Responsibility' of the American Anthropological Association (1971). He quotes; in consideration of the informants' needs, 'protect their physical, social and psychological welfare . . . honour their dignity and privacy', and to build trust, 'it is axiomatic that the rights, interests and sensitivities of those studied must be safeguarded' (p.35).

Although in the situation of a changing world today's globalized climate differs from that of 50 years ago, the basic premise on legitimate human rights survives essentially unchanged. Now extended to include new groups, such as asylum seekers and gay people, all rights are upheld, and research must abide by the moral code of responsibility.

The research instrument—an interview—must obey standard rules of conduct. It is a non-hierarchical, communicative scenario that involves the researcher and the informant. The location is significant: it should be visible to others in order to make both parties feel comfortable. Likewise, empathy between them leads to a sense of concern, a quest for knowledge and the thoughtful treatment of significant issues. Questions that are invasive, too forthright, touch on sensitive issues, or label people are inappropriate. Even when close rapport seems essential to achieve understanding an investigator should not 'go native'—become a member of the case studied and therefore compromise or forgo the academic role. This has relevancy for 'teachers as researchers' (Kincheloe, 2003).

Throughout the fieldwork I took care to remember that all the respondents in my research were virtual volunteers giving freely of their time. It was they who dictated the location of the interview because I was a guest of the environment in which it was taking place. That is not to say that I did not add to the value of their professional work and personal development. I could legitimately expect to display in conversation, and the nature of the research questions, a wider and expert knowledge. This is a commendable consequence of being fully immersed in an exploration of a topic of my own choosing.

The concept of trustworthiness is borne throughout a case study in terms of checkable sources, competent transcribing or interpretation of the data, conclusions sensitively but accurately drawn, and a detailed useful final account of the proceedings. There may be occasions during the research that can arouse unease or disquiet. This is a crucial ethical issue and the interviewer should prepare strategically for any such eventuality. Oliver (2003) suggests several means of reassuring and giving confidence to the respondent in respect of the interview, data recording, involvement severance, divulgence of sensitive information and consequentialism, and the use of ICT. Two recommendations he makes are 'playing back the tape at the end of the interview', and in all communication 'to take care with style and precision of expression' (pp.45–51).

The report of the investigation is required to affirm a commitment to the ethics underpinning the research. Sound presentation of the conclusion is reliant on the researcher's integrity to declare all sources of data; personally obtained or referenced from the work of others. Unquestionably, plagiarism is outlawed and copyright must be observed. There is an obligation to relate negative as well as positive occurrences. The report conveys to the reader what has been learned by the research.

'But all texts are biased, reflecting the play of class, gender, race, ethnicity and culture, suggesting that so-called objective interpretations are impossible' (Denzin, 1998, p.328). Ultimately, 'producing a study that has been conducted and disseminated in an ethical manner lies with the individual investigator' (Merriam, 1988, p.184).

# Chapter 4
# Economic Issues Arising from the Data Analysis

Lifelong learning and the Ufi are each based on certain economic assumptions. That this chapter presents different perceptions of them derives from the data given at interview by the Learndirect providers and students. Their respective views and experiences, many of which are colloquially expressed, are quoted below—the former distinguished by P1, P2, etc., and the later by S1, S2, etc. The responses appertain principally to the world of commercial business then fall naturally within three conjoining themes of employment, finance and marketing.

## 4.1 Business

The Ufi is a strategic partner of the Government working to deliver a vision for lifelong learning. Unique and innovative, it was launched in 1998 to meet the future needs of individuals, employers, and stakeholders in the economy. The Ufi is now established under the Learndirect brokerage—its nationwide e-learning centre network —and thereby has an operating scope within the public service, education, training and private enterprise sectors:

> P1
> Ufi is a very big company; they're the drive in producing vast materials in the form of Learndirect. You have Ufi, then Learndirect, then the providers, then the end users: its one big learning chain. Our centres, our focus and our primary concern in all this is the learner. At the end of the day we're here to help the learner and give them what they want. But obviously behind that we have targets to hit, and one of the targets does relate to SMEs and business courses.

Entrepreneurial leadership, negotiating and management skills among Learndirect providers, and their passion for learning are apparent during interviews. In view of the fact that the Ufi now proposes to fund small to medium enterprises (SMEs) directly to locate Learndirect therein, then responses to the question 'Will manufacturing business accept Learndirect?' reveal varying opinions:

> P17
> I think they will. It's not just Learndirect, it's college courses also . . . because we're combined as a business. We've already got one ven-

ture going . . . a large business, which is BUPA. It's been approached through the college because they offer ECDL within companies: so tutors from this college go into these businesses. They're doing the qualification there, although they have to come to the college to do the exams. Staff do not have to leave the workplace. The college set the centre up; so the company has set time aside. If ECDL comes in to everyone online then in the future employees won't need to leave work and come to the college to do their exams; they will do it straight from their computer.

P15
Learndirect has targeted in the past small businesses through advertising; we've had three or four. We'd like more, but I think Learndirect have realized as well that it's not going to work. I think there will have to be more incentives for businesses. And the main incentive is money.

A strong financial base for ongoing monetary planning is also a distinct measure of success according to one business-orientated learning centre manager:

P10
So we got the funding from the Capital Modernization Fund, a grant of £84,000 to set up the infrastructure . . . the machinery and the kit etc. We have enough money from the New Opportunities Fund over three years, which is Revenue money . . . which is a contribution towards some of it; about £25,000 per year—that starts in June 2004.

Learndirect providers, contracted to the Ufi through the jurisdiction of the geographical, sectoral and corporate hubs, evidently have a major role in driving the organization's mission forward. However, the educational premise of the initiative—readily available, high quality lifelong learning—is sometimes masked by economic imperatives:

P2
I've got the job title of Training Advisor, and we've got quite a few in our Directorate. Basically they're teachers, but also people who can sell training courses. And we develop quite successful satellite businesses in terms of training people in for, say, the chemical industry.

## 4.2 Employment

The restructuring of academic and vocational education, and a blurring of the lines between them, is taking place in the context of changing national policies. A skilled workforce is surmised to be a prime source for economic development:

> P12
> I think a lot of people don't realize that if we don't have the skills as a country we are not going to survive in that competitive market, and life-long learning is all about that—sustainability. Keeping not only us as people motivated and getting the most out of our lives, but for the workbase as well.

The labour market is another changing entity. The demand for lower-skilled employees appears to outstrip any expansion in jobs requiring specialized knowledge. There is increasing flexibility in working and remu-nerative arrangements, with gaps—forced or voluntary—between jobs. Likewise, there is a redressing of workforce career development imbalance 'constrained by the existence of labour market segmentation based in considerable part on personal characteristics, most notably sex, race, age and disability' (Haughton, 1993, p.132). An increase in the quality of the skills base is consonant with, if not necessarily due to, anti-discrimination legislation. With regard to age-associated injustice, new European laws are due on the statute book in 2006:

> P5
> We've in fact cultivated this relationship with disability and employ-ment, and the job centre, so that people can come to us with their needs and we can send people to them with their needs. So it gradually produces a sensible outcome. We give them a Learndirect course called 'Getting a Job' . . . how to present themselves, how to fill in forms et-cetera . . . and then they can go out equipped to do it. And that is what learning is all about.

> S33
> I think that you've got to accept the challenge of a changing workplace in which people are obliged to earn a living.

The learning market is equally transitory in response. Enhancing learners' chances of employability is a way of dealing with social exclusion. Advantaged by the learning provision on offer—in terms of updated work-related skills and knowledge, and bolstered self-esteem—people are able to secure, re-enter, share or change jobs, collaborate in teams, develop career prospects and seek promotion. The greater the number of programmes delivered and undertaken, when coupled with 'keeping abreast', innovation, best practice, and change on the job scene, correlate directly to opportune personal and professional development:

> P15
> I used to be a trainer in a big company. I think some of the courses are great, even work based things. There are a lot of decent courses on employment law, like disability awareness, which even small businesses are going to have to brush up on . . . should have already but seem hampered by paperwork overload.

One ideological construction of the interrelationship of education and the economic community is a competitive 'free' marketplace of provision. Based on this approach, Learndirect is promoting lifelong learning as a job related commodity:

> P1
> I think that the main focus of Learndirect is to get people back into work. So they're looking at the computer packages where people can actually learn new computer skills and use them in the workplace. And the second thing is they are looking at people with basic skills needs. So numeracy and literacy are those key areas to get them on a work tone programme, and I think Learndirect is great for that kind of work.

In the geographical research area there is diversification and growth in employment. New light industries, for example, supermarkets, call centres and online banking, recruit mostly returners to work part-time, flexi-time, job-share or short-time contracts. However, this is usually after individuals have brought their education and skills to the required level of aptitude for them to partake. Career trajectories, forced by economic change, are a long running trend in upward social mobility.

Workforce development contributes to a competitive economy by increasing productivity and, in turn, employment, personal income and the family budget. The dissemination of educational and training provision brings wide benefits. An age diverse learning workforce is a business asset, and moreover a sensible one, in the light of the increase of non-discriminatory legislation specifying gender, age, ethnicity and disability. Talented young people alert to technology, and the willing and experienced semi-retired, collectively create and share wealth. The work ethic is reflected in the increasing independence and successful career development aspirations of young females:

P3
A lot of people who have come into our centre unemployed have gone on to get employment. Women or men who have been retired come basically to keep up with their grandchildren's schoolwork. Because they can learn it's opened up a new experience.

Nationally there is a 'job-gender-generation' issue. Hart (1992) criticizes the 'prevailing industrial-patriarchal concept of work, its underlying assumptions, its surrounding cultural values, and its larger social and economic context' (p.327). The 'masculine' manufacturing base is disappearing, displaced by an increase in the traditional 'feminine' service sector (Hughes, 1991). Men and women are consequently placed at opposite ends of the spectrum. The former, if they are young or made redundant usually seek retraining, but if they are retired or tired of working tend to opt for leisure pursuits. The latter seem to relish the new opportunity to continue their education and, or, the possibility of becoming employable again in the current environment of distribution businesses:

S1
Where initially if I were in that position to get a job in office work it would help me enormously, but obviously they do have other fields where you can go into banking and things like that.

At the present time the level of demand for Learndirect material from employers is low. The Ufi's ambitious promotional directing of people into continued learning is not complemented by any consistent receptiveness from companies. In an era of rapid change that encompasses twenty-four hour lifestyles—workplaces, utility services and leisure facilities rarely or never close—people take on multi-responsibilities. The self-employed, owners and managers of firms, agents and contractors cope on a daily basis with potentially stressful matters, such as staff absences, insurance claims, insolvency, escalating utility costs, diminishing investments and fluctuating markets. In addition they deal with issues that also concern employed, unemployed and retired people. These include; accountability and meeting targets, distance travel, long or unsociable hours, domestic and nutritional problems, debt, elderly parents, child-care, and the effects of anti-social behaviour and public disorder.

Consequently, if people are not given a chance to train in their work environment then often, time for learning is never found. Despite this consideration, the General Federation of Trade Unions believes that studying in an educational environment remote from the workplace revital-izes employees. Also, their 'different' experience, extra knowledge and gained aptitudes beneficially infiltrate the business. The 'Skills for Employ-ers' portal (DfES, 2004), designed to encourage better communication between the Department for Education and Skills and employers about the inconsistency of staff training, further embraces this notion. A Learndirect provider agrees:

P13
People do actually leave the workplace to come into our centre. Because it's a two-way thing the employer is investing in their people and their personnel, and they're pleased to actually think they're getting some commitment back from their employees. So it has worked.

The extent of the employers' contribution—willingly or otherwise—to the success of continued learning, and of Learndirect, directly by paying fees or indirectly by granting paid leave, is still far from clear:

P17
It isn't going to work because SMEs aren't going to want to pay . . . aren't going to take the time out. Well, the vast majority of the companies that I've worked for previously . . . yes, they want their em-ployees to be knowledgeable and to learn valuable skills, but they don't want to go down the Learndirect road. I have not stayed away from SMEs but have realized that this Learndirect centre is for the individuals, and if those people who work for the SMEs want to come then they're more than welcome . . . if the boss 'lets them out'. There's a couple of

guys who are given time out of work, and that's fine, but I won't go looking for them because it's a waste of my time.

Furthermore, there appears no evident immediate prospect of companies seconding workers to learning centres and actually paying to do so. This situation raises questions around the topical issue of the SMEs' alleged imminent acquisition of public money to set up there own Learndirect centres. One provider is adamant that the system is unworkable:

P21
Because you get someone who's got two jobs, perhaps a secretary or administration assistant, and they're expected to do the Learndirect as well, and they can't. No-one can do two jobs unless there's a clear divide. We have BT (British Telecom) onboard at the moment and they cause problems. With the best intentions in the world the fact that if the lady who enrols is off sick, or on holiday, then nothing happens because there's no backup.

Conferring with small to medium enterprises on this funding issue is not within the remit of my research. However, to widen its scope in the future and consult employers about lifelong learning and the Ufi could be interesting. If SMEs become self-learning organizations they might contribute to the long-term effectiveness of work-related educational theory and practice.

## 4.3 Finance

Government money was used to set up the Ufi. The Department for Education and Skills (DfES) committed £76 million to the first developmental year of the Learndirect network. The Learning and Skills Council (LSC) established in 2001 oversees forty-seven local LSCs whose remit is to plan post-compulsory education and training in their designated areas. Of the sixteen members who sit on each council, six must represent expertise from industry and commerce. The LSCs' responsibilities include distributing the money allocated at national level and partnering relevant agencies—for instance, National Health Trusts—and liaising with influential learning providers, such as Local Education Authorities (LEAs) and Local Learning Partnerships (LLPs). Together they negotiate and agree budgets in a competitive bidding arena for funds.

One noteworthy point resulting from this system is that the financing of, and the payment of fees for, lifelong learning are important concerns for the providers and students alike. Hence, they inquire into, and draw from, as many monetary sources as possible:

P10
Because we were coming into a building that was having money poured into it by the local council, and by ERDF (European Regional Development Fund), we were able to claim a third of what we spent from ERDF. So we had about £43,000 ERDF money, which bought things the Capital Modernization Fund couldn't fund. It bought the furniture . . . it bought the desk, the chairs, the crockery, the machinery, the drinks machines etcetera, so that we could create a complete centre. So we are a diverse centre: we are a community learning centre, but we also have a room to rent, and our facilities are available for hire because part of the project is that by the end of June 2004 at the centre we should be self-sustaining. So effectively we are a small business.

The Ufi generates income by supplying its patented learning materials. It operates a financially planned strategy. Money is passed through the regional Learndirect hubs to localized management to operate each learning centre. A significant part of their budget is allocated to the purchase of Learndirect products. In order to secure this essential attribute of spending public funds, providers must meet the LSC's quality assurance standards. At the same time, learners need to pass through identifiable stages of progress:

P2
There's connectivity to funding because it is a little difficult to keep up to date with . . . say the pricing. Ufi's pricing policies . . . they take a little bit of staying in touch with.

P19
So the decision to do Learndirect courses was made for us by our executors because I think they saw it as a self-funding thing. If we sold enough courses we could keep the centres running. The amount of older people we got in to pay for the courses would be ok and we could keep the money coming in to keep the centres open. As it's turned out is that we've never had money from our hub for the courses that we've

sold because we don't hit our targets. They set us very high targets. We don't get the throughput of older people here.

In extreme cases being contracted to the Ufi can be financially disastrous. For one particular Learndirect centre, an audit set up by their supervisory hub has led to closure; a move perhaps due to its ineptitude in cross-matching the Ufi's required levels of material and human resources to fiscal balancing and budgeting. This unfortunate state of affairs is deemed sadly premature for the centre's manager who had already contemplated Learndirect as an attainable learning source for forthcoming students:

P2
I'd just like to finish by saying that the college has come to a decision to stop Learndirect from today. We are withdrawing Learndirect, and it's mainly been a financial decision because when you start Learndirect you have to put resources in people like myself . . . access to computer systems. And because they involve a minimum cost, and that minimum cost starting from scratch, we won't recoup that for two, maybe three years. Until you develop a client basis and an official organization; a system which actually starts to generate significant numbers of students . . . and while ever you're in the throws of growing that situation you're always at risk of not meeting financial targets, and in fact that's what's happened to us.

In view of the repercussions of learning venues dismantling due to financial failure, I wonder if other providers could comprehend such a predicament. A Learndirect manager gives his reaction:

P6
Yes I can quite strongly! We have got experience of this because we are taking on a number of learners from just such an operation. The general feeling that we have got is that . . . one mistake is that it is a commercial operation for them. And the more we talk to learners the more we realize their actual learning needs have been secondary to the financial gain from the training operation. And so, sadly it's this unfortunate mixture between learning and money, and ner the twain shall meet. It's as simple as that. We are a charity; we are already funded for a given period. We have to keep the operation going. The more successful we are the better: that suits us fine.

Any easing of such situations by virtue of financial links with business clients appears unlikely. The proprietor of a small business may reason that learning during 'working' hours is an ill-affordable monetary indulgence or practical impossibility. Another learning centre manager elucidates that specific logic:

P14
Also employers really, do it for their own ends. But it depends on the size of the outlet really, because the small employer can neither afford to let people go in terms of time or money. They won't do; their whole philosophy is really not to do that. If you say to a small employer 'can a certain person go out for three hours' they say 'well why, who is going to do the job while they're away, and who is going to pay them? I'm not going to pay for the course, I want someone to pay me to let them go.'

Therefore, should employers want monetary reward to sign a training code to give their employees time off to acquire basic skills, then it is possible that workers' free entitlement to education and training will be become statutory. Or perhaps employers may volunteer incentives to those who practise more efficiently: they might give, for instance, paid leave for employees to take Learndirect courses.

The LSC already operates a fee remission policy of subsidizing courses for eligible means-tested participants. The price paid by an adult student of Learndirect is usually determined by where they live, and it might be made affordable in relation to their age or economic standing.

P21
We are making money because we get grants from the Government for everyone that we get through a course. So I think we're up to our 112th learner since May. There's a difference between people who go to the college as opposed to those who come to the library. Paid courses are enrolled at the college basically because we don't want to walk around with money, because some of the courses are £100. So we tend to do basic courses in the libraries because the libraries insisted that they're free. Some of the courses in other places there is a charge too, but not in Wallis. The basic courses are free in Wallis. All the courses are free in Wilken.

It is evident that the concept of funding lifelong learning embodies the need for change in the attitudes of potential practitioners, both providers and students. The indications are that people from low-income backgrounds, apprehensive about bureaucracy and stigmatization, are less likely to be aware of, or benefit from, the financial help on offer. A report 'Learning for the 21st Century' (NAGCELL, 1997) states that 'all providers, sponsors and funders of learning should review and modify their practices to ensure that these stimulate a far wider group of participants and do not constitute barriers to lifelong learning' (p.9).

> P11
> The reason we use Learndirect in this centre is because the courses are either free or cut-price . . . usually funded by the Government. It means that people who are on benefit or people who are not able to access courses, or people who aren't able to go into a college, can come here whenever they're available to do the course. Learndirect in this centre would mean a course that would probably cost a person £600 . . . it would cost something like £11.

If this last quotation bears out the Government's pledge to increase and widen participation in learning by ensuring high quality lifelong provision, then there remain certain financial peculiarities.

The Ufi is the implementation of an educational policy. Learndirect programmes can only be funded within the framework of that government directive. In the wider sphere of post-compulsory learning, assistance with payment for education and training courses is available for students only up to the age of fifty-four. Moreover, part-timers are, irrespective of age, a totally excluded group. People who retired early or were made redundant may face financial hardship. It would be a challenge to the Government's commitment to a learning society to attract these very cohorts to Learndirect, ultimately to retain them as lifelong learners, with targeted monetary support.

## 4.4 Marketing

Marketing is defined as the process of identifying, anticipating and satisfying customer requirements—profitably and, or, effectively. The Ufi has a triple mercantile strategy for its Learndirect product: it is promoted in affiliated learning centres, through the free telephone Adviceline, and by national media advertising—mainly press and television. One mode might precede either of the other two, or they may work hand-in-hand. Provision, thus heavily publicized, is targeted to enrol students. It is necessary to outline the Ufi's marketing policy before one can ascertain how this impacts on lifelong learning.

The Adviceline, launched in 1998, is an attractive, user-friendly, energetic and productive marketing tool. It gives out information about the extensive range of courses, whether job related, basic skills or recreational, available throughout the UK; supplemented with details of local learning venues and support mechanisms. There is no obligation to commit to Learndirect. Instead, by virtue of making a phone call, advice given and taken during a conversation is presumed the most easily digestible, and hence highly likely to entice people to learn. The service is operated by advisors who use their inter-personal skills for encouraging people to partake of learning opportunities through Learndirect. Prior training in Ufi policy and product knowledge means they can help with queries about course content, career pathways, and ancillaries such as fees, childcare and transport. Nevertheless, it is difficult to attract new non-traditional learners.

Disaffected students often begin their process of disengagement from education in primary school. If their efforts are not appreciated, or do not lead to success, they develop an early fear of failure, and a poor sense-concept of ability (OECD, 2000). As disadvantaged adults they may benefit from personalized computer-based work which allows them to proceed at their own pace and correct any mistakes without further diminishing their sense of self-worth.

Bourgeois et al. (1999) argue that the significance of the concept of an 'essential university' lies in the extent to which it meets the 'needs and wants of socially excluded categories . . . women . . . the working classes . . . diverse minority ethnic groups . . . also an emergent 'under-class' . . . the well-qualified, middle-class newly unemployed' (pp.161–162). The Ufi obviously markets itself as an open access university organized to facilitate participation for all adults, and statistics do show (1.8 million calls by July 2000; Dent, head of Ufi learner information) that initial curiosity in Learndirect is aroused by this agenda and does lead to enrolments.

Nevertheless, the majority of people accessing the Adviceline have previously established some rapport with learning in general. No student that I interviewed admitted using the Adviceline phone-in facility, or being swayed by television advertising. It appears that unexpected enthusiasm to continue learning is in many cases initiated verbally:

P10

A story came to us of a lady stood at the bus stop talking to one of our learners. She said 'I'm just going down to Stinton College to enrol on a course'; to which our learner said 'Oh, you don't want to go there, you want to go to Hollins Mill, it's just down the road. UK Online did a survey of our learners and the result came back that 78% had heard about it through word of mouth . . . and that is our best form of marketing. If somebody goes out of here after a rewarding experience then they talk about it.

Similarly, family referral and local advertising campaigns are repeatedly formidable marketing hotlines:

S16

How did I know to come here? It was my daughter; she saw an advert outside.

S24

When it was first advertised in the paper this was the number that was given, so I rung up and I found out it was actually in Harewold.

S33

Well I'd read about this new venture Learndirect in the papers and I was sort of stimulated by what it offered.

The Ufi actively publicizes its saleable merchandise—Learndirect courses—in the education and training market. One provider believes that this strategy is too aggressive, and thus ineffectual in promoting lifelong learning. He voices some caustic comments:

P14

Like anything in learning in this country at the moment, it's about 'bums on seats'. And the marketing campaigns that Learndirect have had, have been atrocious. I think if they concentrated on showing the population what skills they can gain . . . focusing on what the learner can get out of it, instead of gimmick adverts . . . then we'd have a lot more people doing Learndirect rather than doing community courses or sitting on their backside watching tele.

A contractual obligation of being a Learndirect provider is following written-down branding and marketing guidelines. Displaying materials and promoting services in their surrounding area is the foremost requirement. Also, tantamount to securing ongoing custom for a commodity is to first target the most loyal and likely clients in a familiar marketplace—

> P19
> I'm just in the process of writing a newsletter to all our current and previous learners to let them know what's going on and to invite them back.

—then diversify and expand to include other cohorts, or enter new fields of learning by establishing relationships with partners—for example, provincial enterprises, national headquarters and large employers—for referral and business matters:

> P1
> I've started to do some business networking as well. We haven't had the opportunity to do it beforehand for other constraints, but now I'm beginning to get my face known out there within the local business community and get Kinesmere known as a training company.

> PI9
> I've met the Chief Executive of Learndirect and she said to me 'how do we get a centre into Age Care in Millar Kearns where my father lives'. And I have put her in touch with our website manager . . . who's also managing the BT project . . . to see if we can get some national link between Age Care and Learndirect.

Many innovatively-minded staff members dedicate a great deal of time and energy to new ideas for promoting lifelong learning through Learndirect:

> P18
> What we did in the summer . . . we had a stall in the local market. We gave people 'goody bags' . . . and in that goody bag was college courses, Learndirect courses, balloons, pens and all sorts of little 'freebies'. From that we've enrolled learners who were generated on the market, and then thought they'd come along to see what was on offer. We've done the BBC bus yesterday . . . the GMR bus (Greater Manster Radio) . . . so we were showing people how to use the Internet, promoting the college there. We even leaflet in the community door-to-door.

P21
To attract learners the college and the libraries have a huge signpost 'Learndirect this way—Sign In'. Because the libraries run free taster courses . . . at the end, everyone who's come through just to learn how to switch the thing on automatically gets a pack saying what's available. We do go to all the Trade Fairs in the town. We have a stand in 'Education Week'. Several special interest magazines . . . 'Angling Times, Shoots and Roots' . . . we do articles for because there are courses that would benefit people with those hobbies. They're very good because they want copy to fill up their magazine with something that's interesting. We do say to them that it's low tech. advertising, but it's a good route that . . . well it gets to the people who are local . . . it gets to the people that are interested in the things that you're advertising.

Learndirect centres on contract from the Ufi are recruited via its partners—the network of 'hubs'. The resulting venues are set up as entities in their own right under proprietorships, like Bespoke Training, or under the umbrella of a known organization, such as Age Care. One respondent is far from reticent about portraying the unique credentials of his centre's service relationship with the hub, including matters of accreditation of advisors and networking:

P3
We're very successful, very competitive . . . a lot of internal and external marketing . . . won several awards . . . inspection in 2002—best in the country for Learndirect provision . . . dedicated 'Skills for Life' team . . . won the award for Best Performing Centre in the North West . . . 11,000 courses and 6,000 new learners.

The contrasting dynamism with which centres market Learndirect is exemplified by how differently, in fact 'hardly at all,' three other providers somewhat lethargically narrate details of their practice and performance:

P2
We've not been going that long that there's ever an effective marketing plan. But I would say we are attracting mainly the individual either from information from the Job Centres or they've been referred back from Learndirect itself. Or maybe they've heard of people coming in asking about courses and those people have said 'well this is available at Learndirect'.

P15

The Employment Exchange occasionally sends people to upgrade their skills. I think we could do more with that.

P14

The other thing that I would say I do is marketing of the centre, which I haven't done much of since the beginning because this particular centre is a joint venture between a private company and the school.

Marketing strategies must hold awareness of personal differences and legal obligations. They should be tailored to suit age, gender, ethnic and disabled groups, and comply with fiscal, educational and environmental statutes. The Ufi, backed by political and economic resourcefulness, has the power to incorporate all such measures. One provider is happy to agree with their position as justification for his own interpretation of the concept of lifelong learning:

P3

People are now realizing countrywide, not just by us but by national campaigns, that as soon as you left school that was it . . . that was the end of your education. That perception's changed now that anybody can learn at any time. I think Learndirect has been a big influence on changing that with their national campaigns. And I think the Ufi's approach is based all around that: it's really been pushing learning for everyone . . . especially I think 'Skills for Life' learning.

The fact that the majority of the data leading to the above findings comes from provider respondents, not students, suggests that the Ufi's delivery of lifelong learning is primarily in the control of the political economy. Learners show little, if any, interest in, and exert minimal influence over, Learndirect's commercial affairs They concern themselves instead with the personal offshoots; mostly aspects of a socio-cultural disposition—for example, how to afford fees or timetable their job, study and leisure. Such issues are imperative to the Ufi's success as an educational initiative. Accordingly, this economic discourse has argued that the Ufi determines curricula and will, therefore, widen participation in learning.

# Chapter 5
## Findings within a Socio-Cultural Paradigm

## 5.1 Background

Of the five themes generated from the data analysis, 'socio-cultural' emerges as the one most affecting both lifelong learning and the Ufi. The general consensus from the interviewees is that, in a multi-cultural, multi-faith society of linguistic diversity, awareness of other people's ideas, feelings and needs is a vital element of harmonious living. The process of guided intervention means acquiring knowledge and behaviour appropriate for understanding the multiplicity of cultures. It equates to being educated about their differences and commonalities, and dealing with their frustrations and aspirations.

Discrimination is a widespread issue. It is essential to combat discrimination on the grounds of disability, race, gender and age. In 2001 the National Institute of Adult Continuing Education (NIACE) objected to the terminology of the Learning and Skills Council's long-term plan for education and training provision—explicitly targeted at 'the entire working population'—on the basis that it 'discriminated against older people's learning needs' (p.3). Nonetheless, three years later a survey of 1,843 adults found that ageism is the most common form of prejudice in the UK (Age Concern, 2004).

It is, however, possible for individuals to overcome problems by focusing on the requirements, which they have in common with many people, for improving their lives. It is necessary to learn basic skills in order to avoid being disadvantaged—for instance, economically. In most cases good levels of literacy and numeracy lead to higher income jobs and contractual periods of employment. In addition, Clarke and Englebright (2003) stress that information and communication technology (ICT) must be accepted and taught as the new basic skill because, for two of many reasons, 'it has and is changing the way we live our lives' and 'is a powerful means of developing social relationships' (p.46). Essentially, ICT is being used globally; both commercially and to keep dispersed families and friends 'in touch'.

Principally, by definition, a family group is related by blood or marriage, and mostly integrates or lives together as a unit. However, family structures extend in several ways, and the word 'family' can be used in context for 'domestic partners, carers, guardians and other surrogates, including interested adults from the community' (Ofsted, 2000, p.5).

Relationships within families are not naturally close and reflect the members' characteristics and aptitudes. These take positive and negative forms that can impact on each other: anti-social behaviour is often handled by helpful approaches. Unemployment or absenteeism that might occur in successive generations can cause frustration and passive attitudes to learning. The DfEE (1999) states that 'children who do not attend school without authorisation are putting themselves at risk' (p.17). It recommends early intervention through multi-agency working, and prevention by home-school agreements.

Generally, people strive to live in a harmonious society. At the same time they wish to, and do, preserve the values, attitudes and practices of their cultural background. Sargant (1996) draws on two surveys to evaluate the variation in educational aspirations between minority ethnic groups and the overall UK population. The former—to a greater extent than the latter—choose to study vocational subjects for job- or qualification-related reasons, and rely on conventional provision rather than studying in the workplace.

There are evidently divergent issues affecting people's lives. In the company of one's contemporaries, however, the cultural and social dimensions of learning are facilitated and supported because ideas are listened to, and views can be freely expressed. The data that I collected from the Learndirect providers and their students reveals how conscious they are of functioning within a socio-cultural framework. The successful implementation of lifelong learning and the Ufi appears to depend on the way the elements of that paradigm fuse together.

## 5.2 Access and Participation

Widening access to lifelong learning involves searching out those people hardest to reach. The shy, reclusive, nervous, poor and the disabled are traditionally under-represented or disadvantaged groups whose 'experiences associated with learning may have been negative ones: failure, a sense of not belonging, low-esteem' (Wallace, 2001, p.95).

Increasing participation means identifying reasons for involvement and non-involvement in continued education. It requires finding ways to narrow the gap; that is, striving to eliminate the current polarized situation—the 'learning divide'. The Learndirect providers recognize and work to fulfil these obligations:

P10
I had a learner in yesterday . . . she's been out of work looking after the kids; not the brightest penny in the batch, but she did a word skills check and the area she did came out as 'no limit'. So she doesn't really need to do any brushing up if she doesn't necessarily want to. And then I explained to her how it fitted into the adult curriculum and you saw the confidence come out of her, and she was encouraged. When she first came in she felt she was quite dejected, like 'I don't really want to do this . . . but if I want to do that, I'm going to have to do this'. It is confidence building.

One student has also found a way to try to increase participation in learning:

S14
Sadly my wife died a few years ago and it does leave a void. I decided on this (Learndirect). It was new and I saw it advertised, and I just came along. In the early days there was only three of us. And what I decided to do in order to encourage people to . . . particularly people who came in at grass-roots level . . . was give a prize of £100 to the student who, in the opinion of the tutor over a certain period of time, made the most progress. When we do it, we'll have a bit of a do . . . a buffet and so on. I've provided that just as a small incentive for people to learn. But one thing about this, you make a load of friends.

The concept of access to, and participation in, continuing education is not just about increasing the number of students. Practitioners want to bring about a change in society in order to make lifelong learning more inclusive. It is an approach sympathetic to the Ufi's attempt to satisfy the needs of individuals, local regions and the national economy.

A powerful discourse of widening educational participation is that it is 'a key issue in national policy, guided by the Government's incentive to modernize the welfare state' (Burke, 2002, p.62). Success is assured if routes are constructed into, and through, education for people from marginalized backgrounds, with support along the way. Access courses dissolve negative perceptions of organized learning by dispensing with barriers and moving boundaries. Although many non-traditional learners belong to a culture of dependency and low expectation they have ample understandings of life outside the mainstream. They have developed a different way of acquiring knowledge, becoming receptive to new ideas through the application of their critical thinking skills. By further using these skills in access education they could participate actively in social transformation.

The Learndirect initiative is designed to smooth the transition from a static current existence to an increasingly flexible lifestyle, by adding a non-pressurizing learning dimension. It allows for the management of people's own discreet plans; time-scales to fit into their daily routine of work and home life:

P15
Learndirect offers an opportunity to learn to people who might not necessarily access it. We've done a lot of research locally. Learndirect was reasonably easily accessible and it offered a variety of courses that appealed to us. We were their first centre in Askmore; so it's getting on for three years now. And the reason it was set up was because it was thought to be an instant, flexible opportunity; a commitment to the community to fill a gap in that community by offering varied training which could be a basic introduction to computers.

P18
It's more flexible learning . . . distance learning so that people can access a course at any time. The brilliant part of it is that people who work shifts can access their course within twenty-four hours of their day.

P16
Learndirect enables individuals to learn at their own pace and in bounds that they are happy with, and when they want to learn. Courses tend to be bite-sized chunks.

S11
I can go whenever I want, not at a specific time like an appointment.

Learning is an empowering experience. It is about understanding life and one's relationship with the environment and other people. Returning to learning after gap years would be psychologically gainful. But making this 'real'—the decision to enrol on an educational access course—is for many individuals a huge mental and physical effort; a task often permanently postponed.

## 5.3 Motivation

Thorkildsen (2002) defines motivation as a multidimensional construct. It is a dynamic system of ever-changing forces, never inert, that activates and maintains behaviour over time. It is also a response to the complex needs of individuals in different contexts. People's positive perception of learning tends to come into play alongside momentous life events. Relocating job and moving house, changing partner or occupation, having children, bereavement or retirement; these events can trigger a yearning for increased earning power, easier quick communication, appropriate support, personal satisfaction and more leisure time:

> P3
> I was an unemployed welder at forty, and now I'm here running this Learn-direct centre, so I can say 'well, you can actually do things and change.'

A perception of lifelong learning is to turn a vision into reality: to guarantee a better quality of life by addressing the troubling, and enjoying the optimum, moments. Self-motivation is a vital component, but one rarely simple to practise because the willingness to approach, and avoid, certain learning tasks oscillates:

> S1
> I can sit there and study it until I get it right, and if I don't succeed first time I will continue until I get 100%. And that's what Learndirect means to me. It gives me 100% and I try and give 100% to the learning that I want to learn.

> S32
> Well I just saw the computers here and I asked about it, and I said I was interested in having a go and I got involved.

> S33
> Do I think this experience is going to be continued into the future type of learning for people? Well, that I think is down to me ultimately. If I can get over the initial stages of learning it all, I can build on that experience.

Some people, for various reasons such as a poor level of basic skills, are lacking in self-confidence, maybe wary of adventure. Motivating them is reliant on other people making them feel in harmony with a learning situation:

S24
Coming here has given me a lot more confidence . . . a lot more confidence. It's opened a whole new world for me absolutely. Everybody wants to help me. Since I've left school I've actually only been sort of a housewife. I have worked as a shop assistant, but that didn't really take any learning because it was only pressing the till and taking the money.

In effect, learning ascends from the melange of instrumental and intrinsic motives injected with debates about academic education or vocational training, and formal certificated or informal non-certificated learning. Furthermore there is the complexity of choice-controlling factors such as, age, job, gender, health, ethnicity, educational background, location, politics and funding. Respectively for instance, retired men and women might be driven by social orientation—like personal disposition and interests—into learning for a hobby. Likewise, unemployed people may be influenced by economic necessity—for instance, the rising cost of living index—to update their skills:

S18
I've learned so much I'm very happy. I started to come to a class and just listened to people while they were having coffee talking about it. So I thought, I'll work with the class at the side, which I think is the best thing to do. I know a lot of people don't like it because it's just clicking and things. It's a lot better now we're getting these books to work from and you can go ahead with it.

S35
Learndirect is a start; it's putting people on that track. If you have a gaol, you can get that bit more out of it. And I think it doesn't do any harm, because as I say, every day of your life something's new. It's a pretty flexible thing because you can stop and start when you feel like it.

Postmodern theory seemingly has a fascination with individual self-worth. In 1994 Blair (elected Prime Minister of the UK in 1997) proposed 'ethical socialism' which embraces a set of beliefs 'committed to promoting the needs of the individual and of enlightened self-interest' (Chitty, 2004, p.58). Kumar (1997) contends that the eclectic features of this contemporary society are based on self-referentiality. He says, nevertheless, that:

> Post-modernism has stuck a chord among much of the educated population of the western world. It appears, that is, to speak to their condition—or at least to their subjective experience of it.
>
> (Kumar, 1997, p.97)

There are implications of this within educational developments within the under-society. How does one start learning; manage to pluck up the courage to see it as a possibility, and then make a commitment to experience it? Increased motivation runs parallel with the satisfaction of receiving the correct advice and appropriate guidance. These are part of an expected provider support engine for the learners' accelerating acquisition of social and personal skills—for example, self-esteem, self-efficacy, peer-group and team membership, and problem solving dexterity:

P10
The learners they see Learndirect and they think 'oh I've seen it all over the place, is it about learning, I'll come and find out'. Then once you actually start sitting down talking to learners they're amazed at how much flexibility there is and . . . although yes we do need commitment from them because they're signing to do a course . . . the friendliness and approachedness of the centres . . . not just us, I've seen it in other centres . . . come over strongly. And I think that affects people because that increases their enjoyment of the service level experience because they might not want to go back into a traditional classroom base . . . it may even feel old . . . stuffy. They've had a poor experience of school, or even college: they're not wanting to go back into that environment . . . that's history and demons. And it does affect them in a positive way in that they feel they are taking ownership.

Nonetheless, for two students fulfilment can be greater or less than they initially envisaged:

S24
There was a little piece in . . . I forget which paper it was in . . . and I looked at it one day and I thought, should I have a go. And I thought, well yes I'll ring up. So I rung up, and they fitted me in for a session, but I was so nervous I got to the door and I actually nearly turned round. I

was going to go home and ring up and say I can't do it. But I came in and sat down with Paul and he just made me feel so at ease.

S32

I mean you're on your own; you're not coming with other people. 'How did you go on with your homework?' . . . I'm never asked. Can I ask the lecturer something or other . . . no you can't. So really you're kicking yourself off to walk down here.

'In the market place' is a frequently used modern idiom in education. At the point of product sale the customer is totally motivated to learn, especially if their personal situation demands skills-updating or professional development. At this time, therefore, information about possible funding becomes an alluring factor:

P21

It's a lottery postcode as to how much you get charged for a course, and it just happens to be that round here people are very well off because it's free. But if you move further south where some of the basic courses are . . . they're not great prices . . . they're £10 or £20 . . . but nevertheless there is a charge to them.

It is keeping the motivation going that proves difficult: Even if learning doesn't cost money, it is never 'free' of constraining elements, such as dissatisfaction with content that's possibly too advanced, or changed circumstances due perhaps to sudden illness. Detecting the reasons for, and curbing, dissolution tends to those providers who emphatically declare to support the 'student experience'.

## 5.4 Support and guidance

When one ventures into an unknown educational arena then support equates to being in an environment of willingly given advice about how, what, where and when to learn. Some students with high support needs are catered for according to the theoretical interactionist overview of guidance. This means that their development is sustained amongst peers in a vibrant and cohesive student group organized to foster each other's desire for learning.

The providers' resolution to furnish support is put into practice with the initial assessment of their students' prior learning experiences, in order to facilitate the appropriate guidance being offered at suitable moments in the learning proceedings. An extensive programme of professional help then becomes available. It can take the form of group face-to-face academic support directed at discipline-based or key skills—

P11
We've always got two members of staff on. I hope ever to have a ratio of one member of staff to fifteen maximum, usually twelve. We operate a completely flexible drop-in arrangement. When somebody comes to the door and says 'Can I come in now?' we advise them to see if there is a machine available, and when they are leaving make an appointment for when they next want to come. So that keeps them ticking over. We are open five days a week, one evening and Saturday morning, and from October we will open another evening, and that's purely and simply due to demand. We can't cater for all the people who want to do evening work. We have a very, very flexible adaptable staff who will rearrange their life to fit around students' needs—and to all extents and purposes pastoral care or counselling to deal with personal study obstacles:

P20
For our clients in particular it goes too deeply; it's just too involved. They're not going back to work so they don't want it at that level. And this is partly why we start them off with one to one sessions anyway before we even suggest they go on a course, because a lot of them . . . dare I say . . . are as frightened as a mouse . . . frightened that if they push a key they're going to break it.

The students' prior reasoning for continuing their education does not take into account 'to increase self-confidence'. They are unaware of this benefit until it happens. A student interviewee talks about his self-image and self-esteem; how both have been improved by supported learning:

S5
I actually have done three courses since the summer and I want to do some more courses because I enjoy going into Mersha in the daytime, because I meet people. Jane helps me do the course . . . helps me to learn things. I feel more interesting to the family because I can talk on a

one to one basis with them about computers and things I've learned. And it's got to be of more use than sitting and watching the television.

In contrast, for two other students the Learndirect occurrence is not socially inviting, nor is it a pleasant change. They view some people's exuberance about it as a misconception, and describe instead a state of negativism—like learning in a vacuum. For one, it is a solitary dispassionate way of learning compared to his past involvement. For the other, it is not conducive to educational progress:

S32
Well it hasn't changed my experience of learning because I've had . . . you know I've done full-time education when I qualified in my profession. And I've done night schools and I've done . . . when I was in the forces . . . that's another experience I had . . . when I was 'called up' for my National Service I did the correspondence course. And I don't like it (Learndirect) . . . there's not enough personal connections.

S36
I was given the chance to be a Learndirect student. I started a word processing course called Office. I followed the directions through headphones. I found it remote and frustrating. There was no opportunity to repeat and therefore learn from what I had just done. In addition it was noisy and distracting. Sometimes poor staffing levels meant waiting a long time for help.

Organizational support and organizing support combine to be a rudimentary function within any Learndirect centre. Guidance is to hand, and accepted, from sponsors, partners and stakeholders, chiefly the Ufi, LSCs and the 'hubs'. Simultaneously, guidance is administered to students. One tutor's novel interpretation of support is that, education-wise, it is only weakly sustaining in 'non-educational' environments. Therein it simply becomes a means of guiding individuals through impending political change:

P20
Well I thought Learndirect was a government-sponsored scheme; so it can't be just for making profit. It must be for wanting everyone to become computer literate. And in particular . . . sort of in a way, at a slight angle in some of our centres, because their own district are wanting people to be able to vote by computer . . . so we had that area new. No-

body came to our centre to vote: they didn't have such a good response to that overall in the area.

This contention is not, however, verified. Contrasting guidance networks are displayed, and variance in the degree of support exists, regardless of the type of learning centre. Hanes FE College appears to deny the possibility and responsibility of giving help based on the delivery mode of Ufi products, whereas VDS consider that intensive support mechanisms are vital to bonding with individual people:

P2
The feedback I get is that many of the people who do try and do Learndirect courses don't fully appreciate, or even don't take warnings of, the fact that they are on-line and basically unsupported for most of the time. So I would say their experience is probably one of slight disappointment at about being left alone. We do try and support people, but you've got to remember that people are actually accessing their learning at home, probably alone . . . either at work or at home in a lone environment. So it's maybe not changing the way they've learned in the past, but really it comes as quite a shock as to how it's done.

P5
Support is vital. The idea that Learndirect is an e-learning organization . . . that people are at home away from the conventional institution, and ner the twain shall meet. We have to create the right atmosphere when they get here. I think when you've been turned down and rejected by a lot of places . . . which is what it amounts to, being disabled literally . . . they need a lot of help and encouragement to get back into it. It's about starting off about five stories down; you've got to get back to ground level.

The influence of different people is an integral part of the learning process. 'The single most important factor in the success of our students is good support from their partners, families and friends' (Simpson, 2000, p.104): this is precisely reflected in how two students were urged to attend particular learning venues:

S8
It was my grandson really . . . he came home with a flyer really from school about an open day. So my daughter and I came to the open day, and it just went from there, you know.

S16

Basically I came here first to learn about the computer . . . not being allowed to switch my daughter's computer on and off. And she thought it
would be a good way of introducing me to computers. She herself is an
IT consultant, and really thought it better for me to 'learn direct' from
the experts here.

Although it proves difficult to uncover the full picture, I have little
doubt that some students contend with discouragement from within their
immediate family and other circles. Where 'new knowledge' is imagined
unnecessary, interruptive or threatening—its benefits never acceptable or
convincing without a tangible conviction, for instance, increased earning
power—then learning is contributing to strained relationships.

## 5.5 Exclusion and inclusion

That many young adults become excluded from post-compulsory learning
is the effect of structural and agency causes. Origins of disaffection might
be their own disruptive or criminal behaviour, which inevitably hinders or
legally halts their education in mainstream institutions. Conversely, the
recipient of the hostile act of bullying may be so physically and psychologically hurt that they withdraw from further education. The way to reduce
this marginalizing perspective of lifelong learning is to promote its antithesis—inclusion. Hence, I agree with Hyland and Merrilll (2003) who say:

> Within the framework of the new social inclusion agenda, emerging
> emphasis on citizenship and regional learning partnerships there is a
> foundation upon which to reconstruct the sector making use of a
> communitarian template that gives more emphasis to the values of so-
> cial justice, trust and democracy than the instrumentalist perspectives
> which have dominated post-school education and training over the last
> few decades.
> (Hyland and Merrill, 2003, p.177)

Marrying and matching the Government's policy to combat elitism
and social exclusion to the concept of lifelong learning involves pragmati-
cally, and psychologically, breaking down existing alleged deterrents to
access to education. Research by Burke (2002) finds that examination
systems are intimidating and demotivate non-traditional students: she refers

to Foucault's (1975) interpretation that 'the examination is an instrument of disciplinary power' (p.90). The removal of such a barrier signifies an educational change that maximises cultural progress. It is a process that can be termed excellent holistic provision, and it spells out a genuine future for lifelong learning.

People with mental and, or, physical, health difficulties easily become at a distinct disadvantage if stereotyped, stigmatized or marginalized by society. However, any consequent learning problems they have are extinguished, or at least minimized, through adjustments for inclusion. These include; easier access to transport, and tailored provision in a suitably styled environment—maybe a modernized day centre:

> P5
> The people that are attracted here are not your conventional learners. They're not the people that would go to the local college and enrol. We're talking about the socially excluded, hard to reach, group who tend to be disregarded . . . left in the community without any aspirations . . . without any belief in their own abilities. So Learndirect was about social inclusion more so, from my perspective, than the actual learning.

The Government White Paper 'Valuing People' (2001) outlines proposals for improved resources and opportunities for disabled people: included is developing the function of their post–16 education. Students become empowered to cope with the changes in everyday life and confidently make decisions about their futures if they are treated with greater regard for their dignity, accompanied by sensitive support. For people who have a physical disability, traditional mainstream educational settings have lots of obstructions, like unsuitable equipment. Learndirect, both as a concept and provider of education, can absorb and accommodate obstacles to learning:

> P6
> One of the things that we're trying to use with the centre is to eliminate barriers. We are repeatedly getting new learners in and requiring new pieces of equipment, and I suppose that'll be by the very nature as we role forward. Learndirect was just a tool in which we could maybe get them a) to come in and b) to participate with the computers; but be mixing with people. I think we encouraged one to volunteer with 'shopmobility'. So what we hope is that in the long term we'll gradually be moving people somewhere. We don't know where: the end product may

be employment, and I think we have already had one, and we have another who looks like they're going.

Joint Investment Plans (JIPs) for adult mental health services and welfare to work for disabled people were introduced in April 2000 and April 2001 respectively. The remit of public 'partner agencies'—social, health, education and employment departments, together with stakeholders from the private sector—is to gauge the two specific cohorts' needs, and then assess them against currently-available services. The inadequacies in existing holistic provision are identified, one being the means to sustain independence through lifelong learning. Learndirect programmes contribute to filling this priority gap:

> P8
> The idea is of course that you try to create, or get an idea of, what a person is capable of, what they might be aspiring to, everything about that person's needs in life, and then you try and achieve that personal development plan. So for example, about one of our learners . . . his plan said that we wanted him to move forward to some sort of ability to live independently. He's not going to be able to be looked after by his parents forever. Following a motor accident, he's gradually got back all his skills. We had to teach him from scratch . . . his skills for life, literacy, numeracy, financial acumen and his interaction with people. And now he's at college on an independent living course.

Whilst it acknowledges the present, and expects future, discrimination laws regarding sexuality and religion, the statutory education system also seeks to present an impartial challenge to racism by increasing the status of cultural diversity for the post-compulsory sector. Guided by the DfES, the major players to field a cohesive proactive plan are the Lifelong Learning and Local Strategic Partnerships, LEAs and the LSC. A 'learning society' is an integrated society; it benefits and progresses when it includes all mankind therein.

The discourse of inclusion in learning is forceful, so much so that some people feel pressurized into a 'life-sentence' of learning. However, a self-inflicted barrier of class identity is also in existence: in certain cases it is never eroded. One provider is sceptical about making in-roads:

> P15
> I think there are people like that and they are entitled to their point of view, and if they don't want to do it then that's fine. I think they should

be encouraged, but at the end of the day if they aren't going to do it you can't force them. I think Learndirect and lifelong learning is great because it is there for those people who want to, and if we can spread the word and actually talk to people, and say to people 'look you don't have to be Einstein to do this but it might help you in some way'.

Hence a stance on learning is in place. A minority of people remain adamant that post-compulsory education has no intrinsic value: it simply means abandoning their working class lifestyle, and they 'won't cross the frontier of shame' (Smith, 2004) into an alien environment.

To this end, the Ufi, cognizant of the need to heighten individual educational aspirations, is intent on increasing the quantity of quality provision for unconventional learners by venturing into previously untested territory. A pilot programme run in five prisons has led to the rollout of this new approach in twenty more, so that 'computer hardware and local networks are being installed to allow inmates access to Learndirect courses' (Ufi, 2004).

## 5.6 Environment

Where learning takes place bears heavily on its success. In response to the aforementioned socio-cultural concerns, the last decade has witnessed renewed interest in community learning. Adult learning is one of the engines of the National Strategy for Neighbourhood Renewal which was set up in 2001 to identify and sort out problems in deprived areas. With the accession of the Local Strategic Partnerships (LSPs) combined empowerment is injected into the domain of neighbourhood life. In addition, there is abundant scope via the nominated local LSC to highlight the potency of learning in suitable environments.

Shared vision based on collective interests and measures, strengthened by integrating resources with expertise, can decidedly activate, then build up, a solid parochial learning culture to improve local society. When a Learndirect centre opens in a specific neighbourhood enrolees bring to it a wealth of information; the by-product of localized informal learning. Their commitment to continued education solidifies as befits the community as beneficiary. Some students find the physical conveniences of a learning centre a big attraction. The providers recognize that 'locals' are the potential static cohort—a nucleus of learners to be nurtured if Learndirect is to survive and flourish:

**S17**

I come to this centre because I live in Harwold, so this is the local place. It's handy. It's the nearest one for me. I come twice a week.

**S24**

The one advantage for me really is that there's no travelling. I can walk here from home; that's a distinct advantage.

**S32**

Well, because I live in Lyle, it was more convenient than having to go into Wallis or in the other direction to Alterton outside the area. It's the convenience of coming here; but I think that has overridden some of the advantages really because of the difficulty I've had is booking the courses. But obviously there's a lot of people with the same ideas as I have. There's only so many hours a week that you can use the terminal, so that is limiting. But on the other hand if you can make the dates available then you accept the challenge.

The Ufi fits into the context for the localized regeneration of education. Learndirect provision is demonstrating how adult learning slots into neighbourhood renewal activism:

**P14**

What they offer the community is a chance to get back into learning, and the proof is in the room today. The Learndirect centre serves as a community centre really for learning because the school has no community courses. A lot of schools in the Wilken area do CLAIT courses, lots of IT courses . . . lots of vocational courses: this school does none. This is the only facility they offer at the moment apart from an antiques class on a Tuesday night, and maybe badminton on a Friday. We even draw in a number of the teachers and other people associated with the school . . . governors etc.

**P9**

We've currently got a client list of individuals from the community. Our tutors are also from the local community and have been trained in their fields. The tutor ratio is 10–1: this gives more support and a friendlier approach to those who wish to learn here.

In the education lexicon, 'community' is a potent word because it engenders different dimensions of learning. The notion of community learning becomes more distinct in terms of domain and context (Cullen et al., 2000). Illustrating the former Gilchrist (2001) recommends community participation in social regeneration. She says 'by assisting people to organize themselves into self-help and pressure groups, informal educators help them to have greater influence over decisions that affect their lives (p.111). Kendall (2004) exemplifies the latter in asserting that:

> The natural starting point for any learning is an informal learning community with family, peers, elders etc. With the need for socialization and preparation for economic activity formal learning communities assert their role in the life of the learner.
> (Kendall, 2004, p.158)

In 2000, a report from the Office for Standards in Education (OFSTED) verified a link between the said domain and context. It draws to the attention of local authorities the need to 'plan family learning programmes as an integral part of their strategies for raising achievement, regenerating communities and fostering lifelong learning' (p.9).

The Learndirect interviewees principally interpret community learning in terms of closeness. This is characterized in a mixture of socio-cultural modes—for example, territorial security, compatible relationships and shared activity:

> P18
> We're integrating all the time; the students in the college, and with the community. The Antelope and the Cobbles are National Health Service Trust buildings, so in there they can drop-in and see a GP . . . anything to do with their health. They have alternative therapies in there. In here (college) we have learning centres, so we have six . . . seven . . . eight computers. In the Antelope there's eight computers: Cobbles has got six. So they can access learning as well as other health problems. And it's open all day and one evening at each centre.

Local buildings are the fabric of community life. Traditionally formal institutions can be daunting and impersonal. Even so, physical makeovers can change areas within them into informal ambient Learndirect centres where the atmosphere is less stifling:

P9

There are Learndirect facilities in the local library, but it's an old-fashioned place. The aesthetics of the tuition environment are especially important to the learners. Our building has a homely feel to it, including the décor.

However, most learners ultimately gravitate to what for them is the most mentally relaxing environment. In this respect Learndirect provision exhibits its sensitivity to, and preparedness of, the students' need for 'personal space'—mainly, flexibility of time, pace and help:

S1

I come into Learndirect at least three mornings a week for roughly two hours. I find Learndirect suitable for me because I'm not tied. It gives me the freedom of the time I can come and go to the college, and it helps me. It helps me to learn at my own speed. I love coming here because of the relaxed atmosphere; the support that's needed; how easy it is when you start doing a course.

P1

A lot of people who come into this centre are either terrified of computers . . . terrified. Well perhaps not terrified of education, but expect . . . especially if they are older clientele . . . expect education to be, well, sat at the back of the class, and if you don't know it you are the dunce. Then they come in here and actually find that it's based on one to one training; that we'll advise them . . . that if they want to be left we'll leave them alone.

The Learndirect users want to feel comfortable and welcomed; that is, unthreatened, but not anonymous. They view meeting with other people as a straightforward and pleasant way to keep their minds active. The providers understand their students' fears, so they try to allay any worries by allowing cultural episodes to infiltrate the mental activity. Learndirect programmes are often an integral part of social gatherings—as, for example, when people from the same locality or age group meet in familiar surroundings, such as libraries or community centres—and in essence these dominate the learning scenario.

P13

For us as a charity we're getting this core base of people who are interested in what we do. People are coming in here who are bringing in their neighbours . . . who are bringing in their friends. We've had about sixty learners so far through the centre, and it's turning now into more of a social thing for the people of the village.

S29

It means a lot to me coming to this centre. There are people that I know that don't have the confidence to come out to college. It's a good social thing for elderly people. Everybody can help one another and you can ask anybody, whereas if you're at home it's very, very stressful.

Outreach approaches to education vary; but the overall aim is to contact non-traditional learners by going outside established centres and institutions in order to attract a re-connection with education by inviting input to programmes that can render geographical obstacles insignificant. Disabled people often consider themselves housebound. A provider and a student authenticate that this group—socially excluded in their own home or a care facility—have tended to be ignored by the learning society. Their respective experiences illustrate the domiciliary and peripatetic models of outreach:

P5

David's role . . . the outreach worker . . . what he tries to do is give people a taste of learning . . . and the best way to wet their appetite is by going to the houses and try to encourage them. I can't emphasize enough how big a step it is to actually make that move just to leave the house to come here. His other role is working in the community to raise Learndirect's profile. Geoffrey and David are currently working with a nursing residential home in Winton because there is a need, which is to try to set up some kind of IT learning. We did some research there, and I think every age from nineteen to upper eighties wanted it; even for just using the computer to e-mail.

S19

I go to the day centre. Geoff comes to the day centre one day a week and I see him, and it's opened . . . well, I'm doing courses that I wanted . . . I'd never have done because it's hard getting to college. So he's brought the courses to us at the Littleshaw . . . showed us what courses they do. So a lot of us just signed on a lot of courses, which otherwise we wouldn't have been able to do.

Learndirect aspires to provide a psychologically safe learning environment. The programmes are taken wherever access for students is available. Some people choose to study in their home because they like the familiar atmosphere: it can also be a private, quiet, convenient and cheap venue. Conversely, other students find it a distractingly cluttered or isolating environment. This way of learning is dissimilar to, though sometimes confused with, 'family learning'—that which takes place in the context of family life, and whereby younger members might rekindle learning in adults:

P2

We are moving more to people taking CD ROMs home, and coming into colleges for accreditation where they can sit the tests. It's an option for the students who don't like the pressure of a classroom type of environment. A lot of people who come in for Learndirect do exactly want to do that . . . work at home without being in front of other people and making a show of themselves if they get it wrong.

Alternatively, 'New Library: The People's Network' (Department for Culture, Media and Sport, 1997) recommended a plan for the public library service to utilize the capacity of ICT networks to improve the availability of learning opportunities.   Different providers have expressed a variety of views about how best to deliver Learndirect. It is evident that those who continue to succeed place much emphasis on making their centre's mode, and its material environment, attractive to the learner. Without this factor of effort clients will fail to come forward despite the availability of electronic material suitable for their needs: the possibility that interest in online learning is waning should not be dismissed. Ultimately it appears to be the case that all providers must deliver their courses in an atmosphere conducive to encouraging the students' increased knowledge. This will be borne out of a learning environment that promotes a community spirit, which in turn fosters conversation and debate leading to understandings of the world.

## 5.7 Gender

Adults do not form a homogeneous cohort in the field of lifelong learning. Gender equity in, and through, education attracts much discussion. According to Klein et al. (2002) it means:

Achieving equitable outcomes for females and males in all that is of value to individuals and society, as well as rethinking what we value to include frequently neglected strengths and roles traditionally associated with women.

(Klein et al., 2002, p.4)

Women are often getting their first real chance to learn for pleasure as well as train in skills, and so gain self-assurance and assertiveness. This concept has tokens of the objectives of feminist pedagogy and the educational theory of Freire (1971) which, underlain with suppositions of oppression and historical change, dwell upon visions of social transformation. Two Learndirect students suggest that women are more likely than men to make themselves aware of, and partake in, the lifelong learning opportunities on offer:

S31
My husband's a total technophobic: he won't even switch the computer on. And I think it's such a shame. I've tried to get him just to use Britannica or something. I revel in it me; it's just opened up a whole new world for me.

S24
I've allocated every Tuesday from 11 to 12 at the moment: I can extend it to 1 o'clock if I want. I used to do an hour and a half . . . but the reason being I do have to pick my grandson up from school in the afternoon . . . and I mean we're both retired my husband and I so he wants to do other things during the day.

Two other women students lack their partner's support but will not be deterred from continuing to learn. They remain proud of their efforts and become more determined to reach their goal. They 'let slip their frustration' at interview by asking me to stop the recording while they were talking about this issue. The general personal feelings they convey are that, despite having received previous job-related training, at the end of a workday, or his working life, a man's interest in learning wanes. He seems less tolerant, and 'set in his ways' he is uneasy about adjusting to change. Anticipated criticism or an image of failure may even prompt some men to exit before it happens. Yet I found no evidence to suggest that when men are made redundant, become unemployed or retire, they cease to learn.

A socio-cultural gender gap is also manifest between age groups. To-day's older women had less educational opportunity, more domestic commitments, little involvement in financial affairs and more unfulfilled ambitions than the current young female population. Many issues have intervened to redress the balance, among them the concept of lifelong learning. One student explains her situation:

S18
My son has done it at university, but he hasn't the patience and he's flying through the pages and things. I think that as we've got older we can't remember things. But everyone's different. Yes, I do I think it's better for the young ones. I do think you can't get anywhere now without all this education. It was different whenever I was getting jobs. But I got to the stage when I thought I should because everybody's talking about e-mail and things . . . doing things online. So I do see a future of carrying on. I'll always be here.

The findings from the collected data—outlined thus far—repeatedly point to the fact that many people aged 50+ and 'unqualified' are very appreciative of a re-engagement with learning once they settle into the Learndirect system. They relish the chances, and thrive on success. They declare their intention to take on new challenges, progressing through more, often higher level, courses. I am, therefore, intrigued to find out if this is a scenario replicated across the demographic field.

# Chapter 6
## Demography as an Interpretive Paradigm

## 6.1 General issues

> It appears that a 'demographic time bomb' (Haughton, 1993) is ticking. Birth rates are falling, the proportion of older people in society is increasing, and there is the potential situation whereby they outnumber the young. According to the 2001 census the numbers (thousands) of people in the United Kingdom aged 60+ in 1901, 1951 and 2001 were 2873, 7869 and 12,141 respectively (Office for National Statistics, 2003). The proportion of the 'oldest old', those aged 85+, rose from 0.8% to 1.8% of the population during the twentieth century.
> (Coleman and O'Hanlon, 2004).

Named 'the population implosion' (Girling, 2003) this trend, which is a decidedly Western phenomenon, presents an economic and social challenge to mankind. It places an uncompromising burden on people of employable age to support an increasingly older cohort. It seems inevitable that productivity will be reduced, unemployment will rise, pensions will be delayed, and the situation of education will be affected.

The '2.4 children statistic'—that is, the average of 2.4 children born per family every generation needed to maintain a stable population—is not being reached. Measures are being taken to combat this imbalance in 'replacement fertility'. The demographic changes now affecting socio-economic balance require solidarity of learning across generations. As the number of young people is decreasing it would be irrational not to tap into the often under-utilized talents of a more mature age group. Hence, older people are being targeted in order to engage them in work—paid or voluntary—and learning, and thereby benefit society from their continued efforts and experience.

Marmot (2004) professes how to 'Learn—to live longer':

> Education may improve health because it leads to higher positions in the hierarchy and because it is likely to arm people with what they need to exert more control over their lives and participate fully in society.
> (Marmot, 18.06.04, THES)

The Ufi is attracting a cross-section of people into learning. All age groups over the ability range are taking Learndirect courses. A provider and a student define lifelong learning. They echo its ageless aspect:

P11

Lifelong learning does have a meaning because we've had learners that have been 90 years old believe it or not . . . so for them they're learning late in life. So it is life long right from 19. Learndirect is 19+, so it's from 19 to the grave. People can continue learning whatever their age.

S17

I've always been keen on learning. When I was fifty I did two 'A' levels because I always had an interest in learning things, and I just said to my-self 'you're getting lazy, get on the computer course', and it's been great. I'm a great believer in learning . . . absolutely. Lifelong learning means you don't stagnate; you achieve, progress . . . you keep up with everybody.

Two more providers expand on different features. The first reinforces the lifelong dimension by giving credit to Learndirect's concentration on the delivery of technologically-based learning. The second explains how the schema of Learndirect consists of a post-compulsory educational package, and therefore people younger than 19 years, require official approval prior to becoming a user:

P1

Learndirect offer a lot of computer skills. The kids that are coming out of school at the moment . . . the 16–17 years olds . . . can do it with their eyes closed. A generation of, I'd say, 40 years old+ don't have those computer skills, and they're coming across jobs, and they're wanting to change careers or wanting to do less hours; wanting to work part-time in an office for example, and they haven't got the IT skills. So they come to Learndirect. They realize that learning didn't finish at 16 years old, and they have to retrain or find a new skill. And Learndirect offers that.

P14

I've taken a few 17–19 year olds on, but the rules are that I've got to make sure that they are actually in employment and not at school. That has to be done in writing to the Learndirect Hub in Wilken.

The most popular age group of students drawn to Learndirect can vary according to the different types of local environment, learning venue and teaching approach:

P15
The population is kind of polarized. You've got the very young, the elderly . . . you don't have a lot in between. So what was attractive for us is that typical people who may go to further education in some areas are not around here. If you can make learning applicable to go with their lives then you are likely to attract a wider audience in this area.

P14
The Collegiate enrols a lot of young people, but not through the libraries. They're mainly retired people we get through the libraries. Some of them aren't that old . . . you know, early fifties . . . but are people with generally more time on their hands who go into the libraries anyway.

It is impossible to escape the fact that ageing is universal. The desire and ability to continue learning as people live to a rarely achievable elderly age is understandably talked about with pride. These students expressed their feelings with wisdom and dignity:

S26
Being age 75 is no reason to stop learning. I share the learning experience with people of a similar age.

S28
At 83 I am still learning, but more slowly.

S18
But then again, I'm one of the slow ones, and I've had people sit at the side of me in a class that are older than me, and they're slower again. But if they can cope and come, so can I. You learn something everyday.

Doubt remains, however, about whether the implementation of Learndirect can adequately accommodate a presumed ageless concept of learning. The principal demographic find from this research into lifelong learning and the Ufi is that the majority of Learndirect students are older people. This pioneering educational opportunity helps the 'grey revolution'—the terminology for the influence of older adults within an ageing population (OU, 1995)—and thereby improves the quality of life of the 19.4 million people in the UK who are expected be aged 60+ in the next two decades (Onofri, 2004). This statistic includes a likely proportional increase from black and ethnic minority communities.

## 6.2 Older people

There is a presupposition that ageism is about pensioners. In fact, in today's society the boundary is drawn closer in. 'Older people' is a distinguishing term—not a definition—for those aged between 50 and 75. Its general usage derives from its deployment by specific or charitable organizations, for example, Saga and Age Concern, who work solely with this age group. Similarly, those people aged 75+ are called 'elderly'. 'Ageism is the notion that society, as a whole, is generally prejudiced against older people' (Victor, 2005, p.333): it infers being on the periphery of postmodern life—colloquially known as 'past it'. Advancing age can engender marginalizing labelling like 'cannot learn', or rankings such as redundant, inactive and dependent.

Nevertheless, most human beings are resilient to criticism. Third-agers are not usually deterred by misunderstandings. Instead, they regard any further achievement as a bonus, and are happy to take their time to repeat, re-learn or master new things. Despite increasing numbers of people leaving employment reluctantly, anti-ageist policies attract, and help, them back into work. The New Deal 50 Plus (1999) and 50+ Challenge (2001) are government initiatives that offer the incentives of a tax free Employment Credit and a Training Grant.

For many people entry to the Third Age is the celebratory dawn of fresh opportunities. They have time to travel and keep fit, to pursue hobbies and enjoy culture. So, to likewise guarantee maximum practical benefits and mental satisfaction in life's latter years, older people are being persuaded to extend their education. Arguably unprecedented longevity is the guarantor of a lifelong learning concept. People are living longer than in previous generations and can, therefore, be encouraged to prolong their learning. The advancements in knowledge of the ageing process have led to an abundance of associated literature and advice on financial, occupational, medical and educational matters. People are able to make short or long term informed choices about leisure arrangements and travel plans. Thus there are plenty of reasons for continuing to learn.

Protected opportunities abound for students through 2004–revised DfES affiliated initiatives. These include the ASP (Association of Learning

Providers), the Adult Basic Skills Strategy, FLOP (Financial Literacy for Older People) and the Age Positive campaign to tackle workplace discrimination. All of these are instrumental to a forward-looking delivery of education, as is the National Learning Network—it is currently training E-Guides. Another enterprise, under particular research scrutiny here, is the Ufi. One Learndirect provider promotes this particular supply of learning as an up-to-date individualized facility, though not without reservation:

> P18
> It is different because the selection of courses and how they are delivered through books and CD-ROMs are accessible whenever they want to learn. Plus it's online rather than just paper-based learning. And it comes with sound . . . which is fantastic . . . so people don't have to read the information; they can hear the information. From our point of view, we seem to feel that you either love it or you hate it . . . and if you hate it, that's it . . . and if you love it, you just go on and on. We have people who have done . . . six, seven or eight courses . . . gradually progressing or expanding their knowledge for their own particular use.

In spite of the better general profile now attached to older age, longer life expectancy still signals health impairments ahead—audio and/or visual being the most common. Therefore, a good supply of learning is only as good as the degree to which it adapts to, and backs-up, individuals' needs. Whatever the ingredients—large print and landscape format, correct lighting and strategically placed power points, hearing aids and audio tapes, precisely designed furniture and mobility apparatus, or arranged transport and trained staff—they can gel together for effective personal development. It is unrealistic to expect such modifiability and still connect online to Learndirect from home, whereas in intentionally equipped centres it is possible to match the specifics of provider delivery and student need.

The facilitative aim of educators is to improve access to, and increase, widen and maintain participation in, learning through innovative practice. The Ufi, by means of its Learndirect network, is achieving some success in the field of lifelong learning, especially with one main age group.

The majority of people I interviewed were by chance Third Age learners. Bearing this in mind, I can reflect on the links between an agenda for learning in later life and three main factors. These are: first, the type and length of initial educational experience; secondly, the differentiation in occupational status, namely professional, white-collar or manual, and thirdly, the disproportionate recruitment of those of working age to those retired. Furthermore, if someone finished their schooling at the statutory age of 14, 15 or 16 years then the chance of them participating in learning, especially formally, as an older person is minimal (McGiveney, 1993). If my research, explicit of the Ufi, is not diffusing these theories then it must inevitably be contributing to changing them.

Many older people have difficulty managing their money, especially at a time when the processing of fiscal affairs is becoming more reliant on ICT. Tackling the financial literacy of online banking, credit facilities, re-regulated insurance policies and pension plans, in addition to juggling fixed incomes to pay taxes or utility and food bills, demands a certain level of patient and competent handling. Even the closure of a local post office can be a worry as some people cope uneasily with the loss of familiar personal contact and friendly advice. There are also situations where older women, raised in previous generations when females did not earn a wage or handle the household accounts, find themselves executing wills and distributing, or receiving, legacies. Changing circumstances are also a daunting prospect for one male student:

> S34
> I do think that people my age . . . a lot depends I suppose on your back-ground . . . what sort of a job . . . but there's a great fear in my mind that on a certain date I won't be able to do certain basic tasks. It might be paying the telephone, gas and electric bills . . . to make it simple. I don't worry too much about e-mails . . . sending messages . . . I suppose I could live with that. I could always write a letter, although it's not going to be as quick.

The type of learning location is meaningful to older people. If they feel comfortable, and are not put under pressure or patronized, then their achievement and retention is maximized. I certainly found no evidence of this particular age group of students working in Learndirect centres where a climate of curiosity, agility and amicability did not surround them. Silken Summers Age Care facilitators, who meet only students aged 50+, have constant empathy with that cohort. A mixture of dedicated personal input and sympathetic delivery of programmes supports a broad teaching and learning agenda geared to the peculiar problems and anticipated progress of older people.

P20

They thought setting up Learndirect in this centre would be a way of getting older people using the Internet . . . but here in particular because it's sort of a less frightening experience. Some of them have tried college courses; even 'Computers for the Terrified'. And they've found that although it's supposed to go at their own speed . . . they've found that there are youngsters there as well that a) are faster and b) catch the tutor's attention more than they can . . . then the tutors go to them more than the older people, because they're slower.

JIPs were set up in April 1999 for older people. They present an opening for registered agencies and voluntary organizations to partner health and education authorities in order to ascertain the needs of local people against locally-available services. Age Care are not 'joined up'; but in view of the active management of their centre, a small part of which is the competent formulating and dispensing of learning programmes, they would make worthy learning consultants:

P19

We've got a gentleman whose wife bought him a computer, who says 'why should I sit at my computer in my back bedroom frustrated when I can come here, talk to nice people, have a good cup of coffee and do the newsletter for the health group' (he has a breathing problem). He started on Learndirect to acquire, and then use, skills . . . he's now using our expertise.

From aged 50 years onwards people's participation in academic education in formal learning environments decreases to a minimum in Further Education, and virtually none in Higher Education. The respondents' quotes are all the time disclosing the bases of new theory. In the later life stages they are inclined to find learning too stressful to outweigh any necessity to undertake certificated courses. There is no guarantee of improved self-concept or economic reward, and their effort or success may be little appreciated outside academia. Consequently, for some older people Learndirect is an appealing option because it also offers 'interest-only' study programmes:

S33

Well I think we're all learning as we go along. I'm astonished how little I know. But if you ask me am I now at my stage of life . . . remember, you know, I retired . . . considering doing something which requires some major input—no, I'm not going to do that. But it'd be different for somebody younger.

P21

In the libraries I have several learners who are in their eighties. I think it's very useful for older people who have never touched a computer to be able to get on to a computer, and with the beginners' courses be competent in a relatively short space of time. And also, not to be too worried about being in a 'class situation'; having to keep up with other people, or having to do exams . . . because they don't have to.

However, it is not found from the fieldwork that the decline in learning necessarily coincides with finishing employment. Most of the courses being taken by Third-agers are vocational; only a few are accredited:

P10

The majority of our learners are retired; people who have never used a computer before. So 80% of people are really starting from scratch. We are attracting a few learners who are looking for job improvement, but they are a small minority. As the centre matures it is increasing: we are getting more who need it for work or who feel they want to get back into work, or who also want a qualification.

Retirement marks a change in lifestyle. For some people being excluded from the world of work leads to negative self-perception; for others it engenders versatility and they feel free to take on new, or previously curbed and suspended, challenges. In either case it means taking on the responsibility to break down physical and psychological barriers, and adapt to change. A provider and a student agree that learning can lead the way:

P15

Women or men who have been retired are basically wanting to keep up with their grandchildren; because they can learn it's opened up a new experience. They come in saying 'oh little Joey can do this, and I feel stupid'. And you say 'look now it's alright don't worry'. And we get them on the net and they're e-mailing their friends in Australia.

S34

I thought at my stage of life, now that I'm retired . . . I felt that if I wasn't careful life was going to pass me by unless I accepted the challenge to try to learn more about computers.

National organizations, like the Older Peoples Advisory Group (OPAG) and Help the Aged, and community based groups, such as an Over 60s' Club, can represent, inform, guide and care specifically for older people against adversity at the often vulnerable time of their transition from work to retirement. These associations realize the benefits of continued education, including its potential to work like preventative medicine, and are happy to partner providers of lifelong learning—for instance, the Local Skills Councils—to ameliorate understandings.

Nevertheless one organization specific to older people, having welcomed Learndirect into their centre, now openly criticize it. With expert knowledge of the later life stages, and sensitised to the requirements of their clientele, two members of staff can rightly express their opinions about the learning content and expected mode of delivery:

P19

The Learndirect courses are fine if people have a basic understanding of computers. But even the Surf Direct course that Learndirect do is not suitable for older people because they have to spend maybe three to four weeks with Sheena and Paul who are our tutors here to get them to a level where they can switch the machine on. They can move the mouse . . . they do not know what a drop-down menu is. We had the idea that courses for Learndirect would be very basic . . . we could just say 'here's a computer . . . here's how you switch it on . . . here's the course'. It hasn't worked out that way. We've had to design our own introductory courses for them.

P20

We've got one particular lady . . . I think she could type because of her previous work in the police force. She's in her seventies now. I think she's quite involved in the church, and she wanted to send letters to people in the church. So we put her on a Learndirect word-processing course and it was just far too advanced, and it was covering things that she didn't really need. So it's put her off and she doesn't come anymore, which is disappointing. So now we're looking at doing different things.

Hence, the apparent strong view from P19 and P20 is that the Ufi's philosophy is not targeted at continuous learning. Instead it is a commercial venture to produce, market and sell learning materials. These providers cannot find any tie-up of Learndirect to lifelong learning for older people. Another respondent agrees:

P21
We've struggled with Learndirect courses here because, well, they're not geared up for older people at all. We are dealing with people who have very good basic skills because they've been through the old-fashioned education system where the 3Rs were very important. And particularly for this target area with people who may be retired profession-als . . . retired ICC workers who had to have a basic level of education to get into ICC, the main employer around here. Also a lot of our older people don't want to do formal courses; they want to see computers as a hobby thing. They don't want to think 'oh, it's difficult to get through this and I have to complete this section of the course'.

Although Learndirect does bestow changed experiences from those that people have been used to, one individual explains why the decision to become a student seems sensible and inevitable:

S34
I've obviously been brought up in a different era to the present genera-tion. I feel that if I don't accept that challenge to learn something new I'm just going to be left behind, and it's only by talking to children and younger people in business that you realize that it's the modern idiom of communication as well as learning. Within a few years time we may find that people of my generation who haven't learned the computer are go-ing to be really stuck.

For another student, increasing age has led to increased satisfaction, to the extent of excitement, for learning:

S14
And I'm that keen on it that . . . you'll see a thing I wrote for the local paper . . . that's my photograph there.

Once enthusiasm and curiosity are thus established, then permanent engagement with learning becomes a reality. Many older people tend to have routinely organized lifestyles and can fit all their commitments into a tidy schedule. They attend Learndirect centres punctually and regularly at prearranged times to suit both parties. If, usually unexpectedly, forced to face life's tribulations, they refuse to give in to them and eventually recover their strength of purpose for learning. By way of illustration:

> P15
> This morning an old gentleman . . . he's 70 years old, he enrolled at Wilken, and he's been on and off courses due to health problems for the last couple of years. I'm so glad he's come in today because he wants to start again.

Third-agers who want to share an experience that adds to the quality of later life can find fulfilment through Learndirect. However, some of them will not ask for help; maybe pride is involved—not wanting to appear 'stupid'—and, by not doing so, become frustrated with an unfamiliar support mechanism. A potentially traumatic learning situation can be diffused if a tutor assesses a student's prior formal and experiential learning:

> P19
> Everyone who comes is given advice. Sheena will talk to somebody— 'what do you know already . . . what do you want to use . . . what do you want to use it for . . . is it for your job . . . do you want a qualification?'—and get all the information from them, and then suggest what we think is the right course. And for some people it may be that Learndirect is exactly what they are looking for.

> P6
> What Martin does with a new starter is go through first a pre-fabricated on-line test of a persons likes, dislikes, needs, aspirations, capabilities etcetera . . . and it produces a full profile of the person.

The escalation of information and learning technology has heightened related social issues for older people. It is a previously unknown educational domain for many individuals. They are soon fascinated by a computer, become adept at its manipulation, and thus have more frequent in-depth communication with family and friends. Older people happily spend many daytime hours in Learndirect centres, but often, because they do not wish to venture outdoors in the evening, some prefer to operate from the safety and comfort of their homes:

> P9
> The eldest Learndirect learner I have had the pleasure to help and support is now at the age of 80. He has gained valuable skills in using the Internet and attachment facilities. He was a bit technophobic at first, but is now fully conversant with the Internet—a wiz with e-mail. He is now in regular contact with his daughters in America and Australia and receives pictures of his grandchildren . . . at any time of the day or night.

The final data allocated to this demographic category—and most pleasing for me, as an older person, a lifelong learner and a teacher, to record—is that, alongside escalating advancements in the field of information and communication technology, combined personal and professional development seems limitless. It is possible to practise new skills as a qualified educator to the benefit of local society:

> P3
> We've had a guy come in here . . . 62 now . . . 60 when he came . . . literally didn't know what a computer was. From a basic course . . . went on another course . . . another course. He's now just got a teaching qualification and a job as a technician with colleges in the community.

The life-experiences that Third-agers bring to the learning situation are regarded as valuable or problematical (Bourgeois, 1999). Some discourses are conducive to their inclusion, for example, the social sciences. On the other hand, 'attitudes may become entrenched by life-experiences, often in a narrow way' (p.121).

Despite this polarization of view, it could be argued that the majority of my older interviewees have gained and earned many of life's most meaningful attributes. Through their sustained efforts, and experience, at home and in their job, they appear to be wise people who, according to research quoted by Coleman and O'Hanlon (2004), have:

> Greater intelligence and maturity (Sternberg, 2000); greater ego development, autonomy and psychological mindedness (Wink and Helson, 1997); better psychological heath (Ardelt, 1997; Erikson et al., 1986);

greater success in dealing with life challenges (Kramer, 2000); and more
successful ageing

(Baltes et al., 1992)

(Coleman and O'Hanlon, 2004, p.55)

Older people are, therefore, responsible and respectful mature citizens
deserving of the pleasure and rewards of lifelong learning.

# Chapter 7
## Technological Issues Drawn from the Fieldwork

People today live in the Information Age. They interact in a society perpetuated by globalized communication, and thus face coping with the many changes borne thereof. Should they engage in 'active citizenship' they are seen as rising to this challenge. Ways of pitching this key element of the postmodern era at a general level are continually being sought. Proving a successful logistic for reaching the educable masses is information and communication technology (ICT): increased access to the Internet is a big step towards reducing social dualism. Similarly, the use of information and learning technology (ILT) is currently prevalent in a variety of teaching and learning situations.

### 7.1 Information and Communication/Learning Technology

The nuclei of the Ufi's delivery of lifelong learning are ICT and ILT. Learndirect is the broker of its self-acclaimed high quality learning packages. Their dissemination and monitoring are exercised through government and commercial contracts to purposely laid-out and well-equipped centres. The product hardware and software are subjected to rigorous quality control. Some of the providers express a strong interest in this technological domain, with less attachment to the learning content of, for instance, 'Skills for Life' programmes:

> P17
> I've been very involved with Learndirect for three years . . . since its infancy . . . so therefore . . . for me . . . it's for releasing people's potential. We're getting students who are accessing courses within the college that will come to us to learn something different as well. We have had two students this morning . . . they're doing what's called A+, which is programming and networking. But they need to know more about the technical side, so they come here to use the computer to learn about hardware and software.

Computer mediated knowledge is now a basic life skill needed for sharing in a democratic society. Some people expect to change jobs three or four times in their lifetime:

S36

I come to Learndirect so I can get a better job. I worked at the bakery when I left school but when my little girl went to school I got bored. If I learn the computer I can go to work in an office . . . really I want to work at the hospital.

In order to do that they re-train; especially by keeping pace with leading edge techniques:

P8

As the majority of people have not used a PC correctly, one of the key things they will have to master is a computer, and from that they can learn whatever material is being offered through the PC. I think small businesses are going to have to realize that 'crunch time' has come and, for whatever reason, they might have to close down, and people are not going to get other jobs unless they are computer literate.

According to Spencer (2004, p.197) 'these technologies were developed to help achieve economic goals of training and re-education of adults rather than social adult education'. However, the interviewees display less profundity:

S16

IT is now the third skill which has to be achieved . . . which is quite worrying because only about fourteen years ago you only had one computer lesson in school. The change . . . it's just become that rapid.

Learning courses are geared to the personal computer (PC). They deal specifically with its technical workings, trouble-shooting and maintenance, or they are designed around its uses. Wherever students are access-based to the Internet—in the home, workplace or a learning centre—they concentrate on reaching a level of expertise in one or the other, before both, fields.

P2

There are two situations really here: one is where a student doesn't have a computer at home . . . isn't web linked. They can come into college . . . here we have a learning centre which is equipped with three dedicated computer assisted set-ups accessible between 9 and 9. But mainly the enquiries we get are from people that have computers. In fact computer technology is one of the first things they want to know about. A lot of the courses are delivered only by using the Web. So therefore they've also got to have a computer and be web-linked. But there is a balance, and there are some courses which are delivered off-line by CD-ROM or by word-processing.

The students are obviously keen to seize the chance, via Learndirect, to become computer literate and enlist with e-mail and the World Wide Web. These are two applications within the Internet infrastructure. Both embody extensive facilities that efficiently foster lifelong learning—for example, electronic mail-groups or conferencing, and dual-sense multimedia. All the processes are subject-orientated, explorative, and use interactive multi-media software. If information absorbed by working through differently 'graded' software packages, such as Surf Direct and Sage Accounts, generates rational thinking then the on-line method of learning, albeit a somewhat repetitive mechanical exercise that might isolate the student, is educationally sound. It constitutes a stimulating knowledge base for contemporary democratic argument. Nonetheless, according to one provider:

P16
Most people who come to us are simply wanting to learn how to use the PC, not learning as such.

However, one certain student remains interested in 'learning as such'. His confused initiation to Learndirect leaves him unconvinced of the superiority of technically-aided behaviourist pedagogy over traditional modes of delivering education. Nonetheless, committed to lifelong learning, he determinately perseveres:

S32
I mean . . . if you're starting on the basics all you're getting is a pair of earphones which you don't even know how to adjust properly . . . whether they're loud or soft, or whatever. I mean . . . you're faced with an array of keyboard which you know nothing about . . . an array of the instructions on a pair of earphones . . . long delays between computer instruction items. The courses are not kept up to date. The first part of the course does not always correspond with the end. It's hard-going . . . I think . . . difficult. But yes, I think I'm continuing to learn. I prefer books actually. I read a lot . . . that's the main thing I like. I prefer a book any day of the week to a computer.

People new to Learndirect are usually apprehensive of the word 'technology'. To them it translates as more confusion in an increasingly complex world. Experiencing difficulties with a PC is the dread of many students, indeed tantamount to a panic situation:

S35
The computer had crashed previously, and it wasn't easy to log on. Sometimes the programmes stick.

S24
Before I came here I was literally terrified of the computer. I wouldn't even look at one because I was so frightened that . . . I think well, I'm not quite clever in the brain . . . but I really thought that if I pressed the wrong button I would delete everything that was on it.

Knowing that a complete range of instant expert help is to hand essentially, and effectively, keeps the students' progress on track. Whilst one provider admits to a loophole in Learndirect's deliverance, her counterpart and a student insist that a twinned resources support system of mechanical reinforcement and human assistance is in place:

P9
The minimum feature that I have found with Learndirect is possibly the lack of on-line support.

P21
It's the computer . . . the voice at the other end of the earphones. And while they're with the computer and the earphones there are people alongside who are specialists; who can help them if they get stuck. They do get a tutor, and we do refer them to 'Study Skills' because we quite like them to go into the Collegiate to do their courses.

S2
It's support that's needed. How easy it is when you start doing a course . . . the help that the computer gives you. I just find it such an appropriate way of learning different things; from switching a computer on, to learning about Microsoft Word 2000.

Compared to many learners elsewhere, such as school pupils or undergraduates, some Learndirect students are at the outset technologically unsophisticated. Because of this, providers may appear to them to have an 'off-putting', distant or authoritarian presence. However, the Ufi, in order to harness its vision to fit learning into the lives of individuals, insists in its *Strategic Plan—2002–2005* that the students' tuition requirements and expectations are paramount.

Admittedly the executive summary of the plan reads rather like a marketing leaflet than an unbiased critique of an educational initiative: the Chairman (Greener, 2002, p.4) says, 'through the use of e-learning, Ufi/Learndirect with its partners will continue to expand the learning market'. Despite this singular emphasis I gain the impression that the Ufi is very aware of sustaining the entrepreneurial type of change that it is portraying for post–19 learning. It is not a conventionally-organized university in terms of doctrine and status, but it is nevertheless a self-reliant initiative with the 'institutional capacity to be highly proactive . . . to go on changing itself and adapting effectively to a changing society, one that allows its groups and individuals to become more effective than previously' (Clark, 2004, p.174).

The Ufi has to be, and is, committed to educational professionalism on the basis that: first, as a publicly-privately financed partnership it is subject to quality assurance, and secondly, it is always sufficiently solvent to recruit solely well-qualified ICT tutors, and its policy is to do exactly that— to work conventionally, or otherwise.

P14
I book two-hour slots for the use of computers in community and school libraries. They're static centres . . . it's me that's mobile.

Mentoring is widely accepted in the current education service that supports lifelong learning. 'Huge emphasis is placed on voluntary and informal processes in a culture that supports coaching and mentoring' (Hargreaves, 2004, p.42). Nevertheless, a dictum from the Ufi is that Learndirect centres should not retain volunteers. This runs counter to the view of many community organizations that value the volunteers' complementary role to teachers; often because they cannot consistently pay to the latter's salary scale.

The provision of accessible e-learning is indispensable for disabled learners. This is a requirement of the Disability Discrimination Act (1995). As a tool for socio-cultural inclusion, 'access technology' is a growth area: its potential to uphold learning is exciting. Virtual environments, known as 'virtual reality', are 'computer-generated, three-dimensional environments which respond in real time to the activity of their users' (Standen and Brown, 2004, p.97). They specifically allow for people with learning difficulties:

> First . . . to learn by making mistakes but without suffering the real, humiliating or dangerous consequences of their errors. Secondly, virtual worlds can be manipulated in ways the real world cannot be . . . constructed in any way the designer or teacher requires. Thirdly, rules and abstract concepts can be conveyed without the use of language or other symbol systems.
>
> (Standen and Brown, 2004, pp.98–99)

Dedicated staff members who work alongside disabled people often get involved in the design and development of adaptive apparatus. They naturally become exited about thus guaranteeing the successful execution of a variety of learning programmes. The stimulation of the students' physical abilities and mental assertiveness leads to applied 'worldly' activities, such as their gainful employment:

> P6
> We've got . . . for physical impairments things that just drag balls with large and small controls . . . for visual impairments the big keyboards in various different forms, screen magnifiers, screen readers . . . which actually translate what is read on the screen into the spoken word. We've also got some software specifically for stroke and aphasia . . . because those obviously change people's perception of how they see and understand things . . . special stuff to make sure that they can communicate and learn to understand better.

> P7
> There is piece of software called Learndirect Teacher . . . it's a sort of skills matching. So you look at what they have and haven't got; what they can and can't do . . . and you look to fill the gaps. And then you can actually feed them into the system armed with the sort of information, skills and needs that they can actually use to go and get something. And then they can match the job opportunities that are up on the advertisements.

It is apparent from P6's and P7's responses that the technological era is impacting strongly on the nature of learning. Yet, I question if, at the same time, effort and initiative are being diminished, and intuition and creativity being replaced. Based on my analysis of the collected data these concerns seem unlikely to materialize. The integration of economic, socio-cultural and demographic influences on learning is a powerful life-changing force, and technology is here to join them. At one Learndirect centre in particular there are socially-positive arrangements in place to integrate technological growth with the joint endeavours of business and gerontology:

> P19
> We've just started a project pilot with British Telecom—'Home Compu-ting'—who are looking at developing their area of computing and older people. We are offering quite good rates of buying computers for older people . . . so the basic computer starts at £450. Part of the package is that the BT engineer comes to the house, sets the whole thing up, puts all the wires in place, sets up the Internet connection, sets up the e-mail, maybe spends two to three hours with that older person, and puts all the icons on the front screen that they want. And then part of the package is that they have a three-month telephone helpline support. The laptop is £750 . . . and the prices have come down since we started the pi-lot . . . and you can buy an optical mouse—that's £30 extra.

Hence, technology is being used in an unrestricted environment of gregariousness. The computer is prolific in maintaining and extending people's socio-cultural circle. It changes their methods of communicating and getting information:

> S22
> I always thought I'd never send e-mail letters to people. I'd rather type letters, or write letters, and put them in the post and that . . . and now I'm inclined to do that only for older people.

There are innumerable user facilities: utility services include banking, bill payment, 'round-the-clock' food and hardware shopping, and ticket bookings for travel, sporting events, conferences and cinema/concerts with an e-mail confirmation amenity. Individuals frequently access—in order to keep-up correspondences and make new acquaintances online—Instant Messenger, Friends Re-united and 'chat-rooms'. Additionally, search resources like ArticleFirst and Google are perused to obtain deeper knowledge of, for example, science or the humanities, and to gather extensive information about, maybe, leisure pastimes like genealogy and natural history.

By briefly describing some 'common' applications of technology I have indicated that the majority of the postmodern population have some interest in e-learning. In fact, global technological infrastructures allow for increasingly rapid cultural transmission (Oliver, 2005). I have also alluded to the idea of a connection between ICT and the concept of lifelong learning, but this relationship is not straightforward. Information and communication technology is not used by people who find it too difficult, consider it to be of no value, or who suffer from Technophobia—fear or anxiety about ICT—a condition that affects half of the UK population (Wheeler, 2005).

Since lifelong learning begins at birth most children are initiated to technology through curriculum delivery in the primary school classroom, especially in literacy, numeracy, science and music (Wheeler, 2005). However, at secondary school level Leask and Pachler (1999) advocate a change for the delivery and purpose of ICT by saying:

> We believe that changes in the world around us present us with the moral obligation to prepare young people for an adult life that increasingly requires knowledge, skills and understanding different from those traditionally covered by school curricula.
>
> (Leask and Pachler, 1999, p.xix)

In order to find out if further changes take place at the post-compulsory educational stage in its development, I will now discuss and analyse the e-learning experience in the context of adult learning and the Ufi.

## 7.2 The e-Learning Experience

E-learning is a means of learning by using ILT. It will not replace conventional ideals and practices (Anderson and Garrison, 2003) because it has 'unique capabilities to support asynchronous, collaborative communication in a dynamic and adaptable educational context' (p.22). Dowling (2004) disagrees on the basis that:

> The capacity of technology to overcome temporal and spatial constraints has obvious synergies with the need to learn at a time, place and rate determined by individual requirements rather than formal structures.
>
> (Dowling, 2004, p.123)

Nonetheless, there are varying contemplations, from justification to criticism, of the Government's promotion and investment in e-learning—namely, the Ufi. Those directly involved in accomplishing its objectives—the Learndirect providers and their students—describe, what are for them, the highlights and pitfalls; the pendulum swinging in favour of the former.

It is the conviction of some of the interviewees that the advent of e-learning coincided with 'lifelong learning for all'. This is a debatable point. My investigation has already discovered that continued learning is the outcome of more than one determinant. However, the general view lingers that, prior to the use of technology, access to, and participation in, education were restricted:

P18
It is to bring learning to the masses . . . it's not just college students. It's open for everyone to learn how to use the Internet because even if they're doing a 'word' course they're accessing the course through the Internet. So they're learning how to use the Internet all the time.

P10
Learndirect means to me access to computer courses for people who would not normally have access to them. It means being able to do courses anywhere they want . . . home, in a centre, libraries . . . and it generally means providing support to people where they wouldn't normally get support.

In experiencing e-learning people are trying to fill unforeseen holes in their lifestyles. They learn to manoeuvre around the inestimable changes of the postmodern world. In most cases it is a search for the sense of 'well-being'; an imprecise notion that in some way relates to the extent to which individuals needs and wants are met. It might be perceived as the bedrock and yardstick of satisfaction in a variety of life situations. Beyond the absolute need for physical survival, desires are freely chosen. Personal satisfaction is based on relative criteria—perhaps self-judgement in everyday situations or comparing oneself with other people. Well-being might also be partly measured in terms of educational achievement like becoming computer literate; and thereby, for one student, it is a direct consequence of the Learndirect experience:

S30

You can start at any level in a variety of subjects. There's no limit, but it gets progressively more difficult. Learndirect covers all computer related courses; also word-processing, spreadsheets and databases. But it's a question really of what you need it for . . . for example, for a particular application of accounts like calculating profit, to send e-mails, to formulate pictures and diagrams . . . you can do all kinds of things.

There are individualistic perceptions of the usefulness of the computer. For another student, learning is the bonus to newly achieved skills; or vice versa:

S10

At first I used to write everything down in case I couldn't remember it. Now I find once you start actually using it, and you make your mistakes, you learn . . . you learn on here. And I think that is perhaps the difference in the sort of learning. It's practical because you learn as you are doing it, whereas from books and things you just have to get it into your head.

Two other students believe that Learndirect is the bedrock and yardstick of satisfaction in a variety of learning and life circumstances. Technological 'know how' is a purposeful tool for upholding voluntary duties and cementing family relationships. It fills an emotional cavity by building and sustaining a self-confident approach to learning:

S10

I do a lot of charity work in the sense of treasurer-ships, and I thought well maybe there was some aspect of the computer that I could use to help me in my job.

S17

I've had a computer at home for three years. My son bought me the whole set up, and all I did was play games on it. So when Learndirect came up I thought what a wonderful opportunity . . . and I haven't regretted a minute. When I started a lot of them had already done this CLAIT (computer literacy and information technology) and the 'driving licence' . . . I'm feeling really optimistic so I'll be doing them as well. I'm really into e-mails: I'm in touch with all family down South. It's just wonderful.

An older student, recognizing the swiftness of change, yearns to keep his learning methods up to date. He treads cautiously but steadfastly, anxious to vie with the mounting intricacies of ICT:

S33
I had a computer when I worked in the bank. We had our own branch terminal . . . it's a little bit different to this programme. So I thought I'd like to get in on the ground floor and learn the basics of it, and then when I've gained a bit of confidence I could then decide whether to buy a computer. The one I had in the bank was geared to the banking industry and how to use it within a branch system, and by comparison that seemed very simple. But it's early days. I'm interested in it and I don't want to give up, though I've met a little bit of a minefield at the moment.

One Learndirect provider intimates how technology can proactively respond to the call of a busy lifestyle. Her innovative thinking reveals her commitment to carrying out the mission of her employer—ultimately the Ufi—and her ongoing belief in its theorizing of learning:

P13
We think it's the ideal solution because you know how busy we all are these days, especially in this electronic world . . . get an e-mail . . . you're meant to have a reply within a minute. So we don't have a lot of time to actually come out of our demanding working lives and personal lives. Learndirect has very good potential within the workplace because if somebody has Internet access at lunchtime they can just 'pop-on', do an hour on their course, maybe do some homework when they get home, and just keep their minds ticking over doing something for themselves. They won't benefit only themselves but their companies.

ICT and ILT represent not just a passing trend. They are firmly planted by statute in educational practice to address learning needs at all phases and in all subject areas of compulsory schooling. This situation is not easy to mirror 'post 19'.

The Ufi is manifestly exploiting the potential of technology to enhance the experiences of all students continuing to learn within the scope of its jurisdiction. Of those enrolees who voluntarily gave respondent interviews—in situ in a variety of learning centres—the vast majority endorse this implementation of the Government's educational policy. Even a minor irritation serves to expose the extending popularity of Learndirect:

S18
The only thing is, there's not enough computers for everybody. So it's got to the stage when you have to book them, whereas before I could just get up and wander back in, like a drop-in centre. It's not like that now; it's changing. There are so many people now—which is good.

The multiplicity of technological application is universally acknowledged. It has the 'ability to dissolve boundaries, whether between countries or between subject, teacher and learner' (Florian and Hegarty, 2004, p.1). It also responds to people's increasing need for skills in finding, using and handling information, particularly in an electronic environment with courses such as MOSAIC (OU, 2003)—'Making Sense of Information in the Connected Age'.

There remains, however, scepticism about certain aspects of technologically-orientated learning. Brown and Duguid (2002) question whether virtual learning locations can displace physical ones. Indeed, notwithstanding the ongoing research in many fields of education there is still no known proven means of comparing e-learning with traditional teaching methods in terms of successful outcomes. Conversely, van Weert and Kendall (2004) make the evidential claim that the changing lifelong learning environment of the digital age is sustainable only if it is supported by ICT. Perhaps the analytical theorizing from the field data gathered in my case study can at least go some way towards altering this state of affairs.

# Chapter 8
## Educational Aspects Induced by Grounded Theory

### 8.1 The Nature of Education

Education is not something that happens only once—by law, between the ages of five to sixteen. Education today continues on a long and wide pathway of teaching and learning, and though not automatically available post-compulsory, can be lifelong.

Revised understandings of the andragogical model—the art and science of helping adults to learn—give credence to the fact that educational change is ongoing (Knowles, 2003). Three of the original underpinning assumptions distinguishing 'adultness' from pedagogy—these being, an autonomous self-concept, self-diagnosis of needs, and self-planned learning—are now comprehensively construed as self-directed with a facilitator to acquaint the student with the 'need to know'.

The Ufi abstains from the academic debate about pedagogy and andragogy. Instead, its overall concern is the provision of '19+' learning. Many Learndirect students simply acknowledge the existence of an imposed physical educational boundary, but having crossed it, continuing their education and lifelong learning become synonymous. Their succinct common interpretations of the concept blanket the many unpacked elements that lie within:

S12
It goes on through life so you can embrace new technology and ideas.

S15
Continuing to improve your knowledge and keep one's brain working.

S16
To study something that is to my advantage for many years . . . and benefit from one level to another. Information I can use to make life easier.

S4
Always looking to learn new things every day: it means that it's never too late.

S22
To get the best out of life one needs a challenge like learning a new skill.

S35
Lifelong learning is something that can give you a better quality of life.

Therefore, in this dominant lifelong form, education has come to be known as an infinitely available interdisciplinary commodity. It also attracts the analogies 'changeability' and 'possibility':

P3
Lifelong learning changes people's learning experiences for the positive. It changes the perception of education, and how it can be beneficial for them. I think it's a growing area. People now realize that because you're retired, or because you're unemployed, education doesn't stop. I think a lot of mature people—which includes myself . . . I'm 50 years old . . . I came back to college when I was 40 . . . got this job—are now realizing countrywide . . . not just by us but by national campaigns . . . that . . . as soon as you left school that was it, that was the end of your education unless you were clever enough to go to college . . . that perception has changed now.

Distance education (DE), a constantly evolving area of practice, is currently attainable by a wider number of students in the mode of open distance learning (ODL). The terms 'lifelong education' and 'lifelong learning', normatively approved in policy discourse, are reciprocal and interrelated (Field and Leicester, 2000). Yet some features of the latter apparently run contrary to dependent conventional education. The freedom of choice of learning styles and pathways, and no formal entry requirements, mean that ODL enrolment is open to all. Wedemeyer (2003) says:

Wherever learners may live, however remote from instructional recourses, whatever their socio-economic condition, the ancient restrictions to access derived from a space-time-elite perception of learning can be overcome by various communications media.
(Wedemeyer, 2003, p.343)

Two Learndirect providers appear not to connect education to their own delivery mode of learning; the inference being that education is, for the one more orthodox, and for the other symbolic of statutory schooling:

P9
Learndirect is an opportunity for people to actually take on board any thoughts or ambitions that they might want to pursue. It's flexible learn-

ing; it's accessible . . . that's how I see it. I don't see it as a traditional means of learning.

P10
I think we have to address the whole issue of our education in the UK. You go abroad into Europe . . . and the schools there, and the kids there . . . they seem a lot more switched on.

Despite these differing notions of lifelong learning there is an indication, evidenced by another provider's interview response, that continuing to learn results from a desire for personal and professional development. People struggle to free themselves from anonymity, to assay their true originality and assimilate their potentialities. The Ufi claims to offer greater scope to each individual. It asserts its ability and readiness to cater for the wants of a greater diversity of people by delivering education through the Learndirect network—a manner designedly less ruthless that that imposed by compulsory schooling:

P11
I believe you never stop learning. It doesn't matter if you get a course book . . . you get a CD-Rom . . . you get a tape . . . you're learning even when you're coming over any pedestrian crossing never having used the buttons before . . . you're always learning. Lifelong to me is people continually developing themselves, whether they need to for career purposes or whether for personal reasons.

P2
I guess the big move behind it is it fits in with one of the college principles of raising the achievements and aspirations of those in our community. And I think the Ufi's principles are very much in line with that, in terms of enabling people to move jobs and trying to get numerous improvements in the borough.

Moreover, educational institutions as repositories of social justice and civilizing values can liberalize people's access to study programmes that meet their needs or fulfil their ambitions. At this point, therefore, I am led to question if, within traditional colleges, the set-up of Learndirect is a distinctive approach to lifelong learning. Alternatively, are they entities with dissimilar objectives?

P3

I'd say at the moment lifelong learning and Learndirect operate as two different philosophies or systems. There isn't a natural tie-up between traditional college education and Learndirect; mainly because it's a bureaucratic system which sits aside from the traditional college application.

A Learndirect pledge to learners is 'to offer the time, place, pace and style of learning that responds to their needs (Ufi, 2002, p.10) In fact, all the values underpinning the Ufi's combined vision and mission are immersed in the agenda of continuous learning. When the two concepts are deemed to separate it is because the latter translates into pure educational philosophy, while Learndirect appears to function as an absolute commercial venture. The providers try hard to marry the two ideas, but often expose their preferred allegiance:

P2

At the end of the day the colleges . . . they do have to operate in a Learndirect approved . . . in a specific way, and that is poles outside traditional teaching. People who come in for a hobby want to do courses at the same level. We need to grasp them and encourage them to move up, or else we won't get funded. Because we are an educational background we have to make money; that's the 'name of the game' these days. But we're not in it for profit; we like to be achieving.

P21

Some big companies run their own Learndirect centres and I think you may well have a problem there if you're going to link up with academia.

In line with Piagetian theory (1972), the teaching profession associates children's cognitive and moral development with an approximate age range: by the end of formal schooling the two have merged. Therefore, adult educators must expect not only rational thinking, but, in response to students' needs, integrate it with their reflective learning. Successful educational outcomes depend on assisting and sustaining the process of internalized learning, which is a communicative mechanism of knowledge transfer. Individuals might be persuaded to learn by didactic conversation and be stimulated by instructional learning materials. According to Cole (1998, p.34) 'literacy and numeracy are direct extensions of the basic mediating capacity of language'.

## 8.2 Learning Material

The Learndirect model of provision represents a crucial area of educational practice. Acting as human resource developers, the providers facilitate all formal, informal and incidental learning that takes place in their centres. Herein they claim that competence and judgement prevail to accurately negotiate personalized learning conditions that engage each student in deliberate critical thinking.

Learndirect promotes their product as pedagogically-designed, high-standard, cross-curricula e-learning; an acknowledgement to their belief that, to constantly upgrade technical skills is to expand the boundaries of education. Well-qualified experienced providers manage a year-round service not bounded by a constricting educational calendar. They are contracted to deliver the course portfolio to the Ufi criterion; that is, to 'push' learning for everyone, especially the 'Skills for Life' debenture which is a big part of their portfolio, and getting bigger. A provider enthuses when asked how he 'finds' Learndirect products:

> P16
> Very, very helpful indeed . . . marvellous stuff . . . the Skills for Life consists of what we would logically call basic skills. They cover numeracy, cash handling . . . it's very specifically tailored. There's a much greater usage of good software interactive programmes. A lot of it is down to the actual course material itself. The maths Maxtrack for people who require additional support . . . that's just one. We have targets to work to, and we make jolly sure that we do them well . . . in fact exceed our Learndirect contract.

Contrastingly, two other providers when faced in interview with considerations about the certainty of favourable end results—in essence implied doubt—for example, 'But what will be the replacement if you stop Learndirect here?'—quickly answer that the supplementary adult education would be 'tried and tested' learning packages, or the introduction of new ones. Moreover, one of their students is partially contented with that:

> P2
> Well we just still do have a trainee development department which does a lot of the fundamental courses that Learndirect offer by the way of

basic skills, skills for life, or things like computer technology . . . CLAIT or ECDL.

P3
A lot of things in education-wise are going to on-line. College has recently become a testing centre. We do ECDL, but we started off in Microsoft courses. Although Learndirect is the core function, and always will be, we've started branching out into other areas of online learning and training. We've always had a good Skill for Life provision anyway. Ann our SfL mentor has come across to us full-time just to oversee the SfL provision and the tutors. So she tends to offer little classes . . . additional support . . . and like BBC websites . . . and we'll move on into that.

S8
It changes the way people learn. I've not learnt anything for years really. Yes, I quite enjoy doing the new CLAIT and so . . . but that's not Learndirect.

It already appears from the interviewees' responses that the adult learning population is diverse. Individuals face many economic and sociocultural boundaries, and barriers, to continuing their education, including financial limits and the lack of English as a 'first language'. Being of mixed intellect and physical capability people's spirit and motive for learning are thus further conditioned. Job specific training, and recreational and ICT learning programmes, can address their aspirations while fulfilling many purposes. In addition, inspirational managers customize course content while conferring with the rules for operating a Learndirect centre, thus forging a fashioned bond with lifelong learning. One tutor advocates more simplistic user-friendly criteria conducive to the wide issue of ageing:

P20
We are putting on our own courses like 'digital photography for older people'.

We are using webwize materials like 'Alan Titchmarsh: how to be a gardener in eight stages'. So we're looking now at doing more fun things with them.

My fieldwork discloses that tutors who work with minority or marginalized groups are often eloquent—detailed, expressive and forthright—in sharing their views. I find that this is a syndrome of these particular cohorts being previously under-represented in, or ignored by, the traditional world of education and society at large. This point is exemplified in the Vactrum Disability Services centre where Learndirect becomes the final objective; a triumphant symbol of formularized learning determinedly achieved in difficult circumstances. The provider elaborates:

> P6
> You've got to recognize that people who are physically disabled think exactly the same . . . the same wants, needs, aspirations . . . same wishes to communicate. Sometimes people simply . . . they can't do it . . . it's hard to say it, but they're not daft. A lot of stepping-stones are put in place before we can actually get them to do any learning. We'll put our materials together then we can give an official course to do in their own time . . . just get it complete, and have a certificate of recognition. We've learnt a lot of other things on the way and a Learndirect course is a very nice little box to put it in and put a tick against it.

It is, therefore, suggested by the data analysis that the Ufi demonstrates its supply of learning by using technology. Central to Learndirect access and progression is competence in computer skills. There is a sense that growing emphasis is put on the students' attainment of these at the expense of their mental absorption of the learning substance of courses. Thus the ill-defined pedagogy/andragogy of e-learning is a lingering contentious issue. A book still retains its appeal as the ultimate learning artefact: it is aesthetically pleasing to see and touch. In addition, the content is verified by literary professionals—such as authors, academics and publishers—unlike that of its online counterpart.

## 8.3 Curricula

Professional educators know how, and have a paid and moral responsibility, to devise and teach to a curriculum—a specified course of study. Staging academic content with vocational and basic key skills enables a student to confidently make changes in many areas of their life. A wholly satisfying lifestyle conducted on a daily basis is the preserve of few people; but well-designed learning courses embedded across the disciplines and skills are effective aids to its achievement.

Learndirect purports to specialize in the field of high-quality curricular and course provision. They in fact do so with well-informed and experienced teaching staff acknowledging the concept of continued learning through their daily routines.

P3
Throughout the three centres I monitor the use of Learndirect. The products have come a long way from what they were in the beginning, and we've had to go through that tussle to get them improved. We get a new catalogue every twelve months and updates that cut out courses that are not viable. There were 700 at one point, but it might now be filtered down to about 150. I think they're trying to strike a balance.

P12
In the absence of the Centre Manager, I run the centre. So I do the interviews with the students. I enrol them on the Learndirect system. I file their paperwork and then greet them when they arrive the first time . . . do student induction. I take them through their courses and I provide them with assistance and support when they need it.

One provider is making a concerted attempt to devise a personalized curriculum reconcilable to the individualistic aptitudes of every student:

P6
We do a lot of sideline additional work which just incorporates people into their particular interests and skills We've got one learner who's doing his work on Tarzan: all his numeracy and literacy is based around Tarzan, which suits him great . . . he's a happy man! He couldn't do the conventional learning in college because they couldn't cope with his visual impairment. It's a different type of lifelong learning, I reckon we can be bigger and better than lifelong learning: we can create life from their learning.

Many of the student interviewees are receptive of the Learndirect approach to adult education and appreciative of their tutors' support.

S17
I'm doing two separate things . . . one today 'A Way with Words', and one on Saturday; it's a special one . . . it's difficult . . . a ten-week one on publishing.

S30

It's very useful for those who are post–19 that came out of school with no reading and writing skills because we can do basic numeracy and basic literacy. It is set out for you to learn without you finding it hard to do so. And there is no stigma of being in class and having to keep up with people.

Nevertheless, on occasion, a student's first chosen course might be a misfit; perhaps it overstretched their capabilities. With hope and patience a curriculum characterized by traits of originality and convenience is eventually made workable:

S8

The first one I did . . . word processing . . . it was actually quite horrendous. I believe they've had to alter it since. I only stuck it out because I'd got so far into it. I did a 'Check Point', which was punctuation; that wasn't bad. And then I had one 'Better Letters' . . . now this is why I came in the first place. I joined the literacy class just to improve my letter writing. Enid the tutor got me this CD, but I didn't actually do the course I just used it to help as I wanted to use it . . . still do. So I didn't get a certificate.

Learndirect is moving such personal literary aspirations forward, with added benefits for the local community and wider economy, and especially with respect to people whose first language is not English. To develop one's linguistic heritage is to try to perfect the mother tongue then communicate proficiently in foreign languages. A provider realizes the significance:

P16

I'm sure the narrow range of Learndirect courses will widen to encompass most areas of learning as now we have languages, which came on board from August. They've got 'Sage Accounts' coming on in February in some format or other. I think it is essential. I don't think you can generalize as to different groups who get training tool benefits from it. If you're looking into deprived areas then you're looking at 'Basic Skills English': asylum seekers . . . they're looking at just the basics . . . 'Citizen UK', a course now available to them.

It is long accepted in the field of education that academic learning extends opportunity. It continues to do so. In schools, colleges and universities the teaching of the natural sciences, mathematical knowledge, and an understanding of concepts in the social sciences, result in success in examinations, and the qualifications and skills needed for employment. My research project, in analysing the participants' data, has suggested many economic, socio-cultural, demographic and technological issues that impact on, or alter, this established formal format. Learning becomes less systematically organized: it becomes informal, its nature self-determined and self-evolved, and 'focused narrowly on micro processes' (Cullen et al., 2000, Summary).

The Government's centralizing and micro-management of learning—for example, via the Local Skills Councils and top-down provision like Learndirect—are dominant motivational mismatches that create problems for lifelong learning (Evans, 2003). Professional educators may feel demeaned by the accelerating number of non-vocational and non-accredited courses. It appears, therefore, that the pattern of learning is always changing.

## 8.4 Progress and Certification

The student population is pluralistic, reflecting the variegation of communities and society in general. Adult students are any age from sixteen onwards, and differ in educational background, ethnicity and faith. Their reasons for continuing their education also vary—maybe it is to upgrade job skills or learn a foreign language. There is a debate about the unique value of lifelong learning as an end in itself. There may be some doubt whether the Ufi really offers this, or is Learndirect its hidden agenda; a push to advance-on courses for economic reasons of increasing productivity and global competitiveness. It could be argued that through my fieldwork I found some answers.

Clearly-defined monitored pathways of progression lead to more, and a higher level, of learning. The providers know that their students cope best with bite-sized units. They are allowed to work at their own speed, repeating along the way if they wish, and advance at a pace appropriate to their interests, confidence and learning ability:

P20
The lady that's in there now is having an hour and a half because she is slower than most, and then she gets more out of it.

S24
I am slow. I mean I am slow at picking it up, but what I'm not sure of I do go back to it and do it again.

Learning progress can be regarded as a 'stage theory'; meaning that it is a supposition that development or movement towards something better takes place as certain factors arise. In particular, if contextually applied to this case study, progress takes place when Learndirect instigates or furthers educational achievement, in whatever form, and in consequence contributes to singularized lifelong learning and the compound learning society. Two providers express their version of progress:

P2
I think Learndirect is going to connect into life. It's more specific to the individual than the principles behind it. When the principles of Learndirect have been fully understood by students and they start to achieve I think it will promote Learndirect. People we've had so far . . . they're thinking about their next course before they've finished the first.

P6
Not all the learning outcomes are completely specific. Some are what the Learning and Skills Council calls soft outcomes . . . combination things about confidence, communication . . . just people getting generally more into society.

I am now finding that the Ufi's impact on lifelong learning is gradually becoming clearer. Once the students embark on Learndirect's learning trail their advancement is reinforced by newly acquired study skills. At its most intense learning can almost turn into an obsession, albeit a positive one. Conversely, it may grind to a halt:

P9
Some people are very particular about what they want, get it, and then call it a day. Their mindsets may be more about education as a means to an end, not an end in itself. Some you can't get rid of.

Most students, however, view enrolling with Learndirect as a starting point to better their lives. Progressive achievement, demonstrated by engaging with content that leads to the successful completion of a course, stimulates their further involvement in learning. Also, benefiting from continuous assessment, they may choose to advance their education through Learndirect:

P12
Learndirect has three to four levels of courses, so if they have prior skills we gauge their skills and put them on a course that's relevant for their level. If they have no prior attainment we put them on a basic course but monitor them all the time. And we can up them when they're ready to a higher-level course.

Alternatively, the students divert to other options on offer, mainly those provided through college networks:

P3
We tend to see Learndirect as a springboard to other things, whereby people will come in, will use the Surf Direct, then go on to the introductory courses. Most people will be happy with that, but a lot now are looking for qualifications . . . looking to get that back into employment. We have the advantage of course being a college that we can recommend them onto college courses. It's our policy never to turn anyone away without either finding a Learndirect course for them, or if the college doesn't offer it, an educational establishment that will.

The concept of educational progression embodies a practical lead to a given option—to be tested on newly acquired knowledge and skills; that is, a chance to demonstrate and gain recognition for one's proven ability. Informed by pilot research, the Ufi recently decided to introduce the operation of course mapping across to qualifications. Certain centres are currently offering the European Computer Driving Licence (ECDL). Hence providers are urging on, and are excited about, the streamlining of the perplexities of taking examinations:

P17
They can gain qualifications along the way as well if they wish. We're linked with the college, so they send people to me if they just want Learndirect courses and we send people across to them if they require qualifications. Plus eventually we're moving towards on-line testing. We can order their exam; then they can access their exam. It goes straight to the Board to be accredited.

P11

We've got more people showing interest in Learndirect because they can now do qualifications. Of those twelve . . . the lady that's just passed, she'd really enjoyed it so she'll move on now to the advanced and then the expert courses.

The students' need to get qualifications varies from lack of interest, to desire, to urgency. Those who have never passed an academic or vocational examination cite possible reasons for their situation: some have not been given the opportunity to be tested; others have not wanted it for fear of failure. However, once they engage with lifelong learning some students agree that any progress they make is pleasing. Moreover, consistent achievement leads to heightened satisfaction:

S1

I find it excellent for keeping my brain going because it gets me thinking. I'm the type of person that loves to do problems, so for me doing a test my brain has got to be going all the time. I can sit there and study it until I get it right.

S16

Learndirect is being able to come to this centre and get first-hand information on any subject that I wish to study. I've learned lots since I've come here. I wanted some extra-curricula studies and it's done that. It keeps me alert.

Two other students start to think about the necessity of job market specified certification. This might be the means of stepping back into employment, or assisting their future in general:

S22

I am with Standguide Training Centre doing a Modern Apprenticeship. I am using this centre at Ripley Dane College to achieve something that I have not done before like ECDL, which I am doing at the present.

S19

Learndirect courses are excellent. I like computers; but a lot of them in the Littleshaw do other courses. There's college upstairs, but it's too easy for me. So I need something like doing exams at the end of it. You don't

know what's going to happen do you, so I need some qualifications behind me.

Within the new market paradigm of globalization there is current
high profile desirability for the European Computer Driving Licence from
transnational manufacturing corporations and smaller service industry
organizations. On this basis, one might expect to find some of their employees, as employer-funded students, in Learndirect centres on this and
other certificated vocational training courses. The interviewees give no
indication that this is happening.

## 8.5 Virtual or Conventional Education

From a historical perspective adult education has been studied principally
within its cultural context. More recently 'adult education knowledge'
became available due to the impact of psychology, and 'the place of other
disciplines in learning theory, such as sociology and economics, has been
recognized' (Jarvis and Griffin, 2003, p.2). The advent of open distance
learning (ODL) expanded this theoretical belief and became a controversial
issue at the centre of much educational discourse. The two ideas about
education—conventional and virtual—are structurally incompatible.
Distance learning is considered 'industrialized' (Peters, 2003). It is 'the
process of alienation or isolation that can occur when students are con-
fronted with technical artefacts instead of human beings' (Simpson, 2000,
p.156).
Learndirect professes to reinforce lifelong learning. There is, however,
a misconception that the compilation of coursework and its subsequent
online delivery in affiliated centres, though subject to meeting fixed targets,
is a sufficient guarantee of effective education.
Reading large amounts of narrative text online is not educationally
sound in terms of motivating the learning experience. The content needs
to be in graded bite-sized sections, alternating with contact to facilitators,
and interspersed by face-to-face interaction with other students. On whether the online agenda upholds the traditional one, and vice versa, there are
individualist sentiments:

P20
Learndirect certainly seems different to them presumably because it's directly on a computer. But to be honest it's not as well structured as if

they were having a teacher or a lecturer. It's not enough in the way of exercises to consolidate what they've just been shown. You've no chance to try it out . . . experiment, so it's hard to consolidate what you've learnt. We recommend that people keep going back and do another bit again to reinforce it . . . take notes as well because there's no way you can remember it all.

The electronic delivery of adult learning in learning centres has strengths and drawbacks. It is neither better than, worse than, nor the antithesis of, conventional teaching methods in academic institutions. Bulpit (2003) finds that the difference between virtual and real learning environments is usually easily recognizable: the flexible working practices of the former, that include general conversation in open contemporary building with mobile-tolerant zones, contrasting with the required quiet, and restrictions on eating and drinking, in the latter. He asks 'how long will it be before students characterize their course in terms of the portal which they use as a reference point for their activities day by day rather than the lecture room (p.210).

Nonetheless, argument remains over the best form of provision. Some Learndirect students believe that virtual learning is a mediocre substitute for 'proper' education. The product of attitudinal change in teaching and learning, it is rendered inferior as inherently authoritarian, conspicuously closed and anti-social:

S26
The assumption that when I've been shown something I will know and understand it. Sometimes the instructions are very longwinded and confusing. There isn't always someone on the same course as you at the time you are at the centre, so you don't get enough assistance.

S32
I've sat here on occasions . . . . I've only been here a few times, bear in mind that I'm very much a novice . . . and within a few minutes I'm lost; then I'm embarrassed. I might go and ask one of the library as-sistants but they say, 'oh, we don't really know ourselves, and no we're not really here to do this sort of thing'. And they may spend a few minutes to get you started again and then you make another awful mistake. I've done things like signing off. . . . I signed off I think on one occasion I think twice by mistake, and I had to go and ask them to put it back on again. It's all very embarrassing.

There are perhaps too many irregularities between virtual and conventional education, brought about too quickly by political or economic instability, and technological invention, for S32, an older person, to fully understand or choose to accept. He typifies the Third-ager: he makes calculated decisions and takes lifelong learning seriously. After comparative reflection on previously explored methods, he gives his final, but unaltered, judgement:

S32
I think on balance I'll keep on going at this but I think I'd have to do it with someone who taught me properly. It's a bit like a correspondence course and it lacks that personal side which I think you need. I think it does have the disadvantage of it's a solitary learning process. In the past . . . many years ago . . . I've done correspondence courses, and I've also done full-time normal courses, and I know which is best. Well, which is best is certainly ones where you're being taught with a person.

Thus the matter of support arises again. Its centrality in the debate about the shift from a real to a virtual learning environment presents a challenging prospect for avant-garde educators. Vital to integrating the two concepts is an adventurously devised support network. This is the essential median to secure best practice from both learning worlds. Any link-up mechanism, like Learndirect, that supplies the online module of a traditional adult learning course can only embolden participation:

S33
What it means is what it says—Learndirect. I would think . . . I don't expect to get a lot of help: I expect to do it on my own. So that's the way I see it. I don't see it being one where I've got teachers. That's how I see Learndirect . . . which makes it difficult. It's not the easiest thing in the world because you've got no help, no support . . . or little help, and I find the . . . I think I've got a course tutor at Winsick . . . Shelley . . . but I don't know really how to get hold of Shelley, if you follow me.

A provider accedes to the urgency to close loopholes in the on-line learning support system for novice students:

P11
I would say that for 90% of our people Learndirect is the opposite from what they've done in the past. They haven't done distance learning.

They've never had an online tutor. So very few of them are familiar with the concept of not having a tutor with them all the time who knows everything about their subject. We always have a member of staff here to help out, but they're not proficient in every subject. With the general computing problems they're very useful, but when you start getting into specialist areas it's difficult for them.

Another provider is adamant that high-quality successful education—be it virtual or conventional—can only be correctly executed by professional educators of proven capability and experience:

P20

I act as a sort of tutor . . . more of a helper really . . . not what I call a proper tutor because I'm used to the teaching profession. To act for Learndirect we have to sign on as an online tutor, which I'm afraid I don't totally agree with. Because everybody needs a tutor, you have to sign even if you can't do the particular topic . . . which is a downer really. What we do is just sort of sit alongside people for when they get started in their first hour and make sure they're ok using the system and doing the course.

The research produced no shortage of provider interviewees with a counter conviction in this critical argument. The collective view is that the Learndirect phenomenon allows for reciprocation in the facilitation of expertise and of knowledge, and thus augments learning progress. Readily offered are versatile tutoring—for some learners almost to the point of dependency—and a miscellany of courses to continually add to the students' portfolios:

P1

We do have one-to-one coaching available as well as development workshops delivered by our trainers, either in a group or individually depending on the client's preference. We have materials available that can also be used at home or for long-distance learning to support development.

S24

(Have you heard the expression 'lifelong learning'?) Not really no. (Do you think you can see a lifetime of getting more interested in learning?) At this moment . . . yes. As each course finishes I would try something that Paul suggests if he thinks it's something that I would probably be able to do.

Therefore support, given in whatever manner, is indispensable to the establishment of the University for Industry as a lifelong learning initiative. Tantamount to furthering education, support is a vital means of retaining the present learners.

## 8.6 Retention

The increased high profile of lifelong learning, coupled with changing funding strategies to maintain it, has brought about a divergent student body whose retention rate is subjected to careful scrutiny. Adults are usually learning voluntarily, so it is relatively easy for them to abandon unsatisfying situations. There are many causal type factors, such as institution, subject, measurement and reason; but course completion results largely from adequate support networks.

The principles underlying retention work include 'meta-cognition and personal development planning, diversity, individuality and success ethos, learner independence, and recognition of underachievement' (Sellers and van der Velden, 2003, p.17). Given these, more work is finished in totality: personal satisfaction, trust, confidence and enthusiasm levels rise, and retention, along with the capacity for continued learning, is increasingly guaranteed. Kasworm et al. (2002) believe that recruiting and retaining adult students is the responsibility of all educationalists. They describe 'ten retention strategies' (pp.55–58): among them are entry advisement, ICT, and special needs services.

Hence, withdrawing from a course that one considers unsuitable in terms of content, teaching method, fellow students, location, workload or because of unexpected personal circumstances should not be viewed as failure, but part of the overall process of learning. One provider is well aware of this:

P21
People do genuinely . . . we do have some that dropout for one reason or another . . . not usually money . . . more lack of time; or the fact that they may have bitten off more that they can chew . . . related to time. We do screen them to some extent to make sure that they can do the course that they're enrolling for.

Implied by a different provider is that Learndirect do not operate a sufficiently expedient, student-centred approach to tracing dropout reasons. When asked if there are any ways of sustaining students' attention and interest, his reply was:

P2
It's very difficult to judge that because . . . because you're doing remote online learning you don't get that feedback of what a student needs . . . that particular type of stimulation or help and advice. It's only when they themselves actually make their minds up to get that sort of help that you can do it.

A centre manager detects a specific cause of course dropout, and a student identifies another:

P20
Older people need one-to-one tuition. I mean you do tend to go slow up when you get older. And if they're just not getting enough attention so they give up.

S18
A lot of people can't be bothered just sitting, just clicking things . . . it's so boring . . . and I know a lot of people have left because of that.

If Learndirect is to maintain a constant and significant role in post-compulsory education it must build on its high profile promotional strategy and find secure ways of keeping current learners 'onboard'. Thoughtfulness from fellow students can lead to re-entry:

S18
I try to encourage people to come back again, not just sign up new ones. And they have their phone numbers and I say ring them up and tell them to come back because it's not as bad now as it used to be.

A change of learning environment is becoming increasingly instrumental to retaining students. Having access to materials and development packages in conveniently located familiar surroundings enhances the students' chances to succeed in meeting objectives for their better future. Has this proved the case for one physically disabled student?

S19

Well it has, yes. I did go to college one day a week with my sister but I was missing out on too many lessons so I didn't complete the course. With doing this I can do it at home; plus when I'm stuck I see Geoff in the Littleshaw and he can help me. So it's a good thing: I'm getting a lot of support.

Time-honoured school and college buildings are reminders of the constraints of statutory learning and the conventional further education system. More interesting to new students are centres that are purpose-built or adapted to cater for specific needs. They are enticingly atmospheric—a symbol of postmodernistic learning maturity:

P10

Learndirect here is very non-threatening. Once we get them through the public door we don't lose them . . . they are then our captured audience. We've got this very supportive friendly atmosphere for learning which may be completely the opposite of what they've gone through either at school, work or college. Some of our learners would never, ever, step foot in a college for various reasons. They prefer it nice and quiet than having the 16–19 year olds bustling about. And I think that's true of other Learndirect centres that are purely adult, not part of a large college.

Open distance learning is characterized by a higher dropout rate than conventional education. Yet, notwithstanding the learning mode or learning location, for the majority of students the socio-cultural aspects take precedence over economic matters. Students invest emotion in learning: they do not see themselves as detached customers:

P21

There is one school of thought that says that if we did make a charge of £10 or more, people are more likely to complete. We've not found that.

The entwining of support and retention leads to a 'retention perspective' on support for continuing to learn. Severance from education is the result of a multifarious condition. In the interests of lifelong learning it is crucial to examine the unsatisfactory elements then mend or replace them. Alternatively, it is widely accepted that prevention is more effective. Student-centred learning support in isolation from a retention programme is not sufficiently potent. A successful scheme would be one delivered as part of the curriculum, one that incorporates facets such as early study risk assessment, advice on revision, self-assessment and social-liaise groupings.

## 8.7 Administration and Regulation

The Ufi is an independent body funded by the Government. Bureaucratically accountable to government policy are the Learning and Skills Councils, and Learndirect providers and their students. Official administration and statutory regulation is delineated to empower the Ufi's aim to drive up the demand for lifelong learning. One provider seems rather confused:

> P10
> I don't know who is doing the leading here but Learndirect are certainly being drawn into the LSC far more. When they started off . . . record keeping for instance . . . they were poles apart, and as we've gone along the years they have got closer together until shortly it should be one system. The LSC are asking for the same data that they ask from traditional courses . . . the same data from a Learndirect student, and they quality check through about support, advice, guidance and contact every four weeks. But it does throw a lot of . . . it is an awful lot of administrative work onto Sheena and her staff. It's no longer paperwork as it used to be; it's changed . . . it's already on the Learndirect database.

The offer to supply Learndirect products to prospective providers of education is outlined in a contract. When accepted by the latter this suffices as a legally enforceable—after consideration—agreement. The Learndirect document includes structured guidelines for establishing learning venues. One provider finds them less than straightforward. In spite of that he is obliged to comply:

> P14
> I don't know too much about Ufi apart from the shenanigans that we had when we first started the Learndirect centre. I think there's six forms in total that have to be filled in, and setting it up from scratch takes a lot of doing. And we could have had a lot more help from the

hub centred in Wilken, but we didn't. And Ufi were a faceless organization that I literally dealt with by e-smails. I don't think I spoke to anybody, which made the process rather more difficult.

Similarly, officially laid down is that new information and material must pass down to centres in a managerial way either by on-line methods, fax or letter. Frequent changes to Learndirect's administrative system cause confusion that frustrates the providers. They are agreed that there is too much unexpected, unnecessary and duplicated paperwork. So time consuming is it that it detracts from practising education. Two tutors are working under pressure and feel stressed:

P19
We have had to do that much paperwork in a short space of time that at times it has really floored us . . . nearly swamped us. Also our hub has had two inspections . . . one in December 2002 and we've got another coming up this week. We don't really know what we were doing. That's not to say we're not intelligent people because we have to have lots of compliance with the charity . . . we're regulated by the Community Legal Service, so that means a lot of paperwork.

P1
At the moment we're run off our feet, so I haven't got another appointment until the middle of December. I've booked a day off to do paperwork because if I didn't it would go through the ceiling.

Unfortunately the educational benefits of Learndirect are diminished when coping strategies are poor. However, one provider has found her own way of rising to the 'enrolment occasion':

P21
You can do two in a morning if you start at ten and they are either related or friends, because one can be doing the paperwork while the other person is on the computer. And you can do one in the afternoon basically between two and half past three. But you can't do them if there's no connection between them because you can't say, 'oh you just fill in that paperwork' whilst the other's on the computer; it's just not nice . . . not private.

The Ufi is purposefully finely tuned to deliver lifelong learning in an organized fashion. Learndirect providers contracted into managerial positions fulfil their role accordingly, or according to how to they interpret the decree. In this respect, therefore, a contrast in emphasis is found, illustrated here by two individual providers from ostensibly differentiated backgrounds—educational and commercial/industrial. For the former, attending to the students' needs takes precedence; administration is merely ancillary—the regulated recording of the same:

> P9
> My role is to run the Learndirect Centre . . . to facilitate and help the learners when they come in, get them enrolled, get them started on the courses and then give help and advice as and when they require it. And then kind of guide them . . . the learners tell me what they want to learn. They must have a reason for them to step through the door in the first place, and then we try and find a goal that they want to get to, and what I will do is give the learner opportunities and options.

For the latter, systemizing paperwork is a readily accepted integral part of Learndirect. She believes that it is vital, never detrimental, to the learning process:

> P15
> My job . . . it's information, advice and guidance. The other side is the administration; making sure that the enrolments are processed correctly and they go through, and the funding then comes through from Learndirect—but I don't class that as part of the work, it's just something that I do in the background basically.

All of the above responses suggest that, in whatever fashion but always in the interest of education, the Learndirect providers are committed to the high quality management of lifelong learning.

# Chapter 9
## A Linked Category Emerging from the Data

## 9.1 Opening Remarks

The remainder of the findings from the data analysis are now placed in a 'multi-category' instead of 'single categories', thus emphasizing the comprehensive, interconnecting thematic nature of the results. This outcome is derived directly from the more extensive data given in interview by the providers and students of Learndirect. In numerous instances, a respondent's perspective took on the form of a succinct integrated overview of several emerging unifying ideas of relevance to the research topic. The extent of this linkage and overlap bears importantly on the eventual research conclusions.

Both the providers and the students believe that learning, exercised through the media of technology and education, has a positive impact on their economic and socio-cultural quality of life. They benefit from extra work opportunities, and increased self-reliance or self-esteem. In addition, they develop a wider understanding of humankind, resulting from the acquisition of new skills, such as electronic engineering, and advanced geographical and biological knowledge augmented by qualified academic status.

In the light of their very presence at interview it is apparent that the respondents have already been attracted into the arena of lifelong learning. Besides which, they are eager to contribute information about Learndirect. I find their readiness to co-operate in a research project refreshing, and the enthusiasm shining through the revelations is illuminating:

> P9
> Lifelong learning is a multi-faceted concept. It means that every opportunity is given for people who wish to learn . . . no matter their age or ability. So that from the 'cradle to the grave' you are never being afraid to tackle something new; to access what you're looking for, and have the enthusiasm to succeed.

What remains a major task for the Ufi, however, is the drawing in of those people unaware of, or indisposed to, Learndirect's online learning provision. Indeed, a renewed engagement with education in general is difficult to secure.

At the centre of the debate about lifelong learning appears to be the economic and humanistic clash over the issue of widening participation. This can be related to the Ufi's perception of its Learndirect initiative as affirmative for influencing training curricula, and hence a leader to increase participation rates. This view, categorically within an economic discourse, is dismissed by humanistic argument on the basis that employment alone does not guarantee life's pleasures—the foundations of advantage and disadvantage instead lying in socio-cultural structures.

## 9.2 Interrelated Themes

There are numerous associated aspects of lifelong learning that arise in the research findings, all of which are examined in the previous five chapters: 'access and participation' is a prime example. Deemed important enough to warrant a 'named' section within the socio-cultural category, the issue impacts nonetheless on the other concepts and categories.

The extent of participation in lifelong learning is systematically significant given that it depends on 'flexible approaches to research and pedagogy, which are responsive to the diverse contexts of access education' (Burke, 2002, p.148). I define access as 'getting a full range of learning opportunities for individuals to achieve their aims and get maximum outputs'. The more accessible the learning organization, the more attractive it is to the students:

> P15
> Access is the big thing for a lot of people: they wander in here intent on doing something and end up doing something else. Despite people's best efforts to advertise . . . to take it out to the public . . . people just don't know what is available.

> P8
> If the individual has a love of learning they've got to be encouraged and given access to what's available to them. Obviously you might want to do weird and wonderful things, but it's accessing what is relevant and what is on offer.

Traditionally there are dispositional, situational and institutional barriers to peoples' participation in lifelong learning, and in many cases underrepresentation is linked to the wide-ranging concept of equal opportunity.

Respective examples of the three types of powerful constraints to access continued education are: individuals' 'deficit' motivation, either intrinsic or extrinsic—they do not envisage a future of learning for, perhaps, self-improvement or job advancement (Houle, 1972); for older people, and married women, the ability to control their own life being severely blocked by their partners (Hedoux, 1993); the middle-class ethos of voluntary learning (Tett, 1996).

In the UK some policy changes improved matters—for instance, following the Robbins Report in 1963 there was increased access for women to HE establishments. Nevertheless, there remain contentious factors to be addressed if providers are to compete to survive in the market place of lifelong learning (Cross, 1981).

The practical implications of an entanglement of ingredients can make learning a fractured experience. The criteria of age and social class alone significantly impact on the numbers of all students participating (Gilchrist et al., 2003, p.77, Table 4.3). Burke (2002) dismisses a hegemonic discourse of lifelong learning that prioritises the national economy and individualized 'success'; insisting instead that 'access students require a strategy of redistribution of funds (as suggested by Kennedy, 1997) and the recognition of their specific, although heterogeneous, needs and experiences' (p.36).

In essence, restricted access and reduced, or stagnant, participation rates are often repercussions of numerous practical factors. People's educational progress might be interrupted, delayed or halted by illness, disability, family commitments, changed learning locations or transport logistics, and the requirement of vocational training, upskilling and qualifications. Hodgson and Spours (1999) say that 'qualification reform has a special role to play in levering up levels of participation, achievement and progression' (p.145), and argue for an 'all-through', from 14+, inclusive and flexible examination and curriculum system for education and training.

In order to secure open and endless learning for everyone the Ufi monitors these demanding and restraining situations. It is a learning organization that uses line management (Turnbull, 2001) to meet 'the needs of all the participants (employee, manager, client(s))' (p.238.). Learndirect providers abide by credit frameworks contracts, carry out regulatory updates, for instance safety checks, and make supervisory decisions to infuse insightfulness, and implant best practice:

P1
You have to have key skills to be able to go on the computer. Learndirect cannot help people who really do need handholding . . . those who need brush-up courses just to give a little bit of confidence boost. We can't do that . . . but we'll point them in the right direction and send them on to someone else.

P2
We felt that Learndirect best fitted with the part of college which looks outwards really to the community rather than one which relies on students to cross the threshold . . . this has been a big problem.

A successful holistic approach to maximizing individual potential is aware that the ability to participate in learning is compromised by lack of personal resources. This pecuniary obstacle may be linked to the incongruities in the funding of part-time and full-time courses, particularly as the latter need to be paid for by part-time employment. Fortunately initiatives do regularly come along to try to ease the burden of poverty.

The Prince's Trust (1976), the forerunner of many schemes to transform the lives of young people who experience personal and practical restraints to entering the job market, offers training and business start up support. In 2004 the DfES along with key partners—the Confederation of British Industry (CBI), the Trade Union Congress (TUC) and the Small Business Council—put in place the Skills Strategy. This includes the offer of some money to adult learners in priority groups towards the overall cost of full-time FE courses.

However, one provider has no doubt that, whatever the intermediary effort to alleviate disadvantage in educational matters, disinterest and disengagement are deep-rooted in cultural insecurity:

P10
We are post–19, so we're adults only, and we were set up with funding from central government who had the idea that everybody should be able to access information on the Internet. Ok . . . and so that if government were going to go that way then there would be people who would be socially deprived, who wouldn't have access either at work or at home. So they set up UK Online centres all round the country, and we are one. We're based in Redmand: it's an Objective 2 Ward . . . a soft ward . . . so it's classed as socially deprived. We know our clientele . . . for instance we are able to fund people from Brinnith, which is another de-

prived ward of Stinton. But there is a cultural clash . . . it's historical . . . people from Brinnith do not come to Redmond. There's a physical divide in the valley, but there's also a metaphorical divide. So we don't
target that area . . . there's no point. We work with a stakeholder group,
which is made up of community activists.

The NIACE Adult Participation in Learning Survey (2002) confirms
that adult learning and social division is a persistent pattern (Sargant and
Aldridge, 2003). The 'learning divide' (between those people who have
access to take part and those who do not) concurs with the 'health divide'
in the sense that they happen at that same time. For example, in 2001 'the
lowest participation figures were found among those outside the labour
market: retired people (48 per cent) and those unable to work due to health
problems or disability' (p.17).

There is awareness, therefore, that multifarious issues affect adults'
learning or health, or both. Hammond (2002) finds a strong link between
education and mental health. In a National Adult Learning Survey (Dench
and Regan, 2000) a group of people aged 50 to 71 were asked if learning
makes a difference to their life. 'One third reported an improvement in
their physical well-being. This is higher than participation in learning
activities related to sports . . . suggesting that learning has a wider impact
on physical well-being' (p.69). The Ufi supports this view: it is intent on
removing the barriers responsible for this dual divide. Learndirect represents vigorous action by supplying the materials and the environment to
ensure that lifelong learning and health come together as reciprocating
elements of a fulfilling and meaningful lifestyle—translated into the perceptions of two respondents:

S27
Well, the information we have only lasts till we die . . . doesn't it? No
matter how brilliant a person is it's gone . . . hasn't it? On the demise, it's
gone: all the things that we know . . . the crafts, the skills . . . the expertise. So my view is to be as active as I can in various ways. I swim each
day as well.

P21
Well I think for your mental health and your physical health it is better to
learn all the time.

The extent to which the different themes are found to constantly interweave in the providers' and students' responses indicates that their overall perception of lifelong learning and the Ufi is conditioned by the impressions that the varied perspectives make on each other. The interviewees ponder how to give and receive economic support—especially funding; how to make social contacts—preferably face-to-face; how to integrate culturally—perhaps provoke or join focus group discussion in educational environments, and how to master technology—ensure that apparatus is correctly operated, and online pedagogies and curricula are designed to meet users' requirements. All these interlocking mechanisms can lead to successful outcomes in the context of Learndirect's implementation of learning:

> P15
> I would say that it's a fairly remote system. We don't get a lot of personal contact. I do get the impression their objectives are good, but I just sometimes question the methods by which they doing them. And also there's connectivity to funding because it is a little difficult to keep up to date with say the pricing.

> P14
> Courses have now been adapted for speed and accuracy with use on a PC. Books and other materials supplied are fantastic for those who cannot afford to purchase a computer.

Habitually, openings for adults to gain qualifications are calculated around the payment of fees to sit examinations. The charges are subject to adequate attendance and, or, aptitude on academic or training courses held during the daytime or evening at pre-specified times. Learndirect changes or opens up the possibilities:

> P10
> We offer two pathways . . . what we would term a traditional route or a Learndirect route. We are a pilot centre for ECDL. Learndirect will only be able to award certification through ECDL, and maybe through that mapping to CLAIT and CLAIT Plus. But that's what happened within adult education. Colleges couldn't put on non-certificated courses because they couldn't draw down the funding.

Throughout the empirical fieldwork I kept returning to two competing, or perhaps complementary, theories that were emerging about the creation of the Ufi. These reflections are based on intuition. The first is the possibility that the idea for Learndirect was conceived through a new philosophy, one whereby the continuance of learning is deemed efficient only through the medium of technology. In other words, that learners' educational progress is proportional, directly or inversely, to technological advancements. The second is that Learndirect provision is the result of a commercial decision to facilitate the Government's capitalization on the already popular notion of lifelong learning by selling educational material. In the course of my interviewing both theories were unwittingly tested when respondents made richly textured wide-ranging comments:

P21
What happened was that you've got the Open University and I think it sort of struck them that there is a whole range of people out there who would benefit from slightly a lower programme, but using the same sort of technology. Also it coincided with the Government's remit that they want everybody to be computer literate by 2006. They want everybody to have IT as a basic skill, which it is now, by this summer. So I think the pieces sort of came together rather than there being one great bolt of lightening.

The presence of older people in Learndirect centres emphasizes how educational content and teaching style have extensively changed over their average lifespan of 50+ years. They are attracted by the relatively recent initiatives and the facilitative options in place that sustain their return to, or continuance of, education. Elsdon (2001) explores the work of HM Inspectorate of Schools (HMI) and its impact on lifelong learning between 1944 and 1992. The shifts in educational policy emphasis are well illustrated. After the Second World War 'educational development was seriously hampered by the building industry's inadequacy to meet the enormous demands of reconstruction (p.172). By the 1970s 'general studies departments were well on the way to becoming the largest departments of most FE colleges' (p.146). The 1980s saw adult literary prioritized as a need of the multi-ethnic society, and in the following two decades vocational education expanded as a result of 'a growing belief in the overriding value of competition and private enterprise' (p.173).

Older people's memories are long and they often amalgamate interesting facets about learning and life, past and present. A provider talks about a particular student, and the student subsequently fills in the detail—a colourful miscellany of interlinking themes:

P14

Jack sat behind you he's actually 82 years old. When he came into the centre he'd never touched a computer . . . didn't know how to use a mouse. And the guy's gone on to do the introductory courses and a more advanced level . . . what we call an IT2 level . . . and he's doing file management, and he's succeeding. It's great because he comes every day. He uses it as a learning tool. And it's good for him to have a 'natter' basically as well. We all bat off each other. It's very much a social thing . . . nice cup of tea!

S14

Well, I started as green as grass. I have certain things of my own which I would need to be recorded preferably by computer to help me. I have various fairly extensive shareholdings and I need the details. And I wanted it to start e-mail with my relatives who live far away. It's not an easy thing . . . for example, if you make a mistake with a letter it doesn't matter, people understand the sentence; if you leave a comma or a full stop out it doesn't matter . . . leave a dot out of this and it doesn't go! I think the advantages in it are definitely for younger people; but for older people, it enables us in a leisurely way to sort of come to terms with it . . . realizing this is the future isn't it?

'Outreach' as a model of learning is present in all the generated themes of this research. The outreach approach extends and enlightens the mainstream function of the Ufi; this being the delivery of Learndirect provision. The two processes have similar traits. Both act as a marketing device to increase participation by advertising away from the mainstream learning institutions, and both need adequate ongoing finance as collateral to exist. Outreach and the Ufi are each a strategy to target specific cohorts of learning in different places and organizational settings, in which staff work less formally away from the educational base. A further resemblance is their networking—separately—with agencies to draw on local knowledge in order to devise new courses and staged programmes, and offer a technology-based learning service direct to people's homes.

Hence, the numerous perspectives on lifelong learning and the Ufi that arise continually in the research findings, though different, are often linked. Intrinsic and extrinsic factors may also be present at the same time. Ethnic minorities need appropriate learning provision—for instance, language support from linguists or interpreters, due in part to the escalating proportion of older people from culturally diverse groupings in society. Besides which, Lynch (2002) says that:

> An ageing workforce employed in an economy that is characterized by rapid technological change suggests that a detailed examination is merited of our educational and training institutions and how they provide for skills upgrading.
>
> (Lynch, 2002, p.74)

Moreover, educationalists cannot deny that government policy is aimed at raising standards at post-compulsory level. The Ufi's contribution is to formulate new graded accredited courses, with the consequent contractually-binding condition, financially based, on the Learndirect provider to ensure that their students achieve prefixed acceptable levels of competence. The anomaly here is that by thus excluding those unable to reach the stipulated benchmark, participation in learning is narrowed not widened.

# Chapter 10
## Discussion of the Findings from the Case Study

In this case study there are no definitive answers to the interview questions. The interview process is complex in that it is not always entirely clear what views the interviewee is trying to transmit to the interviewer. This has implications for the validity of the data. Sometimes it is necessary to try to explore an issue by using a number of follow-up questions. Even then it has not always been easy to synthesize a clear viewpoint from the totality of interviewees. Kirk and Miller (1986) say that:

> No experiment can be perfectly controlled, and no measuring instrument can be perfectly calibrated. All measurement, therefore, is to some degree suspect. When the measurement is nonqualitative, this reservation may amount to no more than the acknowledgement that the 'accuracy' is limited.
>
> (Kirk and Miller, 1986, p.21)

This chapter is an attempt to draw together the main threads from the research data. It presents a discussion about the dissection of the findings, and a critique about the consequences and implications thereof, in terms of their benefits and limitations for lifelong learning and the Ufi.

The methods used to collect the data, and to evaluate it, should be based on trying to establish reliability, relevance and validity before any conclusions can be drawn from the total project. Already adhered to 'is that research takes place in a context, and needs to make this context visible in order to create knowledge that is accurate and meaningful' (McIntyre & Grudens-Schuck, 2004, p.167).

Before the research began I discussed details of the data collection procedure with prospective participants in order to find a reasonable way in which to conduct the interviews. The interviewing technique is unlikely to be completely reliable, but it may be possible to work towards some element of reliability by, for example, explaining the interview sequence and asking clear questions. There is a suggestion that unhurried, clear questioning often encourages genuine responses, which in turn might allow the interviewer to use follow-up questions. Furthermore, if this process were to be repeated after maybe a few months the responses would at least be hopefully similar, thus strengthening the reliability of the interview technique.

The interviewees seemed happy for the interviews to be conducted in a specified manner. It could be argued, therefore, that the questions asked of the Learndirect providers and students, and their responses—subsequently transcribed—are relevant to a case study of lifelong learning and the Ufi.

Although the issue of how to evaluate the validity of different research paradigms is widely debated (Smith, 1996), 'no criteria have yet been agreed within the community of qualitative researchers' (p.192). It is crucial, however, that the analysis of the data should represent the phenomena to which it refers. In this respect, I used an interpretive approach to analysis to try to discover the interviewees' perspectives of lifelong learning and the Ufi. My aim when applying a grounded theory approach to the data was to keep drawing out from the transcripts what actually happened during the interviews, so that the ultimate validity of the research methodology would be enhanced.

I make no attempt at theoretical inference, that is, the development and testing of theory applied in experimental approaches. Nor do I present claims as to the general applicability of the participants' thoughts and experiences to all other adults. Instead, the relevance of the conceptualized findings from the grounded theory analysis is that a discursive level of understanding about lifelong learning and the University for Industry is available for 'transferability' (Lincoln and Guba, 1985) to other cohorts and situations within the field of education.

## 10.1 Results of Grounded Theory

With regard to the six 'findings' chapters of this book, the first five were purposely named after a single, albeit enveloping, category—generated during data analysis—in order to provide a chapter heading that represents the theorized concepts grounded in the data ascribed to that category. The last one, Chapter 9, brought further findings of a combined type: they relate to the majority of the aforementioned concepts and themes, and categories.

The method of grounded theory analysis of the data kept me constantly close, in a psychological sense, to the fieldwork I had carried out while collecting that data. It allowed me to use my memory in an episodic way. Whilst unfolding the data, or identifying in-built concepts for possible theoretical interpretation, I was able to bring clearly to mind occurrences from each 'Learndirect' visit and interview. These memories were arising at irregular intervals from direct and personal experience. Consequently, and in turn, grounded theory methodology enabled me to report to the reader the 'true sense' of the same. It was a revolving process of refining and re-defining data to ensure the accurate naming of newly-emerging concepts, and their subsequent direction to the right theme and eventual category. The findings from my research represent the outcome of using that analytical technique.

The Learndirect providers' and students' interviews were informative about the implicit and explicit significance of lifelong learning and the Ufi. Their responses imparted data about, for instance, fee charges. In addition, they voiced opinions or expressed anxieties about, for example, proposed objectives like certification. In totality their perceptions were plausible and credible, although the general manner in which the information was made available by the two sets differed.

The providers appear confident and are enthusiastic about being interviewed. Their vociferousness is, on the whole, to be expected, due to their apparent commitment to education and self-professionalism. They answer questions directly; prove very able to reason and to articulate an argument: They are also assertive in expressing their views and unafraid to enter into debate:

> P16
> We have another centre down at Chessen Hurst so we are very active. We've put 16,000 learners through last year for 6,000 courses. Most learners have done three or more courses. We've got an 87% completion rate. I feel that the colleges have been detrimental to Learndirect in that they have other agenda that they prefer to follow. Equally they do not want outside bodies taking on Learndirect. Areas where colleges have been involved are usually areas less successful because they've stopped certain private companies opening up. Here, because of the success of Learndirect we make it our main, if not sole, business. We also offer private courses. The colleges within Cirus Plus & Stinton hub were side-lined very early . . . they were no competition . . . they could not stifle our centre.

It is a contrasting verbal performance to the brief and hesitant release of data by several students—a situation that could sometimes influence a researcher to accept some tacit data. A further gulf is noticed within this cohort itself. Those learners giving interviews are initially reticent and timid, but quickly warm to the scenario and want 'to chat.' Others who send e-mail responses 'come over' as impersonal as the communication method itself:

S18
I come to this centre just because I live near. Well, it's like this morning, I forgot my glasses and I'm only down the road and I could go and get them. Like if I went far away somewhere . . . if I had of done that at the first . . . I probably wouldn't have went anywhere else, but because I've come here and I've learned so much I'm very happy.

S9
It's handy, helpful, friendly, and doesn't expect wonders from me—(e-mail).

S37
I have no complaints, except it's not open on Saturdays—(e-mail).

The skill of an interviewer in steering face-to-face meetings is supportive in that it ensures the lucid imparting of data. On the other hand, when a student replies to written questions they do so independent of any helpful prompting.

Throughout the findings from my investigation 'support' emerges as a vital bonding issue: it might be an asset or a problem in the field of lifelong learning. In itself, the fact that this theme is so prevalent supports the significance that was attached to the motivation and support for lifelong learning in the earlier review of the relevant literature (Chapter 2.6). Targeted and timely; occurring in different facets—financial, emotional, educational, and technological—of the Learndirect experience, this source of strength for progression in learning transpires to be a frequent deliberation for the providers and students alike. The former deliberate about the adequacy of support; the latter take it for granted:

P21
The thing is that to learn you've got to have support; you've got to be taught. And well, I wonder where the support and the teaching come in the workplace. Do the staff do it in their own time . . . so one wonders just how much time, and just how committed they're going to be, or if they feel it's a burden if they have to comply to join these courses. We just don't know.

S27

We are always learning in general life . . . everything we do we learn something new. So at the school learning doesn't finish. People continue on to learn new skills, whether it be just to improve themselves or to improve their job opportunities. Lifelong means that you are always supported, and so you'll always be a Learndirect student.

Distance learners need to ask for support otherwise, if there are time lapses or irregular contact, they become remote from their provider. A variety of media are used by Learndirect to circulate advice and guidance, including the telephone and computers, and written—letter correspondence and information leaflets. In addition, teaching staff foster, and ensure, the self-esteem of students through protective counselling and time-management skills incorporated into course planning. Two vulnerable groups are ethnic minorities and the unemployed, both of whom are under-represented in learning—a point that draws attention to associated issues.

In the Literature Review some authors claim that support is most effective when directed at 'non-traditional' students (See p.58). The findings from the data appear to strengthen their argument.

The data also highlights the relationship between culture and economic power: both impact strongly on access to the provision of lifelong learning. Thus, removing barriers to participation in learning can increase and, or, widen it. For instance, it is usual for women and shift workers to want to study with the least disturbance to family schedules. Therefore, childcare and timetabling need to be moveable not removable elements as the latter may lead to 'dropping out'.

Training is part of the fabric of the UK's future stability and prosperity. Halsey et al. (1997) contend that the quality of a nation state's human resources in a global economy is defined, amongst other criteria, in terms of 'a commitment to skill formation through education and training' (p.188). Evans et al. (1993) refer to in-company or 'alternace' training—a feature of vocational education and training in the European Economic Community, about which they say:

The trainer or supervisor working with the trainee in the workplace has a crucial part to play—not least in maintaining the balance between the practical and the theoretical, on- and off-the-job learning.

(Evans et al., 1993, p.142)

Therefore, the research results appear to re-engage with certain issues discussed in the Literature Review. Among them are that 'culture struggles for serious exposure in an arena dominated by economic forces' (See p.32), and the view that training sessions are the practical interpretation of the concept of integrating the principles of employment and education (See p.34). The latter usually take place within institutional or social frameworks—for example in the workplace or community centres.

## 10.2 Learning Centre Variance

Evident from the analytical processing of the findings is that the amounts of conceptually emerging data vary directly according to the emphasis placed on different themes and categories by the interviewees. The providers, more than the students, display such a leaning toward particular aspects of lifelong learning and the Ufi; a trend that also correlates with the type of centre they operate. One Learndirect centre that caters specifically for older people differs from another venue whose objectives are commercially orientated:

P19
I'm opening up the centre to the WI (Women's Institute), Probus, the Townswomen's Guild and the U3A; all those groups of older people who traditionally meet. We may not be able to provide a tutor, but if they have somebody within their organization who is good at IT training they can just come and use the centre.

P13
We chose Learndirect because we believe it's an excellent concept. It's learning for people who may be afraid to go into traditional learning establishments . . . say the colleges or even a library . . . who feel maybe in some way intimidated by it, or have a low moral and no confidence. So we find that because we're a training company it doesn't matter who they are . . . colour, creed, sex . . . no matter what. If they want to learn something, we want to help them. We've found Learndirect is the best product for that at this moment in time. It's flexible learning: the learner's in charge; they take ownership. We're here to support and see them through to achieve their goal or lifetime ambition, and Learndirect is one of the best tools for making that difference.

It follows that when disparate learning establishments collaborate to sign a contract with Learndirect they do so for sound reasons:

P21
The libraries do Learndirect because it's part of their charter 'Ongoing Education'. Also they like it because if they can get them through the door then they might borrow books as well. They got involved with the Collegiate because as a joint venture it was less expensive for both of them to start up. Also, from the college's point of view you have these centres already up and running with computers, so they didn't have to provide them. And from the libraries point of view they have the whole teaching staff to refer people to. So it is mutually beneficial for both sides.

Educational institutions are for the most part enthusiastic about Learndirect as a learning initiative, possibly because of a likely contribution to educational research:

P10
I can only think that they've gone down the accreditation route because of demand, and, assuming that they've done the research, that proves that that's what people want. I would hope that doesn't override the short bite size course that people could do just purely and simply for in-terest, because they want to keep their brains active, and then put that into practice.

Training outlets tend to be less receptive of Learndirect. Appear-ing as though something would have to be away free—an air of 'what's in it for us'—they appear to show little appreciation or understanding of the significance of an educational link. They seem rather more inclined towards the profit-making or survival aspects of running a commercial enterprise:

P16
The thing with Learndirect is that it's changed: it's more precise since its inception. The advent of the LSC last year has polarized the learning to larger centres rather than the small community, because of the nature of the audit departments. Therefore, the original programme of trying to access deprived areas, and deprived learners, has been negated by the fact of the LSC putting restrictions where learners cannot be supported

in small sites. A small site these days would be fifteen machines, as any-thing less would not be feasible.

A prime requirement to be a learning venue is a business plan for its establishment and growth. Thereon, all the providers anxiously expect to abide by it: some are more successful than others. Learndirect centres do not survive without meeting the LSC's criteria for receiving funding. Well-managed learning, in terms of balanced supply and demand, is crucial in order to warrant the outlay of public money. A reasoned overview of one centre's development explains the current fragile state of its endurance in what is, in effect, an educational dilemma:

> P15
> Learndirect here has suffered a little bit over the last couple of months. When we started here the Ufi and the hub set targets for us for num-bers of learners: we exceeded all of them . . . we more than doubled them. It was easily achievable in the first couple of years, but we were the only centre in Askmore. Now we've got Askmore Library . . . we've got two of the local schools that also have Learndirect. So it's much more accessible for people. And I also believe that people generally have more access to computers at home. So they may come in here to enrol, and then we don't see them again until they've completed the course and they want to enrol again . . . which is fine . . . they still count as our numbers. We've got nearly 700 learners enrolled here, and it's empty today.

The last provider, although responsible for the smooth running of the centre, is apparently blaming its current hazardous state on a fickle and competitive learning market. This indicates that, in order to avoid educational instability, every Learndirect centre should remain alert and adaptable: the Ufi should work to gain insights into, and operate in response to, the everyday changes of the contemporary world.

It is apparent, therefore, that Learndirect centres differ from each other, which is an indication that the data analysis reflects my earlier appraisal of some of the literature on the Ufi and lifelong learning. This tends to be specific: much debate surrounds the Government's emphasis on technology (See pp.39–41) but many authors' enthusiasm for commu-nity learning (See pp.52–57)—exemplified through partnerships, and in diverse environments—could be significant in changing the con-cept of learning.

## 10.3  A model for change

The total amount of interview dialogue from the Ufi providers and the Ufi students was analysed using grounded theory. It seems reasonable to consider this interpretation of the data as valid research evidence. When I repeatedly examine the findings it becomes apparent that a unifying idea is present; namely 'change'. This conceptual strand runs through the documented data given by the fifty-nine participants. It is also a perception that occurs frequently in the literature appraised in Chapter 2.

'Change' moulds the results together in a classification framework, or model. At the same time 'change'—being the core category—allows for the division and allocation of the data into five principal sections which are entitled economic, socio-cultural, demographic, technological and educational. Moreover, the subsequent numerous surfacing concepts recorded across this catagorized banding give rise to, and are placed in, themes—for example, business, motivation, older people, ICT and curricula. These ultimately suggest the allegiance of this case study research to a model for change.

The world is always changing and most individuals, receptive to fresh ideas, are changing accordingly. Some people change by personal choice: perhaps they try to understand other religions, or learn a foreign language, for better socio-cultural communication. Others change through necessity if, for instance, they are required to upgrade job-related skills to secure their employment which relies on its economic viability in an increasingly global market. In all cases, adult lifestyles are being altered as people engage in new or continued learning. The Ufi professes to strengthen non-traditional routes into post-compulsory education, a sector that has witnessed numerous changes in the last few decades. One provider claims that Learndirect does change people's learning experiences for the better:

> P14
> I'll tell you of one particular person that sticks out . . . Alwen who came in and knew a little bit about word processing. And I can see a change in that woman from when she came in. She actually had stopped doing her housework to get on and do her Learndirect course. She's come back and done many courses . . . about six or seven. She does them extremely thoroughly to the highest level and completely enjoys it. I think it's changed her way of life. And I've now encouraged her to do actual academic qualifications at college, and she's going to do it.

In education there are constantly-changing learning trends, none high-lighted more so than the current debate about matching the pedagogy with the technology. Social interaction while studying in a traditional educational institution is stimulating—for example, focus group discussions clarify individuals' intellectual thinking. Yet beyond this environment much learning also happens. The collection and understanding of information, though socially constructed, is often transformed by technology. This might happen at work, in community centres, at sporting events and during leisure pursuits. In developing the communication skill—networking—criticism and collaboration are sought from experienced, knowledgeable and influential people in so many walks of life.

Global changes now occur at a faster rate than the human race has been used to. The older a person is, the more they are likely to have to adapt to change. Conscious of this dictum, the staff at Age Care are intent on promoting and maintaining lifelong learning; but not necessarily through Learndirect. They anticipate options more suitable for their clients:

P20
We're looking at new courses and at extending our opening times. I think what we'd like to see is the centre busy from 9 in the morning till 5 at night, and also in the evenings and weekends. All the time I'm talking with Alice and Paul about what we should be doing next. We've had some con-tact with one of the colleges in South Cherfield who said they would like to come in and do some courses free of charge. If we got this group of people together with our core base of learners it would be great.

Overall, there does not seem to be a genuine clear focus about what is provided, by whom, for whom and why. Although innumerable interesting discussion points arise, the plethora of information produces no right or wrong answers. Policy and ideology are sometimes indistinguishable in education. This is the nature of the discipline, however, and serves to underline the continuous changing character of lifelong learning, and the unforeseeable pattern of its distribution.

Referring back to the Literature Review, one is aware of the almost continuous presence of a model for change. It incorporates social and political policies, and technological and educational strategies for widening participation in learning (See p.59). The extensive usage of libraries is also illustrated (See pp.64–65), as is that of information and computer technol-ogy—regarded as the new basic skill (See p.67).

## 10.4 The Future of Lifelong Learning and the Ufi

The fieldwork results serve as the indicators of the present state of the research topic.

They are also prescriptive in that they contain prescriptions about its future. Many of the respondents sense what lies ahead for Learndirect. The majority viewpoint in lifelong learning scrutiny—founded on multi-type exposures that incorporate qualifications and skills—is one of apprehension; one exemplified here by a provider:

> P21
> I think to have a future it's got to link up with the examination board and that is going to require different types of Learndirect staff. Grade 1 officers . . . they just enrol people, whereas Brenda and I . . . we're Grade 2 officers . . . do support, and we do our own backup system. There's a whole backup system to Learndirect as to claiming the money, and making sure that the learners are up and running, and whether or not they've actually accessed their courses. Grade 2 officers and above need degrees; Grade 1 officers don't. So I think they're going to have to up-skill a lot.

My exploration of the relevant literature in Chapter 2 revealed the potential of technology with regard to the prospects for the Ufi and lifelong learning (See pp.70–71). This is now borne out in the findings from the data, in the words of a Learndirect student:

> S33
> When we get to the cut-off date . . . the date the Government want to change over to things technical . . . they're not saying, well, after that point you're at a standstill. The systems will be ongoing . . . it's only that you won't be able to partake of services and speed up the transmission of information. And they're ploughing a lot of money into the public domain to learn it (technology). And this is the crisis I think, that you've only yourself to blame if you're not prepared to move with the times.

The interviewees' responses reveal that each student's relationship with Learndirect follows a similar course to that of their peers. Many students only gradually become aware of the facilities and opportunities offered by Learndirect, and they need a period of time in which to orientate themselves in order to take advantage of those opportunities. The desire to continue and the inclination to change to study different, additional or advanced level subjects is manifest in the enjoyment of a beneficial outcome. The intention to stop is rarely mentioned. Hence, having embarked on the how, why, where, when and wherewithal of learning, it is highly probable that students will participate in future learning.

On the other hand, providers do not subscribe to a single discernable cycle of events that engages individuals in an ongoing relationship with education. Instead they relate to certain aspects:

P18
Learndirect will definitely have an impact on what people will do in the future, because we feel that Learndirect is the future of learning. Online, accessible, easy to follow in simple terms, and they can go up to advanced and expert levels.

P16
I see Learndirect as very much the future of learning, not only at post 19 but also in secondary schools. It's really down to the material that Learndirect is going to produce as to how successful it's going to be in other areas outside of IT. And there are a tremendous number of retired people who want to keep themselves active mentally, and to that end it has been very successful. I feel as it matures it will percolate down to younger groups who will use it as a learning tool in the school sector.

Another provider envisages a narrowing of the health-education divide. However, a different manager harbours reservations due to the possibility of political change:

P18
So eventually all these alternative health clinics are going to be opening all over the country, and in there they'll be learning centres as well. In the Cobbles there are alcoholics and drug addicts. It's for special needs . . . the Antelope. So the learning centre is there to help them learn as well, and socialize with other people: it's run on a multipurpose basis.

P14
I know it's been okayed for the next three years . . . unless there's a change of government of course . . . that the Learndirect should be

around. Judged on the last three years, I'd say that they're not going to deliver what they promised, because of the money they've wasted on terrible marketing, and the lack of getting the point across to the people. I think it might just break down.

## 10.5 Perceptions of University for Industry Poviders of the Approach to Lifelong Learning and the Ufi

When the Ufi set up Learndirect it aimed to make learners for life. When I embarked on the research fieldwork it was to try to find out if the said government initiative is achieving this. The providers expressed a variety of opinions. In doing so they are indicating that the delivery of lifelong learning within the parameters of Learndirect is not controlled by any one factor: rather it is conditioned by several interactive concepts. There is, however, subtle dissent within this framework. Learndirect centres are bound to the Ufi by a legal agreement. Some providers, although wary not to break their contract, manage to work alternative programmes and routines alongside mandatory coursework. They do this when they are unhappy about any restraint placed on what they believe is their attempt to offer best learning practice.

The Ufi does not incorporate mentors in its operational strategy. Yet it happens that, for certain cohorts of learners, Learndirect is a little too reliant on technology. In one such situation, therefore, unpaid help is a valued complementary aid to lifelong learning:

> P9
> We've got two experienced people to come in as volunteers. One managed a big IT centre in Mersha with about 200 people, and the other one was a specific IT trainer. They are going to do little groups of workshops about the workings of the computer . . . why it does this; why it doesn't do that. And we are going to do it like a social course where we're going to get a group of eight people together.

Likewise, there is a belief that Learndirect is unrealistically marketed financially. For one organization, which represents the needs of older people, the product is not cost effective. They find it difficult to reconcile the differences between their own perspective on the delivery of learning, and the Ufi's remit:

P19

We can't justify giving a course to a person in an Age Care centre where we're charging them £50–£60 for a course that a) is not suitable, and b) they wouldn't be able to do anyway.

Financial concerns are one of many learning issues that are applicable to Third-agers—people aged 50+. The work of several writers appertaining to, for example, matters of physical and mental health, and access to educational opportunities or facilities, is analysed in the Literature Review (See pp.44–47)

Despite exploring the findings from the case study even further, the true purpose of Learndirect still seems unclear. To reiterate this perplexity: I am questioning if the Ufi is promoting theoretical concepts of lifelong learning to camouflage a commercial venture. Should this be the case scenario, then it is trying to stimulate demand for, in order to supply, learning provision. The providers are eloquent in helping me to solve this puzzle: two of them are confident that Learndirect is seamless lifelong learning provision:

P10

It fits in very well with us: it's part of our overall offer. It doesn't matter what the individual is coming to do. So it may be they're coming to learn about computers from the basic, 'I don't even know how to switch it on'. Ok, do they want a qualification? 'No, I don't want a qualification'. So we guide them down Learndirect. Someone who starts on a qualification route may just start with a basic IT course, and then want to progress to CLAIT . . . to ECDL. And we are hoping to offer ECDL Advanced.

P14

I believe in Learndirect, otherwise I wouldn't be sat here. Ok, it's a government-backed initiative but, because of the concept of it all, it is lifelong learning. It's for those learners who are 19+ up to 150. They may have missed out at school for whatever reason, or are at home looking after the kids. They want career progression. They need business courses. You've got the retirement people who want to be able to be able to search the net to find out about their crafts hobby.

Connecting the concept of lifelong learning to the Ufi's mission is based on finding factors that can determine a state equilibrium between the two. The providers' perceptions of the approach to lifelong learning through the launch of Learndirect are a thought provoking, albeit sometimes confused, source:

> P13
> There is a concept of lifelong learning linked from Learndirect. Generally though, I don't tend to see it as a link. I just tend to see learning as a student being provided with the correct learning for them, and continuing them on to other courses that they're going to benefit from. I don't really see the concept of lifelong learning much in this environment; it's a) too busy, and b) you're providing too much support as you go along. It probably does come under the concept of lifelong learning, but I just see it as providing the support.

In fact, P13 is explaining how continued education and the Ufi coincide and overlap. His pragmatic disposition reveals that he never consciously conceptualizes his work. Nonetheless, P13 is effectually contributing to the formation of new learning theory.

## 10.6 Perceptions of University for Industry Students of the Approach to Lifelong Learning and the Ufi

It is already known that most students think that the Ufi exists so that anybody can learn at anytime in their life; that Learndirect offers a flexible learning opportunity to those who require it. However, whether the Ufi's execution of educational policy provides people with a chance to return to, or continue with, their education, regardless of the restrictions in place in postmodern society, and whether Learndirect performs better than conventional delivery options within the field of education generally, are matters for much deliberation.

Perspectives are wide across the spectrum of consensus, and no less individualistic. One older person's interview response thematically draws in together her impression of lifelong learning and the Ufi, in contrast to her recollection of compulsory education.

> S8
> I like Learndirect . . . the atmosphere's totally different. I hated school: I hated every minute of it. But this is so relaxed, and you just do it to suit yourself, and nobody's pushing you. Plus it's free, if you live in Redmand. It makes a difference when your pension's only £46. It makes you feel you're not on the shelf so much. I have got to do this

ECDL . . . but I can't, my memory isn't good enough. The ones I'm doing at the moment . . . I can look things up if I need to. I'm enjoying
every minute of it. So I think when I've finished I might go over to numeracy, and brush up my maths a bit. There are so many excellent
courses . . . you're spoilt for choice, and they're changing and improving
all the time.

A second older person bestows a slightly nonconformist slant on the
same topic:

S33
I welcome the initiative of the Government in introducing this Learndirect. I don't pander to the commercial idea . . . they've already got it in
commerce . . . had it for years, haven't they? So I don't think that was
behind it at all. I think it's a direct policy of government to accept that at
a certain date in the future there's going to be a cut-off point, and all this
tuition and that is geared to that point on the horizon, And they've set
the stall out and said that we want everybody . . . children and
adults . . . to learn how to use the computer. And if you don't, then it's
your own fault: I'm afraid you have to be blunt about it.

A third student dismisses the innuendo that the Ufi has sufficient af-
filiation with lifelong learning. She declares Learndirect's educational
programming not expansive enough:

S17
I mean . . . I'd like to learn French. If they did other things, like languages, I would also sign on for that. It's very limited in that it's only IT.
Having said that, they cover quite a wide spectrum of IT. But I'm
in . . . you know . . . that University of the Third Age; that's smashing.

And finally, the 'exception rather than the rule' amongst the findings,
is total disillusionment from another student. Reflecting on his episodes
with Learndirect, he refutes a perception of lifelong learning and the Ufi
that takes account of their assumed conceptual attachment to each other.
He says:

S32
I don't think they are! I'm not terribly excited by this method. And it
hasn't got any stimulus. I'm retired, so what is it? I mean an afternoon

here . . . but you have to kick yourself off. Would I rather listen to the afternoon play, or would I rather come here? Quite often, I'd rather listen to the afternoon play. So no, I'm not excited by it.

In spite of this comment, educational progress and change are acknowledged—as they were in the aforementioned review of the literature (Chapter 2). The significant area of the findings of this case study is grounded in the collective analysis of the experiences, and emotions, as told by the interview participants. The providers and their students view lifelong learning and Ufi from different angles, but they engage with common features. It is simply that each group redefines the other's perceptions.

# Chapter 11
# Conclusion

## 11.1 Preface

I preface this conclusion by explaining a fine, but significant, distinction between lifelong learning and continuous education. This has been brought about by economic and socio-cultural changes that come into contact with the growth in technological innovation and the fluctuations in educational policy. In addition, informed by the participants' interview responses, a demographic common factor becomes apparent. The cohort known by the current idioms of 'older people, Third-agers, or the 50+', were not, in most cases, given the option to continue with their education post-compulsory. Their longevity privileges them to be called lifelong learners, but the truth is that they are returners to learning.

Conversely, younger people can become permanent learners. From the Foundation Stage through to Key Stage 4 in schools, then in colleges, universities and training centres there is no age limit to lifelong education. The array of provision on offer moulds continuous learning into an attractive proposition. The Government's education policy is strongly directed at choice in the post–19 learning zone, and the introduction of the Ufi's national Learndirect multi-media network is an innovative pathway.

Each of the three aims of this research has been addressed. The first two were discussed in the previous chapter. The final one—the place of lifelong learning within the philosophy of the University for Industry—signified by the interactive in-depth experiences of the providers and students as delivered to them by Learndirect is now dealt with.

## 11.2 The Place of Lifelong Learning within the Philosophy of the University for Industry

In conclusion, the Ufi's initiative for the implementation of education does not comply with all of the prevailing conformities, and ongoing fluctuations, in the concept of lifelong learning. The resulting factual data from my investigation, together with the exposition of incorporated clear strengths and reservations about Learndirect, leads to seven concluding remarks:

1.

There is a model of radical practice in existence to meet the nation's commitment to lifelong learning. A people-focused design, based on critical thinking and learning for transformation, it seeks recognition and promotion through collaborative relationships among providers of education. However, this research project found no innovation truly fostering learners' emancipation.

Then there is an alternative view, that education alone is not responsible for the pattern of people's lives. This is rooted in economic, socio-cultural, demographic, technological and educational issues. The solution to the problem of inequality—progressive change to redress balance in a learning society—is likewise inherent.

2.

Learning is not implemented by a 'demand-led' system. People's desires or deprivation do not dictate a lifelong learning agenda, nor do they invite one. Instead, government policies interpret the concept to their liking: it is the 'supply-side' that determines the provision. The prime role of present-day providers of post-compulsory education is to plan and deliver, within time limits, specific academic and vocational courses. This is a learning structure incompatible with a student-centred approach.

The University for Industry is one such venture. It promotes Learndirect as being disposed towards aiding education and training, by producing high quality learning materials. Some distinctive examples of its intention to 'kick-start', regenerate and lead a lifelong learning drive are—a high profile marketing and subsidized funding system, consistency of functional and environmental balance in its centres, and courses which, whether basic skills, technology, or language, emphasize the Ufi's inclination towards helping business and education by engaging companies and individuals alike. All these measures are uniquely designed to try to break down inhibiting psychological barriers, and eliminate the tangible disincentives, to a new method of learning.

3.

Lifelong learning and the Ufi do have a mutual, purposeful goal—to enrich lives. Separately and together, they succeed. People already familiar with, and those marginalized by the mainstream educational system, enjoy equity, respect and opportunity through Learndirect. Although their corresponding gains differ slightly in alignment—the former group to economic; the latter to socio-cultural—both undoubtedly make headway in terms of learning. Access to continued education is thereby facilitated, and participation is consequently widened and increased.

The foremost advantageous outcomes of the Ufi are socio-cultural. However, a certain related discourse—ethnicity—is conspicuous by its absence from the findings of the case study. I conclude that, in the geographical area of research, people from ethnic minorities are not present, have low demand for, or are not sought out by Learndirect.

4.

Lifelong learning and the Ufi engage with particular cohorts. Young people are motivated to establish themselves in the job market. Enthusiastic older people, mostly female, wish to make up for their lack of basic skills—the leftover deficit of a relatively short period of schooling. Employed people are re-skilled in the workplace, or with training companies. Part-timers—housewives, young mothers, and infirm or disabled people—seek personal development. Moreover, fees remission coupled with their need to update, and improve, communication skills, readily sways retired people, or those in receipt of state social benefits, to enrol with Learndirect.

Learndirect is an ingenious learning policy in that it is reaching marginalized groups, which banded together are a significant proportion of a prospective learning population to capture, and then encourage, lifelong learning. The majority of all types of student find their association therein satisfying and worthwhile. They do not identify any disincentives to learning. Feeling immediately welcomed and safe in a learning environment geared to their needs, they build up tolerance, empathy and self-control. Hence, the Ufi's learning initiative can help to make people's different lives a more fulfilling experience.

5.

A debate continues about the relationship between technology and education; the focus being put on how the former is used in order to procure knowledge. Whilst many people, including academics, providers of education and students, believe that proven traditional teaching methods and learning settings are superior, most of them also recognize, and accept, the increasing valuable influence of interactive ICT and ILT. Media literacy in the pragmatic economic, vibrant social, and pluralistic cultural, world of today is receptive to ever-changing communication skills.

6.

The penultimate point drawn from this case study is that the phenomenon of change influences the concept of lifelong learning, and also exercises control over the functioning of the Ufi. The research is finishing with the understanding that human beings have the capacity to feel, to know, and to change. Individual interviewees confirmed that the 'main areas of change occur in existing relationships; perceived movement between social classes—may be due to increased empowerment and intellectual development' (Dawson, 2002, p.119).

The strength of the Ufi is that it can interact with profound shifts in all spheres of the learning society. It persists in helping to produce the human and material reserves necessary to keep the United Kingdom stable within global changeability. The experiences developed by Learndirect transmit crucial principles that can transform and manage such changes for the betterment of the recipients' lives. For example, where individuals with English as a second language, or modern businesses are affected, online learning and training courses, such as 'ELLIS Middle Mastery' and 'Creating a Continuous Improvement Culture', respectively teach the practical realities of speaking English, and explain how to develop procedural frameworks to increase workplace productivity.

7.

Finally, I refer back to Chapters 1, 8, 9 and 10 where I alluded to some ambiguity about the political and economic motives for the setting-up of the University for Industry. It appeared to be the case that there was some uncertainty about the place of lifelong learning within its philosophy. Despite these original reservations, which were also well-established in the relevant literature, this research now suggests that the Ufi has indeed achieved a measure of success in the delivery of lifelong learning opportunities to a range of people—such as, those in different age groups or with special needs. It further suggests that Learndirect providers and their students do tend to develop a sense of co-operation that consists in the students achieving their education aspirations and goals within the context of the Ufi.

Based on new theory grounded in the empirical evidence from this case study, it could be argued that, even if the Ufi is politically and commercially backed it does promote learning. Therefore, Learndirect is not just about learning ad infinitum: it is about a purpose, because learning is never without a purpose. Learning keeps us alive—economically, culturally, socially, technologically and educationally.

# Chapter 12
# Summary

I embarked on this research project seemingly aware, though apprehensive, of the scale of its pledge to academic achievement, both personally, and in contribution to the field of education in general. The exercise has rewarded me. It has been stimulating and informative, and at times frustrating, but it has never disappointed me. From the inception of the case study there was an enveloping awareness that, as the inquiry process developed so were the ideas about it being continuously refined. I agree with Nias (1991), who says:

> It is important to allow oneself time to think, at every stage from data collection to interpretation. . . . Time spent thinking about other things can also be valuable; not all cerebral activity takes place at a conscious level and ideas can form while left to 'compost' slowly.
> (Nias, 1991, p.162)

Consequently, at this stage of final reflection, I can submit a digest of the main aspects that have led to the completion of my research task.

In totality, this book is traceable back to its philosophical underpinnings. The choice of topic, as well as the research mode and its meaningful execution, depended on my interpretation of those fundamental tenets. This gave a firm foundation that had further bearings on the progress of the investigation.

The rationale for the research was explained. The project was contextually specific. The background to the topic was expanded upon by the compilation of a literature review. A research design was systematically planned. The qualitative research model was sustained throughout the investigation of lifelong learning and the Ufi. The case study strategy was applied, and rested in the Learndirect locations.

Recorded interviews, plus a little observation, followed by transcription and note-making, were carried out. The narrative structure within the reality context of this case study had resonance for analytical inquiry; the resulting data appropriate to using a grounded theory approach. This integrated and logical process first marshalled the collected data into an appropriate initial classification of concepts and themes. It was further assigned to a wider category—one of six, representing economic, socio-cultural, demographic, technological, educational or linked-themed perspectives on lifelong learning.

The consequent complete set of the findings from the case study, supported by evidence, was sequentially presented. The discussion that followed concentrated around the implications of the newly-developed grounded theory, especially for learning in the future. It ensured that concluding remarks could afterwards be drawn about the focus of the research—the Ufi's approach to lifelong learning.

Their interpretation of lifelong learning had been asked of Ufi providers. The responses, when analysed, exposed multiple, but similar, perspectives on lifelong learning. The same questions were put to Ufi students. Likewise, they produced responses that revealed their perceptions of lifelong learning through Learndirect. As intended by the research design, the elucidation of lifelong learning and the philosophy of the Ufi were thus contained by the fieldwork.

My processing approach—dealing with the input, storage and analytical retrieval of the collected data—revealed that a dichotomy of learning for instrumental reasons or intrinsic motives is too simple to contemplate. Individuals' perceptions change; they are in essence complex throughout their lives. In a similar way, the provision of learning opportunities and strategies contains constantly changing outcomes.

The Ufi's vision of learning, derived from a political stance, seems clear enough. However, the outcome of my research is that there can be no finite decision about whether the Learndirect strategy consolidates, or confuses, the lifelong learning model. To balance the results—that is to establish a 'perfect' sense of proportion and discretion—is never easy, but I am confident that the conclusion drawn was critically founded.

In producing this book I take full responsibility for the implications of its content, ever conscious that 'learning is deeply embedded in its social, political and economic context, is not static and will develop as the context changes' (Maehl, 2000, p.34). Ethical issues have been paramount throughout my research: protocol and legal restraints were strictly adhered to. To write the book has been exciting; particularly presenting the results—outcomes I hope are informative for the future of both lifelong learning and Learndirect, and their mutual relationship.

I finish with the belief that the rationale for an inquiry is justified by the favourable consequences of researching the particular case. My aspiration, and intention, is that this uniquely portrayed study of lifelong learning and the Ufi occupies a worthwhile place in the domain of educational research.

# References

Adams, R. (2003) *Social Work and Empowerment*, Basingstoke, Palgrave Macmillan.

Age Concern (2004) *How Ageist is Britain?* London, Age Concern.

Alexander, T. and Clyne, P. (1995) *Riches beyond price: making the most of family learning*, Leicester, NIACE.

Anderson, T. and Garrison, D. R. (2003) *E-Learning in the 21st Century*, London, RoutledgeFalmer.

Ashford, M. and Thomas, J. (2005) Interprofessional education, in H. Burgess and I. Taylor (eds.) *Effective learning and teaching in Social Policy and Social Work*, London, RoutledgeFalmer.

Ball, C. (1989) Should education continue? in *Adults Learning* Vol.1, no. 1: 7, Leicester, NIACE.

Barnett, R. (2002) Learning to work and working to learn, in F. Reeve, M. Cartwright, and R. Edwards (eds.) *Supporting Lifelong Learning, Volume 2, Organizing learning*, London, RoutledgeFalmer.

Bartlett, W., Rees, T. and Watts, A. G. (eds.) (2000) *Adult Guidance Services and the Learning Society*, Bristol, The Policy Press.

Bassey, M. (1999) *Case Study Research in Educational Settings*, Buckingham, Open University Press.

Berkeley, G. (1910) *A New Theory of Vision*, London, Dent.

Berofsky, B. (1966) *Free will and determinism*, London, Harper and Rowe.

Blair, T. (2004) Socialism, in C. Chitty *Education Policy in Britain*, Basingstoke, Palgrave Macmillan.

Blunkett, D. (1998) *The Learning Age: a renaissance for a new Britain*, London, DfEE.

Bourgeois, E., Duke, C., Luc-Guyot, J. and Merril, B. (1999) *The Adult University*, Buckingham, Open University Press.

Breisach, E. (2003) *On the Future of History: The Postmodernist Challenge and its Aftermath*, Chicago, University of Chicago Press.

Bridge, H. and Salt, H. (1992) *Access and Delivery in Continuing Education and Training—a guide to contemporary literature,* University of Nottingham, Department of Adult Education and Department of Employment, Resources and Strategy Directorate.

Brown, G. (1994) *University for Industry: turning the workplace into a centre of continuous learning, discussion paper,* Labour Party.

Brown, G. (1997) Budget Statement, July 2nd, in *Hansard*, HoC, Parliamentary Copyright.

Brown, J. S. and Duguid, P. (2002) *The Social Life of Information*, Harvard Business School Press.

Brown, S. (1984) *Objectivity and cultural divergence: supplement to philosophy*, Cambridge, Cambridge University Press.

Brown, T. and Jones, L. (2001) *Action Research and Postmodernism*, Buckingham, Open University Press.

Bruner, J. and Haste, H. (eds.) (1987) *Making sense: the child's construction of the world*, London, Methuen.

Bryman, A. (2001) *Social Research Methods*, Oxford, Oxford University Press.

Bulpit, G. (2003) Looking over the horizon: a future perspective, in E. Oyston, *Centred on Learning*, Aldershot, Ashgate.

Burke, J. (2002) *Accessing Education*, Stoke on Trent, Trentham.

Cahoone, L. (ed.) (2003) *From Modernism to Postmodernism*, Oxford, Blackwell.

Carlton, S. and Soulsby, J. (1999) *Learning to Grow Older & Bolder*, Leicester, NIACE.

Carr, W. (1987) What is an educational practice? *in Journal of Philosophy of Education*, Vol.22, no.2: 163–175, Oxford, Carfax.

Carruthers, S. and Smith, S. (1997) Challenge of the Information Society, in *Information Services and Use*, Vol. 17, Issue 4: 225, IOS Press.

Chaney, D. (2002) *Cultural change and everyday life*, Basingstoke, Palgrave.

Charmaz, C. (1994) *Identity Dilemma in Chronically Ill Men*, Midwest Sociology Society, The Sociological Quarterly, 35(2), p.269–288.

Charmaz, C. (1995) Grounded Theory, in J. A. Smith, R. Houre and L. V. Longenhore (eds.) *Rethinking Methods in Psychology*, London, Sage.

Chitty, C. (2004) *Education Policy in Britain*, Basingstoke, Palgrave Macmillan.

Clark, B. R. (2004) *Sustaining Change in Universities*, Maidenhead, Open University Press.

Clarke, A. (2000) *The Learning Centre Guide for small and medium sized enterprises*, Leicester, NIACE.

Clarke, A. (2001) *Learning Organizations*, Leicester, NIACE.

Clarke A. and Englebright L. (2003) *ICT—The new basic skill*, Leicester, NIACE.

Coffield, F. (ed.) (2000) *Differing Visions of a Learning Society*, Bristol, The Policy Press.

Cole, M. (1998) Cognitive development and formal schooling, in D. Faulkner, K. Littleton and M. Woodhead (eds.) *Learning relationships in the classroom*, London, Routledge.

Coleman, P. G. and O'Hanlon, A. (2004) *Ageing and Development*, London, Arnold/Hodder Headline.

Collins, J., Harkin, J. and Nind, M. (2002) *Manifesto for Learning*, London, Continuum.

Cowham, T. (1999) *The University for Industry*, Manchester, OCNW/Open University Conference Paper.

Crain, K., Davies, J. and Morgan, W. J. (1995) *Access and Delivery in Continuing Education and Training—a guide to contemporary literature, First Supplement*, University of Nottingham, Department of Adult Education.

Cross, K. P. (1981) *Adults as Learners*, San Franscisco, Jossey-Bass.

Cullen, J., Batterbury, S., Foresti, M., Lyons, C. and Stern, E. (2000) *Informal Learning and Widening Participation*, Nottingham, DfEE.

Cullingford, C. and Oliver, P. (2001) *The National Curriculum and its effects*, Aldershot, Ashgate.

Cullingford, C. and Gunn, S. (eds.) (2005) *Globalisation, Education and Culture Shock*, Aldershot, Ashgate.

Cusick E. (2001) Observation and Discovery, in J. Newman, E. Cusickand A. La Tourette *The Writer's Handbook*, London, Arnold.

Davidson, C. (2003) *Returning to Education*, Oxford, How To Books.

Dawson, C. (2002) *Practical Research Methods*, Oxford, How To Books.

Dench, S. and Regan, J. (2000) *Learning in Later Life: Motivation and Impact*, Norwich, DfEE.

Denzin, N. K. and Lincoln, Y. S. (eds.) (1998) *Collecting and Interpreting Qualitative Materials*, California, Sage.

Department for Media, Culture and Sport (1997) http://lic.gov.uk

Dewey, J. (1916) *Democracy and Education*, USA, Macmillan.

DfEE (1997) *The Contribution of Higher Education to the University of Industry*, Sheffield, HEED, DfEE.

DfEE (1998) *The Learning Age: a renaissance for a new Britain*, London, Stationary Office.

DfEE (1999) *Social Inclusion*, London, DfEE.

DfES (2001) *Valuing People: a new strategy for learning disability in the 21$^{st}$ century*, London, Stationary Office.

DfES (2004) http://dfes.gov.uk

DfES (2005) *14–19 Education and Skills White Paper*, London, DfES.

Dowling, C. (2004) Evaluating electronic learning environments from a lifelong learning perspective, in T. J. van Weert and M. Kendall (eds.) *Lifelong Learning in the Digital Age*, Boston, Kluwer Academic.

Doyal, L. and Harris, R. (1986) *Empiricism, explanation and rationality*, London, Routledge and Kogan Page.

Drever, E. (1995) *Using semi-structured interviews in small-scale research*, Glasgow, Scottish Council for Research in Education.

Drolet, M. (ed.) (2004) *The Postmodern Reader*, London, Routledge.

DTI and DfEE (1999) *Competitiveness through Partnerships with People*, London, DTI and DFEE.

Edwards, R. (1991) The inevitable future? Post-Fordism in work and learning, in *Open Learning*, Vol. 6, no. 2: Longman.

Edwards, R. (1997) *Changing Places? Flexibility, lifelong learning and a learning society*, London, Routledge.

Eisner, E. (1992) Objectivity in Educational Research, in *Curriculum Inquiry*, Vol. 22, no. 2: 157–71.

Eisner, E. (1998) *The Enlightened Eye*, New Jersey, Prentice-Hall.

Elliot, J. (1984) Methodology and Ethics, in C. Adelman (ed.) *The Politics and Ethics of Evaluation*, Beckenham, Croom Helm Ltd.

Elsdon, K. T. (2001) *An education for the people?* Leicester, NIACE.

Evans, K., Dovaston, V. and Holland, D. (1993) The changing role of the in-company trainer, in R. Edwards, S. Sieminski and D. Zeldin (eds.) *Adult Learners, Education and Training*, London, Routledge.

Evans, N. (2003) *Making Sense of Lifelong Learning*, London, RoutledgeFalmer.

Fawbert, F. (2003) (ed.) *Teaching in Post-compulsory Education*, London, Continuum.

Field, J. (1994) Open Learning and Consumer Culture, in *Open Learning*, Vol.9, no. 2: 3–11, Longman.

Field, J. (2000) *Lifelong Learning and the New Educational Order,* Stoke-on-Trent, Trentham.

Field, J. and Leicester, M. (eds.) (2000) *Lifelong Learning. Education Across the Lifespan,* London, RoutledgeFalmer.

Field, J. (2002) *Promoting European Dimensions in Lifelong Learning,* Leicester, NIACE.

Florian, L. and Hegarty J. (2004) *ICT and Special Educational Needs. A tool for inclusion,* Maidenhead, Open University Press.

Ford, J. (1969) *Social Class and the Comprehensive School,* London, Routledge and Kegan Paul.

Freire, P. (1971) *Pedagogy of the Oppressed,* New York, Herder & Herder.

Fryer, R. H. (1997) *Learning for the 21ˢᵗ Century. First report of the National Advisory Group for Continuing Education and Lifelong Learning.* London, Stationary Office.

Fryer, R. H. (1999) *Creating Learning Cultures: Next Steps in Achieving the Learning Age,* London, National Advisory Group for Continuing Education and Lifelong Learning.

Giddens, A. (1974) *Positivism and sociology,* London, Heinemann.

Gilchrist, A. (2001) Working with networks and organizations, in L. D. Richardson and M. Wolfe (eds.) *Principles and Practice of Informal Education,* New York, RoutledgeFalmer.

Gilchrist, R., Phillips, D. and Ross, A. (2003) Participation and potential participation in UK higher education, in L. Archer, M. Hutchings and A. Ross (eds.) *Higher Education and Social Class,* London, RoutledgeFalmer.

Gill, R. (1996) Discourse analysis: practical implementation, in J. T. E. Richardson *Handbook of Qualitative Research Methods,* Leicester, BPS Books.

Gillham, B. (2000) *Case study Research Methods,* London, Continuum.

Girling, S. (2003) *The Great Baby Shortage,* London, The Sunday Times Magazine.

Glaser, B. G. (1978) *Theoretical Sensitivity,* California, The Sociology Press.

Glaser, B. G. and Strauss A. L. (1967) *The Discovery of Grounded Theory*, New York, Aldine de Gruyter.

Glover, D. and Law, S. (2002) *Improving Learning*, Buckingham, Open University Press.

Golding, C. (2002) *Grounded Theory: a practical guide for management, business and market researchers*, London, Sage.

Goodson, I. F. and Hargreaves, A. (1996) *Teachers' Professional Lives*, London, Falmer Press.

Goodson, I. F. (2003) *Professional Knowledge, Professional Lives*, Maidenhead, Open University Press.

Gottlieb, A. (1999) *Socrates*, London, Routledge.

Gray, D. E. and Griffin, C. (eds.) (2000) *Post-Compulsory Education and the New Millennium*, London, Jessica Kingsley.

Gray, F. (ed.) (2002) *Landscapes of Learning. Lifelong learning in rural communities*, Leicester, NIACE.

Greany, T. (2003) What makes an effective lifelong learner? in *Adults Learning*, Vol. 14, Issue 7, p. 19, NIACE.

Green, A. (2000) Lifelong Learning and the Learning Society, in A. Hodgson (ed.) *Policies, Politics and the Future of Lifelong Learning*, London, Kogan Page.

Green, A. and Lucas, N. (eds.) (1999) *FE and Lifelong Learning: Realigning the Sector for the Twenty-first Century*, London, Institute of Education, University of London.

Greenbank, P. (2003) The role of values in educational research: the case for reflexivity, in *British Educational Research Journal*, Vol. 29, no. 6: 791–801.

Gunn, S. (2005) Introduction, in C. Cullingford and S. Gunn (eds.) *Globalisation, Education and Culture Shock*, Aldershot, Ashgate.

Haggart, J. (2000) *Learning Legacies: A Guide to Family Learning*, Leicester, NIACE.

Hall, D. E. (2003) *Subjectivity*, London, Routledge.

Halsey, A. H., Lauder, H., Brown, P. and Wells, A. S. (eds.) (1997) *Education: Culture, Economy, Society*, Oxford, Oxford University Press.

Hamel, J., Dufour, S. and Fortin, D. (1993) *Case Study Methods*, California, Sage.

Hammond, C. (2002) *Learning to be healthy*, Report 5, Wider Benefits of Learning Centre, London, Institute of Education.

Hargreaves, D. H. (2004) *Learning for Life*, Bristol, The Policy Press.

Hart, M. (1992) *Working and Educating for Life*, London, Routledge.

Harvey, D. (1990) *The Condition of Postmodernity*, Blackwell, Oxford.

Haughton, G. (1993) Skills mismatch and policy response, in R. Edwards, S. Sieminski and D. Zeldin (eds.) *Adult Learners, Education and Training*, London, Routledge.

Hazemi, R., Hailes, S. and Wilber, S. (eds.) 1998) *The Digital University*, London, Springer-Verlag.

Headington, R. (2003) *Monitoring, Assessment, Recording, Reporting and Accountability*, London, David Fulton.

Hedoux, J. (1993) Des publics et des non-publics de la formation d'adultes: Sallaumines-noyelles-sous-Lens des 1972, in R. Edwards, S. Sieminski and D. Zeldin (eds.) *Adult Learners, Education and Training*, London, Routledge.

Hegarty, S. and Evans, P. (eds.) (1985) *Research and Evaluation Methods in Special Education*, Windsor, NFER-NELSON.

Hegel, G. W. F. (1963) *Lectures on the History of Philosophy*, London, Routledge and Kegan Paul.

Hillman, J. (1996) *The University for Industry: creating a national learning network*, London, Institute for Public Policy Research.

Hodgson, A. and Spours, K. (1999) *New Labour's Educational Agenda*, London, Kogan Page.

Hodgson, A. (ed.) (2000) *Polices, Politics and the Future of Lifelong Learning*, London, Kogan Page.

Hodgson, A. and Spours, K. (2003) *Beyond A Levels*, London, Kogan Page.

Holton, R. (2005) Globalization, in A. Harrington (ed.) *Modern Social Theory*, Oxford, Oxford University Press.

Houle, C. O. (1972) *The Design of Education*, London, Jossey-Bass.

Howell, K. E. (2000) *Discovering the Limits of European Integration: Applying Grounded Theory*, New York, Nova Science Publishing.

Hughes, J. (1991) A critical overview of labour market trends, employment and unemployment, in K. Forrester and K. Ward (eds.) *Unemployment, Education and Training: Case Studies from North America and Europe*, Sacramento, Caddo Gap Press.

Hutchins, M. R. (2003) The Learning Society, in P. Jarvis and C. Griffin (eds.) *Adult and Continuing Education. Major Themes in Education*, Vol. 1, London, Routledge.

Hyland, T. (2000) Learning, work and community, in J. Field and M. Leicester (eds.) *Lifelong Learning. Education Across the Lifespan*, London, RoutledgeFalmer.

Hyland, T. and Merrill, B. (2003) *The Changing Face of Further Education*, London, RoutledgeFalmer.

Jansen, T. and van der Veen, R. (1992) Adult education in the light of the risk society, in *International Journal of Lifelong Education*, Vol. 11, no.4: 275–86.

Jarvis, P. (2000) Lifelong Learning. An Agenda for a Late-modern Future in, D. E. Gray and C. Griffin (eds.) *Post-Compulsory Education and the New Millennium*, London, Jessica Kingsley.

Jarvis, P. (2001) *Learning in Later Life*, London, Kogan Page.

Jarvis, P. and Griffin, C. (2003) General Introduction, in P. Jarvis and C. Griffin, (eds.) *Adult and Continuing Education. Major Themes in Education*, Vol. IV, London, Routledge.

Jeffs, T. (2001) First lessons: historical perspectives on informal education, in L. D. Richardson and M. Wolfe (eds.) *Principles and Practice of Informal Education*, New York, RoutledgeFalmer.

Jenks, C. (1977) *The Language of Postmodern Architecture*, London, Academy Press.

Kant, I. (2003) 'An Answer to the Question: What is Enlightenment?' in, L. Cahoone, (ed.) *From Modernism to Postmodernism*, Blackwell, Oxford.

Kant, I. and Smith, N. K. and Caygill, H. (2003) *Critique of Pure Reason*, Basingstoke, Palgrave Macmillan.

Kanter, R. M. (2001) *Evolve: Succeeding in the digital culture of tomorrow*, Boston, Harvard Business School Press.

Kasworm, C. E., Polson, C. J. and Fishback, S. J. (2002) *Responding to Adult Learners in Higher Education*, Florida, Kreiger Publishing Company.

Keep, E. and Rainbird, H. (1999) Towards the learning organization, in S. Bach and K. Sisson (eds.) *Personnel Management in Britain*, Oxford, Blackwell.

Kendall, M. (2004) Community Based Learning, in T. J. van Weert and M. Kendall (eds.) *Lifelong Learning in the Digital Age*, Boston, Kluwer Academic.

Kennedy, H. (1997) *Learning Works: widening participation in further education*, Coventry, Further Education Funding Council.

Kidd, J. R. (2003) The Educative Society, in P. Jarvis and C. Griffin (eds.) *Adult and Continuing Education. Major Themes in Education*, Vol. I, London, Routledge.

Kimball, L. (1998) Managing Distance Learning—New Challenges for Faculty in, Hazemi, R., Hailes, S. and Wilber, S. (eds.) 1998) *The Digital University*, London, Springer-Verlag.

Kincheloe, J. L. (2003) *Teachers as researchers, qualitative inquiry as a path to empowerment*, London, RoutlegdeFalmer.

King, B. (2002) Managing institutional change and the pressure for new approaches to teaching and learning, in F. Reeve, M. Cartwright and R. Edwards, R. *Supporting Lifelong Learning, Volume 2, Organizing learning*, London, RoutledgeFalmer.

Kirk, J. and Miller, M. L. (1986) *Reliability and validity in qualitative research*, Beverly Hills, Sage.

Klein, S., Ortman, P. and Friedman, B. (2002) What is the Field of Gender Equity in Education? in J. Koch and B. Irby (eds.) *Defining and Redefining Gender Equity in Education*, USA, Information Age Publishing.

Knapper, C. and Cropley, A. (2000) *Lifelong Learning in Higher Education*, London, Kogan Page.

Knowles, M. K. (2003) Excerpt from 'How My Ideas Evolved and Changed', in P. Jarvis, and C. Griffin (2003) (eds.) *Adult and Continuing Education. Major Themes in Education*, Vol. IV, London, Routledge.

Konecki, K. (1997) Time in the Recruiting Search Process by Headhunting Companies, in A. Strauss and J. Corbin (eds.) *Grounded Theory in Practice*, London, Sage.

Kumar, K. (1997) The Post-Modern Condition, in A. H. Halsey, H. Lauder, P. Brown and A. S. Wells *Education*, Oxford, Oxford University Press.

Kvale, S. (1996) *Interviews*, California, Sage.

Lawton, D. and Gordon, P. (2002) *A History of Western Educational Ideas*, London, Woburn Press.

Learning and Skills Research Centre (2004) *Learning styles and pedagogy in post–16 learning: A systematic and critical review*, Learning and Skills Development Agency.

Leask, M. and Pachler, N. (eds.) (1999) *Learning to Teach Using ICT in the Secondary School*, London, Routledge.

Lee, J. A. (2001) *The Empowerment Approach to Social Work Practice*, New York, Columbia University Press.

Levis, K. (2003) *Why I believe universities should be more like businesses*, London, THES, 28.11.2003

Lewis, J. (2003) Design Issues, in J. Ritchie and J. Lewis (eds.) *Qualitative Research Practice*, London, Sage.

Lincoln, Y. S. and Guba, E. G. (1985) *Naturalistic Inquiry, Beverly Hills*, Sage.

Longworth, N. and Davies, W. K. (1996) *Lifelong Learning*, London, Kogan Page.

Longworth, N. (1999) *Making Lifelong Learning Work: Learning Cities for a Learning Century*, London, Kogan Page.

Lore, A and Hurd, S. (eds.) (2001) *Supporting lifelong language learning*, London, CILT.

Lyle, J. (2003) Stimulated Recall: a report on its use in naturalistic research, in *British Educational Research Journal*, Vol. 29, no. 6: 861–878.

Lynch, L. M. (2002) Too Old to Learn? Lifelong Learning in the context of an Ageing Population, in D. Istance, H. G. Schuetze and T. Schuller (eds.) *International Perspectives on Lifelong Learning*, Buckingham, Open University Press.

Lyotard, J-F. (1979, trans.1984) *The Postmodern Condition: A Report on Knowledge*, Manchester, Manchester University Press.

MacDonald, A., Saunders, L. and Benefield, P. (1999) *Boys' achievement, progress, motivation and participation: issues raised by the recent literature*, Slough, National Foundation for Educational Research in England and Wales.

MacDonald, R. and Wisdom, J. (2002) *Academic research and educational development: evaluation and changing practice in higher education*, London, Kogan Page.

McDonald, A. and Edwards, V. (eds.) (2000) *Widening participation through the University for Industry: how libraries support lifelong learning*, Sunderland, University of Sunderland Press.

McGiveny, V. (1993) Participation, non-participation and access, in R. Edwards, S. Sieminski and D. Zeldin (eds.) *Adult Learners, Education and Training*, London, Routledge.

McGiveny, V. (1999) *Excluded Men*, Leicester, NIACE.

McGiveny, V. (2004) *Men earn, women learn*, Leicester, NIACE.

McGuigan, J. (1999) *Modernity and Postmodern Culture*, Buckingham, Open University Press.

McIntyre, J. and Grudens-Schuck, N. (2004) Research in Adult Education and Training, in G. Foley (ed.) *Dimensions of Adult Learning*, Maidenhead, Open University Press.

McKie, J. (2000) Ageing with technology: adult viability in a technological world, in J. Field and M. Leicester (eds.) *Lifelong Learning. Education Across the Lifespan*, London. RoutledgeFalmer.

Mac an Ghaill, M. (1996) Local student cultures of masculinity and sexuality in, P. Woods (ed.) *Contemporary Issues in Teaching and Learning*, London, Routledge.

Maehl, W. H. (2000) *Lifelong Learning At Its Best*, California, Jossey-Bass.

Mahoney, L. A. (2003) *An exploration into some of the factors surrounding boys' underachievement in writing at the end of Key Stage 2*, Huddersfield, University of Huddersfield

Marmot, M. (2004) *Learn—to live longer*, London, THES, 18.06.04.

Margolis, J. (1973) *Knowledge and Existence*, New York, Oxford University Press.

Marsick, V. J. and Watkins, K. E. (2002) Envisioning new organizations for learning in, F. Reeve, M. Cartwright and R. Edwards (eds.) *Supporting Lifelong Learning, Volume 2, Organizing learning*, London, RoutledgeFalmer.

Matheson, C. and Matheson, D. (eds.) (2000) *Educational Issues in the Learning Age*, Continuum, London.

Matlay, H. and Hyland, H. (1999) Small firms and the University for Industry: An appraisal, in *Educational Studies*, Vol. 25, Issue 3: 253–266, Abingdon, Carfax.

Merriam, S. B. (1988) *Case Study Research in Education*, California, Jossey-Bass.

Millman, J. and Gowin, D. B. (1974) *Appraising Educational Research, a Case Study Approach*, USA, Prentice-Hall.

Moon, B. (1983) *Comprehensive schools: challenge and change*, Windsor, NFER-Nelson.

Morrison, M. (1992) Part-time; whose time? Women's lives and adult education, in *Managing Time for Education* CEDAR paper 3, University of Warwick, Centre for Educational Development, Appraisal and Research.

Morrison, M., Burgess, R. G. and Band, S. (1999) *An Evaluation of Aspects of the University for Industry in the North East*, Sudbury, DfEE.

Morse J. M. and Field P. A. (1985) *Nursing Research. The application of qualitative approaches*, London, Chapman and Hall.

National Advisory Group For Continuing Education and Lifelong Learning (1997) *Learning for the twenty-first century: first report of the National Advisory Group for Continuing Education and Lifelong Learning*, London, NAGCELL.

Neuhouser, F. (ed.) and Buar, M. (Translator) (2000) *Fichte: Foundations of Natural Right*, Cambridge, Cambridge University Press.

Newell, R. W. (1986) *Objectivity, empiricism and truth*, London, Routledge and Kogan Page.

Newman, J., Cusick, E. and La Tourette, A. (2000) (eds.) *The Writer's Workbook*, London, Hodder Headline.

NIACE (2001) *The social, the cultural and the economic case for lifelong learning*, Leicester, NIACE.

NIACE (2002) *Adult Participation in Learning Survey. Adult Learning and Social Division: a persistent pattern*, Leicester, NIACE.

Nias, J. (1991) Primary Teachers Talking, in G. Walford (ed.) *Doing Educational Research*, London, Routledge.

Nomura, Y. (2002) *Lifelong Integrated Education as a Creator of the Future 2*, Stoke-on-Trent, Trentham Books.

OECD (2000) *Knowledge Management in the Learning Society*, Paris, OECD.

OECD (2000) *Motivating Students for Lifelong Learning*, Paris, OCED.

Office for National Statistics (ONS) Census (2003): *National Report for England and Wales*, London, Stationery Office.

Office for Standards in Education (OFSTED) (2000) *Family Learning*, London, OFSTED.

Oliver P. (ed.) (1999) *Lifelong and Continuing Education*, Aldershot, Ashgate.

Oliver, P. (2003) *The Student's Guide to Research Ethics*, Maidenhead, Open University Press.

Oliver, P. (2005) The Concepts of Globalization and Culture in C. Cullingford and S. Gunn (eds.) *Globalisation, Education and Culture Shock*, Aldershot, Ashgate.

Onofri, P. (ed.) (2004) *The Economics of an Ageing Population*, Cheltenham, Edward Elgar.

OU (1995) *Glossary, Course Guide EH266*, Milton Keynes, The Open University.

OU (2005) http://www.open.ac.uk

Palacios Lleras, M. (2004) *Investing in Human Capital: a capital markets approach to student funding*, Cambridge, Cambridge University Press.

Pappas, N. (1999) *Routledge Philosophy Guide to Plato and the Republic*, London, Routledge.

Pattison, M. (1992) in 'Isaac Casaubon', in A. Partington (ed.) *The Oxford Dictionary of Quotations*, New York, Oxford University Press.

Perraton, H. (2000) *Open and Distance Learning in the Developing World*, London, Routledge.

Peters, R. S. (1966) *Ethics and Education*, London, George Allen and Unwin.

Peters, R. S. (2003) What is an educational process? in P. Jarvis and C. Griffin (eds.) *Adult and Continuing Education. Major Themes in Education*, Vol. V, London, Routledge.

Phillimore, A. J. (1996) Flexible specialization, work organization and skills: approaching the 'Second Industrial Divide', in J. Ahier, B. Cosin and M. Hales (eds.) *Diversity and Change*, London, Routledge.

Piaget, J. (1932) *The Moral Judgement of the Child*, London, Routledge and Kegan Paul.

Piaget, J. (1972) *Psychology and Epistemology. Towards a Theory Of Knowledge*, Harmondswoth, Penguin Books.

Piaget, J. (1973) *The Psychology of Intelligence*, Totowa, N.J. Littlefield Adams.

Pigeon, N. and Henwood, K. (1996) Grounded theory: practical implementation in, J. T. E. Richardson (ed.) *Handbook of Qualitative Research Methods*, Leicester, BPS Books.

Pike, A. (2005) *Disciplined Thinking*, London, THES. 19.08.05.

Pilley, C. (1990) *Adult education, community development and older people*, London, Cassell.

Plewis, I. and Preston, J. (2001) *Evaluating the Benefits of Lifelong Learning*, London, Institute of Education, University of London.

Popkewitz, T. S. (1984) *Paradigm and Ideology in Educational Research*, London, Falmer.

Quality Assurance Agency for Higher Education (2004) *The accreditation of prior learning in context*, Gloucester, QAA.

Quicke, J. (1999) *A Curriculum for Life*, Buckingham, Open University Press.

Raffe, D. (2003) Foreword, in A. Hodgson and K. Spours, *Beyond A Levels*, London, Kogan Page.

Rees, G., Gorard, S., Fevre, R. and Furlong, J. (2000) Participating in the Learning Society: history, place and biography, in F. Coffield (ed.) *Differing Visions of a Learning Society*, Bristol, The Policy Press.

Reeve, F., Cartwright, M. and Edwards, R. (eds.) (2002) *Supporting Lifelong Learning, Volume 2, Organizing learning*, London, RoutledgeFalmer.

Richardson, J. T. E. (ed.) (1996) *Handbook of Qualitative Research Methods for Psychology and the Social Sciences*, Leicester, BPS Books.

Richardson, L. D. and Wolfe, M. (eds.) (2001) *Principles and Practice of Informal Education. Learning through life*, New York, RoutledgeFalmer.

Riddell, S., Baron, S. and Wilson A. (2000) The meaning of the Learning Society for adults with learning difficulties: bold rhetoric and limited opportunities, in F. Coffield (ed.) (2000) *Differing Visions of a Learning Society*, Bristol, The Policy Press.

Ritchie, J and Lewis, J. (eds.) (2003) *Qualitative Research Practice*, London, Sage.

Robbins, L. (1963) *Report of the Committee on Higher Education*, Cmnd 2154, London, HMSO.

Robertson, D. (1998) The University for Industry—a flagship for demand-led training, or another doomed supply-side initiative? in *Journal of Education and Work*, Vol. 11, no. 1: 5–22. Abingdon, Carfax.

Rogers, C. (2000) Librarians supporting the Ufi: the Birmingham experience, in A. McDonald and V. Edwards *Widening participation through the University for Industry: how libraries support lifelong learning*, Sunderland, University of Sunderland Press.

Romm, N. R. A. (2002) *Accountability in Social Research*, New York, Klumer Academic/Plenum.

Rubin, H. J. and Rubin, I. S. (1995) *Qualitative interviewing: The art of hearing data*, Thousand Oaks, CA, Sage.

Sargant, N. (1996) Learning and 'leisure', in R. Edwards, A. Hanson and P. Raggart, (eds.) *Boundaries of Adult Learning*, London, Routledge.

Sargant, N. and Aldridge, F. (eds.) (2003) *Adult learning and social division: a persistent pattern*, Leicester, NIACE.

Schofield, J. W. (1990) Increasing the generalizability of qualitative research, in E. W. Eisner and A. Peshkin (eds.) *Qualitative Inquiry in Education: The Continuing Debate*, New York, Teachers College Press, Columbia University.

Schuller, T. and Bostyn, A. M. (1993) Learners of the future: preparing a policy for the third age, in *Journal of Education Policy*, Vol. 8, no. 5: 365–79.

Searle, J. R. (1995) *The Construction of Social Reality*, New York, The Free Press.

Sellers, J. and van der Velden, G. (2003) *Supporting Student Retention*, York, Learning and Teaching Support Network (LTSN).

Silverman, D. (2000) *Doing Qualitative Research*, London, Sage.

Simpson, O. (2000) *Supporting Students in Open and Distance Learning*, London, Kogan Page.

Smith, N. K. (1929) *Immanuel Kant's Critique of Pure Reason*, London, Macmillan.

Smith, J. A. (1996) Evolving issues for qualitative psychology, in J. T. E. Richardson (ed.) *Handbook of Qualitative Research Methods*, Leicester, BPS Books.

Smith, A. (2004) *Who will and who won't cross the frontier of shame?* London, THES, 28.05.04.

Smith, J. and Spurling, A. (1999) *Lifelong Learning. Riding the Tiger*, London, Cassell.

Smith, J. and Spurling, A. (2001) *Understanding Motivation for Lifelong Learning*, London, NIACE/Campaign for Lifelong Learning.

Spencer, B. (2004) On-line Adult Learning, in G. Foley (ed.) *Dimensions of Adult Learning*, Maidenhead, Open University Press.

Spours, K. (2000) Series editors preface in, A. Hodgson (ed.) *Polices, Politics and the Future of Lifelong Learning*, London, Kogan Page.

Spradley, J. P. (1979) *The Ethnographic Interview*, Florida, Holt, Rinechart and Winston.

Stake, R. E. (1995) *The Art of Case Study Research*, London, Sage.

Standen, P. and Brown, D. (2004) Using virtual environments with pupils with learning difficulties, in L. Florian, L. and J. Hegarty, J. (eds.) *ICT and Special Education Needs*, Maidenhead, Open University Press.

Stock, A. (1993) *Lifelong Learning: Thirty years of Educational Change*, Association for Lifelong Learning.

Strauss, A. and Corbin, J. (eds.) (1990) *Basics of Qualitative Research: Grounded Theory in Practice*, London, Sage.

Summers, J. (2002) *Schools are for adults too*, Leicester, NIACE.

Sutcliffe, J. D. (1998) *SATS: a fair benchmark for assessing pupil progress?* Huddersfield, University of Huddersfield.

Tett, L. (1996) Education and the Marketplace, in P. Raggatt, R. Edwards and N. Small (eds.) *The Learning Society*, London, Routledge.

Tett, L. (2002) *Community Education, Lifelong Learning and Social Inclusion*, Edinburgh, Dunedin Academic Press.

The Open University (1995) *Learning through Life*, Milton Keynes, The Open University.

The Open University (2003) *MOSAIC (Making Sense of Information in the Connected Age)*, Milton Keynes, The Open University.

Thompson, J. (2000) *Women, Class and Education*, London, Routledge.

Thompson, J. (2002) *Bread and Roses. Arts, Culture and Lifelong Learning*, Leicester, NIACE.

Thorkildsen, T. A. (2002) *Motivation and the Struggle to Learn*, Boston, USA, Allyn and Bacon.

Tight, M. (2002) *Key Concepts in Adult Education and Training*, London, RoutledgeFalmer

Tileston, D. W. (2004) *What Every Teacher Should Know About Student Motivation*, California, Corwin Press.

Tomlinson, D. (2004) *Working Group on 14–19 Reform Final Report*, DfES, Stationary Office.

Turnbull, A. (2001) Using line management, in L. D. Richardson and M. Wolfe (eds.) *Principles and Practice of Informal Education. Learning through life*, New York, RoutledgeFalmer.

Tysome, T. (2000) *Ufi pockets £84m for autumn launch*, London, THES, 09.06.2000.

UCAS (2000) *Curriculum 2000*, Cheltenham, UCAS.

UDACE (1986) *The Challenge of Change: developing educational guidance for adults*, Leicester, NIACE.

Ufi. (2002) Transforming Learning: Changing Lives. Working through Learndirect to expand the learning market, in *Strategic Plan 2002–2005*, Sheffield, Ufi Limited.

Ufi (2004) http://www.ufiltd.com

Universities Association for Continuing Education (1998) *UACE Annual Conference 1997*, Dublin, UACE.

van der Zee, H. (1991) The Learning Society, in *International Journal of Lifelong Education*, Vol. 10, no. 3: 210–30.

van Weert, T. J. and Kendall, M. (eds.) (2004) *Lifelong Learning in the Digital Age*, Boston, Klumer Academic.

Victor, C. (2005) *The Social Context of Ageing*, London, Routledge.

Vygotsky, L. S. (1978) *Mind in Society: The development of higher psychological processes*, Cambridge, Mass. Harvard University Press.

Walford, G. (ed.) (1991) *Doing Educational Research*, London, Routledge,

Walker, R. (1980) The Conduct of Educational Case Studies: Ethics, Theory and Procedures, in W. B. Dockrell, and D. Hamilton (eds.) *Rethinking Educational Research*, Kent, Hodder and Stoughton.

Wallace, S. (2001) *Teaching & Supporting Learning in Further Education*, Exeter, Learning Matters.

Walsh, P. (1993) *Education and Meaning*, London, Cassell.

Ward, S. V. (2004) *Planning and Urban Change*, London, Sage.

Wedemeyer, C. A. (2003) Open Learning, in P. Jarvis, P. and C. Griffin (eds.) *Adult and Continuing Education. Major Themes in Education*, Vol. IV, London, Routledge.

Weeks, A. (1986) *Comprehensive schools: past, present and future*, London, Methuen.

Wengraf, T. (2001) *Qualitative Research Interviewing*, London, Sage.

Wentworth, N., Earle, R. and Connell, M. L. (2004) *Integrating Information Technology into the Teacher Education Curriculum*, NY, The Haworth Press.

Wheeler, S. (ed.) (2005) *Transforming Primary ICT*, Exeter, Learning Matters.

White, R. C. (2000) *The School of Tomorrow*, Buckingham, Open University Press.

Widening participation through the University for Industry Conference (1998) *Widening participation through the University for Industry—how libraries support lifelong learning*, Sunderland, University of Sunderland Press.

Williams, G. (2000) Paying for lifelong learning: problems and possibilities, in A. Hodgson (ed.) *Policies, Politics and the Future of Lifelong Learning*, London, Kogan Page.

Withnall, A. (2000) Reflections on Lifelong Learning and the Third Age, in J. Field and M. Leicester (eds.) *Lifelong Learning. Education Across the Lifespan*, London. RoutledgeFalmer.

Woodhall, M. (1997) Human Capital Concepts in, A. H. Halsey, H. Lauder, P. Brown and A. S. Wells (eds.) *Education: Culture, Economy, Society*, Oxford, Oxford University Press.

Woods, T. (1999) *Beginning Postmodernism*, Manchester, Manchester University Press.

Wolf, A. (2003) *We should, by now, understand that universities can't produce completely 'work-ready' employees any more than workplaces can take over education*, London, THES.

Wolf, M. (2004) *Why Globalization Works*, USA, Yale University Press.

Wright, A. (2000) New models of learning; The University for Industry—not a University and not just for Industry, in A. McDonald and V. Edwards (eds.) *Widening participation through the University for Industry: how libraries support lifelong learning*, Sunderland, University of Sunderland Press.

Wright, A. W. (2004) *Religion, Education and Post-modernity*, London, RoutledgeFalmer.

Yin, R. K. (2003) *Case Study Research*, California, Sage.

Yin, R. K. (2003) *Applications of Case Study Research*, California, Sage.

Young, M. (1999) Reconstructing qualifications for further education: towards a system for the 21st century, in A. Green and N. Lucas (eds.) *FE and Lifelong Learning: Realigning the Sector for the Twenty-first Century*, London, Institute of Education, University of London.

Young, M. (2000) Bringing knowledge back in: a curriculum for lifelong learning, in A. Hodgson, *Polices, Politics and the Future of Lifelong Learning*, London, Kogan Page.

# Appendices

## Appendix 1
## Autobiographical Account of Lifelong Learning

I never expected to be, or envisaged the joy of being, a lifelong learner. Yet it happened. I belong to a generation whereby an educational pathway for life was invariably mapped out at the ages of eleven, fifteen or sixteen, eighteen, and the 'coming of age' at twenty-one. Hence, this introductory brief life history reads: an '11+' pass into a state grammar school, then GCE 'O' level passes good enough for a place in the 'sixth-form', followed by GCE 'A' level grades acceptable as entry to a teacher training college for a three-year Certificate in Education course. By this ultimate stage, a specific route for my occupational life-chances was virtually mapped. I accepted that it would stay that way, reinforced by the notion of 'education' as a process of infiltration into of form of life; that of taking on the role of developing democratic-minded citizens (Peters, 1966). There remained at the back of my mind, however, a sense of unfulfilled achievement, and a desire—a sense of aspiration—to advance my education.

'Education across the lifespan' is the explanatory sub-title of a book about lifelong learning by Field and Leicester (2000). As a dedicated learner I agree with their interpretation of the concept. After general teaching in a primary school, then specializing in mathematics at secondary level, I temporarily left the profession to have children—a move that coincided with the formation of my business partnership. To date, and over a period of almost forty years as a teacher, parent, employer, and subsequently a 'mature' student, I have naturally witnessed innumerable changes of policy, and fluctuating practices, in both traditional education and vocational training in industry. These often included controversial or widely-debated events.

In the early 1970s there was the introduction of comprehensive schools (Moon, 1983, Weeks, 1986); in 1983 the government funded Youth Training Scheme for the unemployed (16–19), and in 1985 Standardized Assessment Tests (Sutcliffe, 1998). In 1988 the National Curriculum overseen by the Office for Standards in Education was established (Cullingford and Oliver, 2001), and in 1992 General National Vocational Qualifications were introduced. These were among the initiatives that have impacted on my understanding of the parts played in society by two major components—namely, education and industry.

In the continuing dual, but temporally separate, capacities of a company director and a teacher, I retain an ongoing interest in education. My need to learn has been nurtured over time to keep abreast of the variety of swings in practical educational initiatives. In 1998 Technical and Enterprise Councils were established as 'deliverers of government policies on adult unemployment' (Hodgson and Spours, 1999, p.12), with New Deal 25+/50+ following in 1998/1999, then Sure Start in 1999. Becoming aware at the advent of the populist drive to ease access to, and widen participation in, informal continuing learning, and formal further and higher education, I took advantage of the diversity of options on offer. The distance learning opportunities offered by the Open University were immensely important to me. By registering for academic and vocational courses, then channelling my effort and knowledge into practise in different work environments, I achieved qualifications at undergraduate and postgraduate levels, and was awarded training diplomas.

The decision to carry out this particular case study was to proceed along a personal learning curve that acted as a conduit for the deepening ideas and pragmatism intrinsic to the research process. Even the necessary upgrading of a key skill, from assignments written longhand—still a useful accomplishment for sitting examinations—to the keyboarding required for the presentation of a book, can present a challenge.

Examining, determining and developing the philosophical underpinnings of this project constituted the primary intellectual exercise. A balanced use of my abilities and ambitions was important. Plato (427–347BC) maintained that ethics, in terms of the virtues of justice, wisdom, courage and moderation, are the blanket cover for the achievement of happiness by individual human beings, and society as a whole (Pappas, 1999). Essentially, I had the urge to establish momentum through research, to find out if others were similarly prolonging their learning, and moreover, to investigate how, why, when and where, they were doing this.

# Appendix 2
## Interview Schedule

### Introduction

Greet the interviewee. Introduce myself as a 'Third-age' (50+ years old) educational researcher—a light-hearted preamble to relax the respondent.

Give an outline of my study, entitled Lifelong Learning and the University for Industry: a case study.

Say that the interview involves some questions, and that their responses will be confidential and anonymous.

Demonstrate, with the respondent, the recording method. Tell them to stop the tape at any time they wish.

Ask if the respondent has any queries before starting the interview.

### Interview

| Main Question | Notes and follow-up questions |
|---|---|
| **Thinking about the University for Industry and Learndirect—what are the main features?** | Select each aspect in turn—such as, online and/or flexible learning—and ask the interviewee to elaborate. Draw attention to an item that appears to be the most significant—for instance, student support could be problematic/advantageous—and explore why that is the case. |
| **Would you tell me about Learndirect in this centre—the reasons for using it here, and your own involvement with it?** | Are some reasons being emphasized more than others? If so, (I suggest it is likely) use follow-up questions to try to find out if providers and students have<br>(cont.) |

| | |
|---|---|
| | different agendas—for example, are subjective reasons, like certification for job promotion, made distinct from those influenced by extraneous factors, such as providing education? |
| **Can you think of ways in which Learndirect changes people's learning experiences?** | Be guided by the individual's reaction, as this may be a sensitive area based on personal experience. Do not 'force answers', but encourage the respondent to expand on if, and how, Learndirect effects educational aspirations. Any data is valuable—in terms of, for example, class, finance, age, employment, gender and ethnicity. |
| **Consider for a moment 'lifelong learning'—overall what do you think it means?** | Look for positive / negative / ambivalent attitudes to lifelong learning. Encourage the interviewee to relate these feelings to tangible aspects, such as the content and location of learning. By now there may be themes linking or disconnecting the temporal stages of learning—for instance family circumstances. |

| What would be your perception of the approach to learning of the Ufi? | If the respondent is hesitant, use prompts, like relaxed/stressful and distant/drop-in, to try to draw out related issues, such as technologically- and/or community-based learning. By this stage in the interview it should be possible to relate responses back to any, or all of, the responses to the previous questions. |
| --- | --- |

## Interview Conclusion

Ask the respondent if they have any questions.
Say thank you for their help towards my project.

## About the Author

Dr Jennifer M. Fullerty was born in Lancashire, England and qualified as a Maths teacher in 1966. She became Company Secretary of a private manufacturing company in 1978 and later the sole proprietor of a property letting agency.

She currently works as an educational consultant, children's tutor and primary school governor. She is proud to be a member of Soroptimist International advocating 'the best for women.'

Dr Fullerty is married with two children and two grandchildren and currently lives near Cambridge, England.

*Lifelong Learning* is her first book.

Lightning Source UK Ltd.
Milton Keynes UK
UKOW011100190412

191062UK00002B/1/P